Adirondack Kaleidoscope

and North Country Characters

"Hardships of the wilderness were
everyday occurrences for Adirondack folks."
Courtesy of Marilyn Breakey

Compiled, Edited and with
Written Commentary by

William J. O'Hern

Adirondack Kaleidoscope

and North Country Characters

Edited and with Biographical
& Historical Commentary by William J. O'Hern

The book and cover design and typesetting
were created by Nancy Did It! (www.NancyDidIt.com)

Cover: Snowy Mountain stream with floating leaves
by Johnathan A. Esper, Wildernesscapes Photography

Grateful acknowledgement is made for
permission to use Edna West Teall's "Mother Was an Optimist,"
original material that appeared in *Adirondack Tales,
A Girl Grows Up in the Adirondacks in the 1880s*, copyright
Adirondack Life, 1970 and 2001.

In the
Adirondacks

8701 Maple Flats Road • Cleveland, NY 13042
www.adkwilds.com

Printed in the United States of America by Versa Press, Inc.
ISBN 978-0-9890328-0-3

CURRENT TITLES
by William J. "Jay" O'Hern

Thomas C. O'Donnell's
Life in a North Woods Lumber Camp
Edited and with Biographical
and Historical Commentary
by William J. O'Hern
The Forager Press, LLC, 2012

Adirondack Adventures:
Bob Gillespie and Harvey Dunham
on French Louie's Trail
By Roy E. Reehil and William J. O'Hern
The Forager Press, LLC, 2012

Noah John Rondeau's Adirondack
Wilderness Days: A Year with the hermit
of Cold River Flow
The Forager Press, LLC, 2009

Under An Adirondack Influence:
The Life of A.L. Byron-Curtiss, 1871–1959
By Roy E. Reehil and William J. O'Hern
The Forager Press, LLC, 2008

Adirondack Characters
and Campfire Yarns:
Early Settlers and Their Traditions
The Forager Press, LLC, 2005

Adirondack Stories of the
Black River Country
North Country Books, Inc. 2003

Anyplace Wild in the Adirondacks
Self-published, 2000

Life with Noah:
Stories and Adventures of Richard Smith
with Noah J. Rondeau
North Country Books, Inc. 1997

UPCOMING RELEASES
by William J. "Jay" O'Hern

Adirondack Pastimes:
Family Camping and Sporting Adventures
in the Cold River Country with
Hermit Noah John Rondeau (1913–1950)

Adirondack Memories
and Campfire Stories

Adirondack Wilds:
Exploring the Wilderness Haunts
of Noah John Rondeau,
Hermit-Mayor of Cold River City

Discovering the Memoirs
of Emily Wires (1885–1975)
A Window into the
Old Days of the Adirondacks

Adirondack North Country Journeys
and Fireside Stories
Gathered Stories from Foothills
to Mountains

Adirondack and
North Country Reflections:
Journeys from Foothills to Mountains

Gathered Memories and Fireside Stories:
A Celebration of Past Adirondack-
North Country and Upstate New York Life

Logging in the Adirondacks:
The Revolutionary Linn Tractor
and Lumber Camp Stories

Adirondack Echoes:
A Portrait of Camp Life a Century Ago

The Informal History
of the Moose River Plains

Remembering Adirondack Legend
Noah John Rondeau:Following a Hermit's
Footsteps Through His Final Years
(1913–1967)

⋊IN APPRECIATION ⋉

Courtesy Special Collections, Feinberg Library, SUNY College at Plattsburgh

George Glyndon Cole
June 6, 1909–March 21, 2004

George Glyndon Cole's quest to document and preserve historical content brought people together. The archivist-publisher-educator, nevertheless, would have been the first person to say success would not have come about without a dedicated team of volunteer associate editors, the cooperation of publishers, the subscribers, and contributors who selflessly offered stories and poems without remuneration—all for the love of history and folklore.

This compilation recognizes the volunteer spirit of everyone who contributed to *North Country Life* and *York State Tradition* and to all ages who have a curiosity about New York State's rich historical past.

A special note of gratitude goes to the volunteer-collaborators whose work made this book possible. I would like to acknowledge posthumously those who were sharing and selfless. Each person's spirit lives through their writing. ⋊

⹀ CONTENTS ⹀

In Appreciation 4
Preface • *William J. O'Hern* 8
Introduction • *William J. O'Hern*...10

PART ONE: CULTURE, LIFESTYLES AND MOUNTAIN AIR..........15

Collection I: POINTS IN TIME...16
Seasons Come to the Mountains • *William J. O'Hern*................................16
The Hand of Nature Poem • *Mark Hemenway*...22
Summer in the North Country • *G. Glyndon Cole*.....................................23
Mountain Moods • *Frances Boone Seaman* 24
Marcy Kaleidoscope • *Grace L. Hudowalski*...27
A Visit to Adirondack Country • *Samuel Irenaeus Prime* 34
The Sky Was Too Blue—
   A True Tale of the Great Blizzard of 1888 • *Cynthia Smith* 37
Ice Harvest, 1890 • *Author unknown*..41
Lake Placid Childhood • *Leila M. Wells* 43
A Log Cabin Speaks • *Marjorie L. Porter*..49
T.R.'s Midnight Ride • *C. R. Roseberry* 54
President Cleveland in the Adirondacks • *Author unknown* 61
Three Literary Greats on Ampersand Bay • *Lee Knight*............................64
The Philosophers' Camp • *Lee Knight*...68
An 1842 Fishing Trip to Moose River • *Author unknown*..........................73
The Mattesons and Their Sweet Mountain Home • *S.L. Leonard Sr.*.........77
Ice Fishing in the Adirondacks • *Gladys R. Brown*...................................84

Collection II: ADIRONDACK LAND...89
I Remember • *William J. O'Hern* 89
Adirondacks Poem • *Julia Simmons*...96
"It All Belongs to Me" • *Marjorie L. Porter*...97
Our Forest Preserve…A Rich Inheritance • *Ralph S. Hosmer* 99
The First Adirondackers • *W. H. Burger*...103
Adirondack Fundamentals • *John G. Broughton*.......................................106
Verplanck Colvin and the Great Land Survey • *Roland B. Miller* 109
Creation of the Adirondack Park, Part One • *Michael J. Rushman*...........115
Creation of the Adirondack Park, Part Two • *Michael J. Rushman*...........123
Inferno in the Adirondacks • *Harry W. Hicks*...130

Collection III: AN ADIRONDACK PAST 138

A Delightful Mix of Styles and "Voices" • *William J. O'Hern* 138

Rendezvous With Beauty Poem • *Edna Greene Hines* 140

Recollections of the Adirondacks, Part One • *Frederick H. Cowles* 141

Recollections of the Adirondacks, Part Two • *Frederick H. Cowles* 145

Recollections of the Adirondacks, Part Three • *Frederick H. Cowles* 148

Father's Last Decoration Day • *E. Eugene Barker* 153

Mother Was an Optimist,
    Essex County Life in the 1880s, Part One • *Edna West Teall* 160

Mother Was an Optimist,
    Essex County Life in the 1880s, Part Two • *Edna West Teall* 163

Mother Was an Optimist,
    Essex County Life in the 1880s, Part Three • *Edna West Teall*.........167

Mother Was an Optimist,
    Essex County Life in the 1880s, Part Four • *Edna West Teall*...........171

Life on an Adirondack [Fire Tower] • *John Wilkins* 173

The Passing of the Pigeons • *Marjorie L. Porter* 178

The Adirondack Guide Boat • *Roland B. Miller* 183

The Adirondack Guide Boat • *Frances Boone Seaman* 185

Number Please! • *Marjorie L. Porter* 189

Adirondack Medicine • *LeRoy H. Wardner, M.D.* 193

I Remember the North Country Bootlegging Days • *Charles Mooney* 201

The Old Kitchen Stove • *Glenn Neville* 203

Collection IV: ADIRONDACK SCHOOL DAYS 210

I Don't Know B from Bullfrog • *William J. O'Hern* 210

My Friends Poem • *Louella Waterman* 214

An Early Adirondack School • *Edwin A. Juckett* 215

The Country School at the Crossroads • *Carroll V. Lonergan* 220

The One-Room Country School • *Dorothy Pitt Rice* 223

PART TWO: NORTH COUNTRY CHARACTERS 226

Collection V: NOTEWORTHY ADIRONDACK FOLKS 227
Adirondack Souls • *William J. O'Hern* 227
Woodsloafer Poem • *Elsie Wilkins* 232
Adirondack Murray • *Glyndon Cole* 233
Franklin B. Hough, Father of American Forestry • *Ralph S. Hosmer* 237
"Pants" Lawrence in New York City A Poem • *by Helen Hays* 243
"Pants" Lawrence of the Adirondacks • *Donnal V. Smith* 244
Mitchell Sabattis • *L.E. Chittenden* 252
Tom Peacock, Adirondack Guide • *W.H. Burger* 258
Jacques Suzanne—Man of the North • *Terry James Gordon* 263
The Hermit of Cold River • *Clayt Seagears* 267
Adirondack Hermit: Ferdinand Jensen • *Elmer Owen Hoffman* 272
Old Mountain Phelps • *Rev. Frederica Mitchell* 279
Some Conservation Men [of Old] • *W.H. Burger* 283
George Webster—An Adirondack Minister • *W.H. Burger* 291
Old Man of the Mountains • *Emil G. Kraeling* 295
GI, 1863 • *Julia Gardephe Simmons* 302
George Morgan of Raquette Falls • *W.H. Burger* 305
Elkanah Watson, Pioneer • *David M. Ellis* 311
Arthur Couture, the Strong Man of Rouses Point • *Author unknown* 317
Melvil Dewey • *W.H. Burger* 318
A. Fitzwilliam Tait, Adirondack Artist • *Author unknown* 323
The Giant Hermit of the Adirondacks • *Author unknown* 324
Daniel Dodge • *Marjorie L. Porter* 328
This Was Paul Smith • *Gayle Carman* 330
Catherine R. Keese • *Marjorie L. Porter* 334
William Marcy • *Frederick C. Marcy* 336
Father Mac • *W.H. Burger* 336
Granny Rhoades of Early Washington County • *Fred T. Stiles* 341
Ted Hamner, Builder of Adirondack Guide Boats • *Ed Schulz* 344
Seneca Ray Stoddard, a Pioneer Photographer • *Author unknown* 345

Afterword • *Debra Kimok* 348
Postscript 350
Acknowledgements 352
Contributors 354
Sources 361
End Notes and Sources 364
Index 366

⮛ PREFACE ⮛

One of the most popular regional magazines from 1946 through 1974 was George Glyndon Cole's *North Country Life*, later called *York State Tradition*, compiled and edited by the historian-folklorist-archivist. Throughout New York and across the United States, fans made the quarterly digest a much-anticipated periodical, keeping it in publication for twenty-eight years.

The reason was simple: People were as smitten then as they are now with the magic of the North Country, and Cole's quarterly gave them a delicious dose of that magic in the form of stories, articles, poetry and folklore.

Cole delighted his readers with personal recollections, amazing stories and informative histories about the Adirondack waters and mountains. He reprinted interesting old newspaper and periodical stories, true backwoods tales, pioneer stories, military history and much more.

Hundreds of readers asked Cole to assemble a collection of stories from his magazine in book form. If all of their requests were laid end to end, they might well stretch to the peak of Cloud Splitter, the translation of the putative Native-American name for Mount Marcy—New York State's highest mountain.

Cole never did compile a book-length collection, but with so few of the magazines still in existence, now seemed the time for me to take the project on. When I met Glyndon Cole in 1989, I found him to be humble, kind, and extremely intelligent. He shared my imagination and gave his blessing to my proposal that one day I would like to represent his years of work in book form.

Adirondack Kaleidoscope and North Country Characters: Culture, Lifestyles and Seasons in the Adirondacks collects the memories of North

Country natives of the past and present as well as information gathered by historians and journalists. It comprises a fascinating picture of the people who first blazed trails through the wilderness and of those who followed them. We learn about life in the first isolated settlements, and see what the region meant to all sorts of people—from crusty old hermits and guides to famous writers, politicians, and city-bred "sports."

North Country Life, was published from 1946–1974.

Adirondack Kaleidoscope and North Country Characters finally fulfills Cole's readers' wishes that decades of articles, stories and poems about their beloved Adirondacks be brought together in one place. It also continues my practice, begun in *Adirondack Characters and Campfire Yarns*, of sharing stories about North Country natives and those lured there by the promise of everything from prize trout and game to fortunes in trapping and lumber to merely wanting to bask in the peace and quiet.

Illustrated with rarely-seen photographs, *Adirondack Kaleidoscope and North Country Characters* offers a wealth of enjoyment for readers and fans everywhere. ■

⋑ INTRODUCTION ⋐

When I decided to take on the project of compiling Glyndon Cole's work, I wondered how I would begin such a large undertaking. What would be the best way to share the memories of so many story-tellers? Perhaps I would begin by reaching back into my own memories of days spent in the place I love best, the Adirondack wilderness.

On a river bound for somewhere, I shaded my eyes as I turned toward shore, steering my boat into the mouth of an unfamiliar tributary. An insignificant opening in the brush that hugged the low riverbank caught my attention. I've always had a sense of belonging to solitude and wilderness, as do the rocks and trees, the scents of balsam and wild animals.

Drawing closer to the tributary, I realized the opening was either a narrow footpath or game trail.

Many would have found it inconsequential; I found it interesting. I was in a state of mind removed from reality, a comfortable state in which I often find myself when I am out and about, so much so that I nullify the reality that surrounds me. My real purpose for going out on the water, camping in the woods, or climbing a mountain is to experience some primitive ways. I enjoy recapturing simplicity. The pathway was just another adventure and an extra taste of freedom. I had earned the trust afforded by my parents and grandparents to leave the protective cocoon of my immediate kin to ramble the waterways, woods and fields surrounding Camp Oasis, my grandparents' riverfront retreat. My boat and bike, the water and rural countryside vegetation, frosty temperatures and stormy weather—in them wilderness always sings to me.

The autumn color was at its peak in the first week of October. Maples, in diverse shades of red, covered the banks on either side of the waterway. Beyond my range of sight the highest peaks of the Adirondacks lay about 140 miles northeast as the crow flies—but the roads definitely do not go as the crow would.

The mountains were not yet old friends, but I had already fallen in love with them during years of summer family camping trips and weekend getaways during spring, autumn, and early winter. Having an active imagination, I tried to resurrect the pleasant "Going North" memories of my earlier childhood. It was wonderful to think of the places of joy and belonging in the North Country that I had known.

I continued up the creek and drifted into a tiny cove near a submerged wooden rowboat whose gunwales poked above the waterline. I beached my boat and leaped from the bow seat, nearly clearing the mire that hugged the shoreline, but without the force to avoid the muck that sucked one loosely-laced high-top sneaker off my trailing foot as I landed.

As I slapped the mud-covered sneaker against the trunk of a tree, I heard a voice yell "Hey kid!" I didn't know if I had invaded posted property, but somehow I knew by the sound of the voice I was not in any danger.

Turning toward the direction of the voice, I noticed an older man stepping off the covered stoop of a derelict wooden tarpaper shack. A fishing shanty or trapper's cabin? It seemed as natural as the adjacent territory. I'd read the voice right: He proved to be a friendly stranger, one of the first who shaped and changed my life. We spent a pleasant half hour or so talking about the many black water snakes that hugged the shoreline and the beautiful fall color and the oncoming winter, but mostly I listened, fascinated by the stories he told me about his life here in the Adirondacks. Throughout the ensuing years, I've found great pleasure in encounters with interesting people I came to call "characters"—people who seemed to enjoy sharing their stories as much as I enjoyed listening to them.

They were ordinary mountain folk. Plain people, true natives connected to the land from birth, and they calmly went about their work of living from day to day, doing their best to get along. Not one of them was singly consequential on the national or even the local scene. Not one of them wanted or tried to be "important." Nevertheless, to me, they were consequential, because they were champions of the character and ideals and virtues upon which the United States was founded.

The sport of my youth was day-long rambles far from home, well beyond the boundaries my mother ever suspected I would breach. Family camping trips to the Adirondacks and summer vacation at my grandparents' camp provided more opportunities to explore, fish, build huts, and join forces with fellow "river rats."

As an adult, I still spend a majority of my leisure time out of doors.

I was never much of a reader in grade school. A local history book titled *Among the Hills of Camillus* was the catalyst that launched me into years of exploring around my then-rural community. By middle school I had discovered old issues of *North Country Life*. The covers were simple, but spoke to my outdoor desires. The contents often warmed my wishes, the way sitting before the open flames of a campfire can do with comfortable stirrings of vague dreams of romance and adventure in some far-off place.

"Fishing Piseco in 1850." Jacques Suzanne. Noah John Rondeau. "Adirondack French" Louie Seymour. "Pants" Lawrence, navigating on the Black River, stories along the Fulton Chain of Lakes, Bloody Island, William Johnson's retreat to Canada across Raquette Lake. Ethan Allen and the Green Mountain Boys. Folklore and more. The quarterly magazine was the best motivation for a once-unmotivated reader to finally poke his nose between the pages of a book.

Bushwhacking led to finding a book about the people and places in the Adirondack Park. Finding little in print about born-hard Adirondackers' histories—swept aside by stories of wealthy outsiders or their ilk—I sought ordinary mountain folk and those who trekked through the mountains and paddled the waters to fill a historical void with portraits of life from a past time. My findings provided a front-row seat to an earlier era.

The warmth and companionship of good books like Peter Freuchen's early 20th-century northern polar expeditions and trapline trail stories sparked a flickering firelight in my eyes that illuminated times past. The authors' words evoked wonder about earlier times and places that could be satisfied only through reading. Reading established a link to the past and its people and events.

These were some of the things I shared with Glyndon Cole when I met him in 1989. I wanted to tell him how much his magazine had meant to me as a youngster. As we talked, he confessed that as a historian, his publishing efforts forged links to the past in his memory too. In fact it was just for that reason that he had started the publication. He and his like-minded friends shared a connection with the North Country's past. As those who followed the Revolutionary War-era frontiersmen and pioneers moved from the forests and mountains to the protection of villages, northern New York's development began to unfold. Some of the earliest fortunes were made with the abundance of natural resources. Mining, logging, millwork, farming, and the modern tourist attraction were the main sources of income for the native inhabitants.

In the face of this development, Cole wanted to rebridge the gap between past and present. He felt a historical connection to his homeland was being lost. By the 1940s, some longtime natives were relocating beyond the North Country. A younger generation needed a sense of belonging to the expansive Upstate New York real estate, and tourists and summer camp owners could find within the magazine's pages a resource that made them feel they were in some measure a part of the mountainous chunk of Adirondack North Country. Cole wanted to reach back to a time when existence was simple, and he wanted to share the present virtues of the region as well. Founding *North Country Life* satisfied that desire.

The lives and journeys within the 113 issues of Cole's long-out-of-print magazine document the North Country's men and women, and places of interest. They are a tangible representation of Glyndon Cole's lifetime effort to document and share a large portion of the Adirondack North Country history gathered over his lifetime. *Adirondack Kaleidoscope: and North Country Characters*, is my effort to share and preserve his amazing masterwork. ◼

⋝ PART ONE ⋜

Culture, Lifestyles and Mountain Air

dirondack Kaleidoscope deals with such absorbing topics as mountain childhoods, literary greats, ice fishing and ice harvesting, Colvin's land survey, Adirondack fires, guide boats, old-time medicine, bootlegging and country schools. It presents a panoramic overview of much that made this charismatic region home to hard-working folks and a vacation magnet for tourists since the mid-1800s. ⋜

Deer meat was a staple in the diet of early Adirondack families. The Conklin family of Wilmurt, N.Y. *Grotus Reising, photographer. Courtesy Edward Blankman (The Lloyd Blankman Collection)*

PART ONE

Culture, Lifestyles and Mountain Air

➡️**COLLECTION ONE**
Points in Time

COLLECTION TWO
Adirondack Land

COLLECTION THREE
An Adirondack Past

COLLECTION FOUR
Adirondack School Days

Photograph by George Hoxie. Courtesy Meredith Ferlage

SEASONS COME TO THE MOUNTAINS

By William J. O'Hern

Although I could just as easily open the door and poke my head outside, I decided to defer to the Internet and The Weather Channel's *NEW* TruPoint forecast to provide the details for 44.29°N 73.97°W —Lake Placid, New York.

> *Sunday, March 28, 2010, 6:51 am ET. Point Forecast right now: 22 degrees F. Feels like 13 degrees F. Wind is from the SSW at 7 mph. LEARN MORE. Click Here for DETAILS.*

I did and I found so much more! There was humidity and wind speed, an hour-by-hour forecast; a school day forecast (but there is no school today); Top Weather Stories; Cold & Flu Maps; and Smart Travel Tips. There was even additional weather if I chose to click again. If I did I would be privy to a 10-day forecast, and the predicted coming month's weather. I could even view Doppler radar maps.

It all seems like so much overkill.

During the previous century, snuggled in a tiny hut positioned deep in the Cold River valley among the High Peaks surrounding Lake Placid, Adirondack hermit

Noah John Rondeau had the right idea. It was as simple as my first inclination. Open the door and poke my nose outside.

Here is what the hermit recorded in his daily journal for yesterday and today, sixty-four years ago:

Wed. Mar. 27th. 1946. At Big Dam Cold River. Sunshine and Mild Temperature and Breezy. I replant 30 plants and sow 2 packets Tobacco seeds. Plant Fox Gloves and Daisies at Cabin and Caboose doors. Walk around little V. Saw One Grouse.

Thurs. Mar. 28th. 1946. At Mrs. Rondeau's Kitchenette. Perfect spring sunshine continues. I transplant Pinks and Pansys (50 plants). I haul 30 loads Wood.

Pretty simple. Not like the clever overabundance of Weather Channel data. I think all the Internet information is amusing, but I am enough of an old-schooler to agree with the Adirondack hermit's point of view.

I can imagine what his reaction might be if he were able to access what's available at a point-and-click in this Information Age.

"Yes sir, I guess there's plenty that's *come to the finger tips!*" the man of the mountains might have remarked with dizzying lack of interest. "This past January 15th it snowed heavy overnight. Spruce trees were decked in white come morning. Beautiful sunset in lake of fire red that evening and then on the 27th a three-day storm settled in. Cool January weather. I even set out a Buck's head for my Chickadee neighbors to pick on. By the end of February I'd seen new snow most the month but felt the temperatures moderating ever so slightly. Nice winter days in the mountains. Sure have plenty of things happening here daily."

Rondeau also had an interest in the aftermath of World War Two, political doings and scientific breakthroughs; but they were all rather insignificant to the isolation he lived in. The weather was his main concern. It dictated how his day would be spent.

Weather was mankind's earliest, most callous adversary. Freezing temperatures could kill. Droughts could wreak havoc on lives dependent on rain. Weather could only be overcome by outfoxing it with manmade things like shelter, fire, and irrigation. And weather will be the single thing still hanging about if and when human life on earth comes to an end. We don't know what it will be like, but there will be some kind of weather. Interest in the weather sensibly comes before other worldly matters, but possibly people who have never lived close to the soil are more apt to find folks' talk of weather and the business of farming merely amusing—or the last bit of conversation they would ever think of.

The only real fitting way to look at a meteorological forecast is to become a weather forecaster oneself, and the *only* way to do that is to live in one place long enough to become skilled at every subtle change, every faint trace of Nature's voice, and to read accurately what is seen and heard. This skill goes further than learned logic. Most outdoors people are able to predict the weather pretty closely, especially when they are operating in their neck of the woods. When, without knowing why, you squint skyward and recognize a change coming when there is no apparent sign at all, if you're out on a big lake and you sense that a gathering storm is hiding behind the semblance of fair weather, you turn your kayak toward shore before the water turns to nasty seas in order to save your life. When you become weather-wise, countless subtle signs of nature are always present and can register unconsciously on your mind and in the very marrow of your bones.

The old weather proverbs I've learned are sheer poetry to me: "A red sky has water in his eye." "Sound traveling far and wide—a stormy day will betide." "The higher the clouds, the finer the weather." It's all good poetry. The proverbs remind me of the many experiences those who gained that knowledge must have had: "Clear moon, frost soon." "Sky red in the morning is a sailor's sure warning; sky red at night is the sailor's delight." "When grass is dry at morning light, look for rain before the night."

The browned grass is dry this early morning. In spite of the wind chill it was still possible to dart out in my tee shirt, grab a few chunks of firewood from the pile near the door, and never get chilled.

In those bygone years, a bit of Halloween entertainment was called for at Meredith's grandparent's Red Camp in the Adirondacks. *Photograph by George Hoxie. Courtesy Meredith Ferlage*

My cats know a few things about the weather, too. "When the wind's in the south, the rain's in its mouth." They just know what to expect when they poke their noses into the wind.

I know the good weather is not going to last. The grass was dry this morning. The sky is 70% overcast. The official weather forecast is calling for a 40% chance of showers after 1:00 PM, 100% by tomorrow. The leafless maple, beech and ash stand ghostly against a gray sky. Evergreen boughs wave gently. I truly feel the urgency to accomplish all the outdoor tasks that I want to finish before the afternoon closes in. I know, too, that the old proverbs have much to do with the color of the sky and the appearance of the sun, moon and stars, for it seems reasonable that changes in their appearance mean changes in the atmosphere itself— changes that usually come before one or another type of weather.

That's what Nature's weather reports do for me.

You could say the Adirondack Mountains and woodlands are an observation station for naturalist-at-heart breeds.

When the calendar says, "Spring at Cold River"
among Lofty Major Adirondack Peaks,
And hard packed snow is four foot deep.
After the Winter, the Sun and Earth change node,
It takes half of Springtime, to melt the snow.
The day is longer, the sun higher than before;
And the first bird to arrive is the crow....

This is how Noah John's "Spring Time Scramble" poem began. The poem dragged on for pages. He drafted the original version on site, at Cold River, throughout the spring of 1944.

Outdoor lovers consider the sound of water rushing over stones or wind in trees a sort of pleasing natural symphony. Otters splashing into the water at the end of a chute down a bank or the sight of moose before dusk pulling green shoots from a marsh can be more affecting than the greatest painting. To chance upon the first wildflower blossom of the spring seems an irrefutable and essential right. We are the ones labeled "nature lovers," "tweety bird watchers," or better yet, "tree huggers"!

The truth is that we don't love nature any more than anyone else is keen on breathing, drinking or eating. All four are simply things without which a rewarding life would be impossible—there would be no benefit to living. Life without the sight of reddish soft maple buds together imparting a purple cast against the major Adirondack peaks, life without spotting elder buds the size of sparrow's eggs—that would be appallingly mediocre.

"Nature lovers" are not trained naturalists. They have amassed no notebooks filled with statistics, put forward no intellectual philosophy, made no central contribution to the body of botanical, zoological, or geological data. They lean toward being absorbed by the awe-inspiring and diverse natural world into which they were born, and easily fritter their time away smelling, looking, listening, and feeling. How else can one spot the rapidly-flapping ruby throated hummingbird hovering in mid-air before it darts with a whirl? They find comfort and inspiration— maybe even refuge—in natural objects, but most of all they find interest and enjoyment. Nature lovers may be a rather hopeless lot, unmotivated and tending to be somewhat emotional over bunches of shad flowers with five long white petals looking as bright as laundered cotton, or noting poplar leaves spinning like coins hung by strings. But even birds with family cares don't cease to sing! Perchance nature lovers are a little too innocent, easily distracted by simple things like water turtles coming out on the bank in trusting sunshine to lay their eggs in the sand, or following the movements of tree swallows with their clever speedy long wings, soaring in a stiff wind to catch flies. But for all their shortfalls, they're innocent and they are content.

I know because I'm one of them. ⬛

On their boulder perch, the trampers stared at the small dark shapes that whizzed like water-bugs across the lake below. Mountain birds made day-songs on the ends of evergreen boughs. The blue sky glitters with reflected sunlight from little kettle puddles of water in the rock. *Courtesy Jane Ritz*

Taken along the trail to Beaver Lake, Moose River Plains, 1938. *Author's Collection*

❄ THE HAND OF NATURE

The thrush will return to the thicket,
The bobolink back to the marsh,
As Winter's cold grip loosens
And horizon seems less harsh.
The beauty of the living
Returns to meet the eye
In the glamour of a sunset
Beneath a summer sky.
Along the roads and by-ways
The hand of Nature weaves,
As she gathers up each remnant
And magically retrieves.
The bounty of the harvest
With heaps of golden grain
Gives proof each year to all mankind
That life is not in vain.

—Mark Hemenway, *North Country Life*, Spring 1955 ◣

SUMMER IN THE NORTH COUNTRY

By G. Glyndon Cole, *North Country Life*, Spring 1958

Summer is perhaps the most delightful season in the North Country, and the North Country in summer is one of the most delightful vacation lands in America—as thousands of vacationers have long since discovered.

For Northern New Yorkers, including those who have adopted the North Country for their summer residence, there is little need to mention the features that make this a popular vacation land. Moreover, that which lures one vacationer may not be what brings another, for this summer Northland abounds in holiday opportunities. It may be the sunny days that appeal—days made for lazy hours of fishing, drifting in a boat, sun bathing, hikes or horseback rides along shady trails, or a refreshing dip in river, lake, or pool. It may be the cool nights conducive to sound, restful sleep. It may be a North Country fair or the annual pageants, or it may be special occasions which lure the vacationer northward.

Thousands of scenic spots beckon: cool, blue lakes, tree-lined rivers and creeks, quiet retreats to soothe frayed nerves and restore the sparkle of life. Gay cities and villages with their many entertainments, the thrills of flying, mountain climbing, horseback riding, motorboating, waterskiing, swimming in crystal-clear fresh waters—all these call the vacation seeker to a summer of happy relaxation.

Yes, there's a wealth of summer fun to be found in the North Country. There's adventure and excitement, or there's quiet rest and relaxation—all of which will furnish happy memories for re-living during the long, dull winter months.

There are all these things and more that could be said about summer in Northern New York. We dare say, however, that it is not alone the North Country's many and varied opportunities for recreation and entertainment which cause so many to return year after year. It is, we believe, as much the friendly, homey atmosphere which the sojourner finds here that makes him want to come again. Though many of us may be reluctant to admit it, we have no monopoly on scenic beauty, excellent fishing grounds, recreational opportunities, or good entertainment. But here one does find an unusual friendly atmosphere.

Northern New Yorkers, an unsophisticated, plain-living, and happy people, are eager to make the stranger forget he is a stranger. Though the visitor may have come first to see such attractions as the Thousand Islands or historic Fort Ticonderoga or the beauty of the Adirondack Mountains, he comes the second time because he discovered on his first visit North Country hospitality. It is indeed this neighborly atmosphere which makes the North Country a good place to live not only in the summer but the year around. ◣

MOUNTAIN MOODS

By Frances Boone Seaman, *North Country Life*, Winter 1953

Whoever has come to know the Adirondacks and traveled not only their labyrinth of highways but taken up pack basket and map to hike the less accessible trails, to him has been unfolded the heart and moods of this great region. One spot above all others may be favored, yet one doesn't feel that it belongs to him, but rather that he belongs to it. Whether that be a favorite high peak or only the view from a fire tower, a winding stream of great beauty or even a sunny sand beach on some quiet lake—all have their special charms.

For me, that favored spot is Long Lake in the heart of the Adirondacks. Here from childhood I have come to know and love the lake, the forests, and the mountains.

On a calm morning in summer, the lake is like a gem when, with sunshine suffusing all, one's spirits cannot help but soar. The very woods sing with their myriad bird calls and humming insects, and every leaf becomes a glistening canopy of dew drops. Occasionally a heavy fog over the lake tends to delay temporarily an enchanting spectacle, but it assures that the day will continue to be beautiful.

My fondest memory of such a morning reverts to my teens, when I preceded the sunrise one morning in July to go guide-boating. It was foggy and chilly, but passing along the faintly discernible shoreline was exhilarating. After a half-mile row, I decided to cross the lake and head into the fog. The occasional glimpses of sunlight through the swirling mists were my only guide. After fifteen minutes of being "in the fog," weeds and grasses began appearing, and I knew I had reached the familiar Big Brook Marsh across the lake.

By this time the sun was beginning to burn away the fog and the immense marsh began to take shape, yet the surrounding hills and mountains remained undisturbed by sound. As I sat drifting and marveling on the mirrored waters, the beauty of the place seemed unreal. Across the lake thin wisps of fog lifted off the water against the shadows of the dark shoreline, and far down the lake a solid white fog bank hung over the outlet with the rising blue peaks of the Seward Range shimmering above.

Before long a ringing bell broke the spell, its melodic tones echoing back and forth between the hills. In a few moments a Chris Craft sped up the lake, and from summer camps the sound of voices floated across the still water. Reluctantly, I ended my reverie as I came back to reality.

Sunrise in winter time is much different. A native seldom, if ever, gets up merely to see the sunrise. If he should have occasion to enjoy the sight, it is in the line of some duty involving any early rising. I am an early riser and have no excuse for missing nature's colorful displays since I live by the lake shore and have only to look out of the window for an unobstructed view of the sunrise lighting the Seward Range. On such mornings, the temperature is usually at zero or colder. By seven o'clock there is a white column of smoke rising high in the air from many of the houses in the valley.

As the sun rises, long shafts of sunlight play across the shadowed expanse of the frozen lake, increasing gradually as the sun tops each new ridge and mountain top. Winter also has its charms.

In learning to understand the nature of the mountain seasons, there are certain signs one comes to expect and anticipate each year, such as the black-fly season, the turning of the leaves in autumn, and the spring break-up. We have found from unforgettable experience that the black flies make their appearance between the middle and last of May, depending upon how early a start spring has had. If one spends much time out of doors during the following month, he is mighty glad to welcome some good, hot weather, for that is the best natural exterminator of the little pests.

Mosquitoes put in their appearance about the middle of June and join the black flies in making life miserable. This is unfortunate, for in other respects June is one of the pleasantest months in the mountains.

In July the gnats have their innings with their wicked little sting. But by the arrival of August, most of these unpleasant pests are gone, if the summer has been fairly dry. These calculations are made without considering the new chemical sprays which are becoming more generally used in this locality with telling effect. August is the month for camping. In June, when canoe parities have passed determinedly down the lake, I have wondered if they knew what they were in for in making camp that night.

Autumn in the mountains! That means a cold but glorious, short but brilliant season. The hardwoods are usually at their peak of color during the last week of September, and nowhere are the views more beautiful. Standing on a high hill one can often see some body of water sparkling like a diamond in the forest of colors.

On a clear day in late September, when once I walked to the top of an overlooking hill, the waters of Long Lake stretched like a winding blue ribbon far into the distance toward Saranac Lake. The brilliant foliage of the hardwoods intermingled with the dark green of the pointed evergreens, both changing to a soft mauve in the distance and the clear, blue, mountains looming in the background made it a picture to be long remembered.

A neighbor on the lakeshore, Wallace Emerson Sr., whose father was one of the early settlers, was seated near the beach among some of his guests when I happened along one evening in the summer. It was an exceptionally pleasant evening, and our talk naturally turned to the effect it had upon the surroundings. The sun had recently set, the wind had ceased, and the lake, then motionless, reflected every tree and mountain top.

I remarked about the splendid pines growing across the lake. They were like sentinels standing in grandeur, their huge, gnarled branches like folded arms upon their chests. A light green marshy spot along the water's edge furnished enough contrast to make the scene enchanting against the evening sky. It was all enhanced by the appearance of a deer that came down to drink there in the shallows.

Mr. Emerson made a remark, the truth of which I think few of us have realized. He said, "The shoreline of this lake is a lot prettier than it has been in a long, long time, perhaps 65 years." I looked incredulous, and he explained, "When this region was lumbered of most of its virgin timber, the most accessible and some of the best trees lined these shores. Only during the last few years has the lake reverted to its former beauty."

Mr. Emerson had come to know and love the lake, too. ◼

▓ MARCY KALEIDOSCOPE

By Grace L. Hudowalski, *North Country Life*, Spring 1954. Reprinted from *The Ad-i-ron-dac*

Mountains are there to be climbed. And the highest one in any range, area, state or country becomes an added challenge. The reason varies with mountaineers: to explore, to be first, to climb the highest, to get the view, to enjoy the lure of the unknown, for fun, and as George Leigh-Mallory said of Mount Everest, "Because it's there." There are other reasons, too, but these will serve as to why people have, since August 5, 1837, been climbing Mount Marcy, New York State's rooftop.

It was William C. Redfield, a scientist of the highest rank, who first recognized the mountain for its true worth. On a trip to the Adirondack Iron Works in 1836 with the idea of taking an interest in the ownership and management of that property, Redfield saw the mountain and called it the "High Peak of Essex." The following year, a party headed by Ebenezer Emmons, a New York State geologist, climbed the "High Peak of Essex" and promptly called it "Marcy" for the governor responsible for the jobs of certain members in the party.

Old Mountain Phelps and his wife seated in front of their mountain home in 1888.

A Seneca Ray Stoddard photo. Courtesy Maitland DeSormo Collection

Charles Fenno Hoffman, the English poet who visited the Iron Works the same summer, later referred to the mountain by the Seneca word "Tahawus," interpreted as "it cleaves the sky," a word which curiously has nothing to do with a place name. It is, rather, from the Seneca-Iroquois council phraseology and refers to declaring an expression of truth so powerful that "it cleaves the sky." So much for the names of this mighty mountain.

Verplanck Colvin, leader of the Adirondack Survey, placed Bolt 1 in the summit of Mount Marcy in 1872 and later in the year, by means of the theodoloite, barometrical observations proved the mountain to have an altitude of 5,333 feet.

However, more than twenty years prior to this, a colorful philosophizing man was taking summer people from Keene Valley up mountains as a hobby. Orson Schofield Phelps, affectionately called Old Mountain Phelps, boasted of having climbed "Mercy," his favorite "mounting," more than a hundred times. He had blazed the first trail to its summit in 1849 and a year later had successfully guided two ladies to the top of Marcy and back. The fact that these were the first women to make the difficult ascent brought him considerable fame.

In the years that followed, different personalities came and went, but perhaps no one event so catapulted the mountain to fame as the climb of Vice-President Theodore Roosevelt, who literally became President of the United States in 1901 while on a climbing and camping expedition on Marcy.

Credit for the first winter ascent from the west goes to Gifford Pinchot, destined to become governor of Pennsylvania, who reached the summit alone; his companion, C. Grant LaFarge and guides were forced to turn back at timberline because of the intense cold. This was February of 1899, during what was eventually recorded as the beginning of the "Blizzard of 1899."

And so the great and near-great take their respective places in Marcy's kaleidoscope, all of which is background to personal impressions of a mountain which stands out as my indoctrination in mountain climbing.

It was 1922. Dad had taken the Mountain View House in Minerva. With school over in Ticonderoga, I, too, went north, where I was promptly invited to join a three-day safari to Marcy via the old Iron Works.

My blanket roll was ready days ahead of time (it was years before I was to know the joy of Bergen!) and I was continually slinging it over my shoulder to get the feel of it. My voluminous bloomers were carefully pressed; my middy blouse, complete with the large red square of a tie (twice the size of today's kerchief), hung in readiness on a hanger. Dad was too good an outdoorsman to let me go in the woods without the facts of life. I was, therefore, told to "walk softly and reverently," to do my "share and a little more," and to "be cheerful, no one wants a grouch around." "The last pull up Marcy is tough," Dad concluded. "It is not important whether you reach the top of the mountain, but it is important how you make the climb."

The trip in to Lake Colden was perfect. The wonder of it thrilled me beyond words and the added delight of that incomparable view of Mt. Colden from the Flowed Lands took my breath away. The rains, which descended during the night, failed to dampen my spirits and I was on my way up the muddy trail early the next morning, reveling in the cascading Opalescent rushing down the mountain alongside our path. We were all pretty wet when we paused in the old Feldspar Lean-to for a breather.

From here on the trail became steadily worse. It being the end of June, we caught up with the black flies, which have a way of getting in eyes, ears and down gasping throats. The trail was steeper and muddier and we often took one step to slide back three. We were tired and wet and hungry, and all of a sudden Dad's famous last words ran through my mind: "It is not important whether you reach the top of the mountain, but it is important how you make the climb." While I may have wondered what he meant, I certainly had no time to speculate.

At Four Corners, while we ate before a sputtering, useless fire and discussed plans, I was faced with three alternatives: I could wait while the rest went on (too cold for that!); I could retrace my steps down the mountain: ("It is not important whether you reach the top …"); or I could go on: (…but how….!) Without realizing it, I was face-to-face with a fundamental of life.

I chose to go on. It was tough, and once the summit was reached we couldn't see a thing. Clouds swirled around, engulfing us. Then, for a fleeting moment they lifted, revealing Lake Tear of the Clouds, three quarters of a mile away.

By the time the Centennial Climb came around in 1937, I was keeping a yearly tryst with Marcy. Unfortunately, that climb was scheduled during the middle of the week and many of the Troy hikers with whom I usually climbed had to work. As was the custom, though, we filled the car. Arriving at Heart Lake the previous afternoon, we took possession of the old "cow shed" in back of the Loj and started up the trail at daybreak. Two in the party had never climbed a mountain, and one of them was a courageous housewife of about 45 who had been led astray by our glowing accounts of mountain climbing. While not as encumbered as the woman of Old Mountain Phelps' day with Turkish trousers and skirt, hat with veil, and equipped with an umbrella, she was far more suitably dressed for a walk in a park that didn't have the word "Adirondack" in front of it. But we were all too happy to be concerned over what were to us inconsequential matters.

An older hiking member remained behind as guide and companion for our aspirant. The younger climbers raced on, eventually catching up with the struggling, panting optimists who were attempting to tote heavy radio equipment up the last half mile of Marcy's summit for what turned out to be a very inadequate broadcast.

Hikers swarmed Marcy's top, basking in the sun, taking pictures, enjoying the view and greeting old friends. Occasionally we kept dropping down the side of the mountain to a vantage point where we could see climbers struggling up from timberline. I shall never forget with what joy we greeted the older members of our party and how unsuppressed tears of happiness rolled down our cheeks to see that one woman—housewife—literally crawling! A lot of things about that climb stand out in my mind, but paramount is the daring courage of that unsuspecting woman… back in her own home late that night she was obliged to crawl upstairs on her hands and knees, and it was more than a week before she was able to wear shoes. There were, however, no complaints. Likewise, there were no other mountain jaunts for her, but she understood better why we wanted to climb every chance we got. Her reward was the state's "High Peak."

In August of 1939, after scaling the highest summit of each New England state, we decided to climb Marcy to see the sunrise from its summit. Leaving the Loj at 1:30 AM, our way was lighted by a magnificent display of the Aurora Borealis. Climbing that night was fun until we reached Plateau. The cone of Marcy was enveloped in mist and the air was cold and damp. By the time we reached timberline, the mist was so dense that cairns were hard to find even with strong flashlights and the leader dared not move from the line of vision of the person behind, who stayed in sight of the last cairn. And then, without warning, we were there against the ledge and the bronze centennial marker. We put on every item of clothing in our Bergens and huddled together for warmth, taking an occasional sip of coffee from our thermos bottles.

All of a sudden—as wind blew the mist away—the day began! Tinted in shades of palest pink to deepest rose, the eastern skyline appeared. Sundogs stretched themselves out until there were six vari-colored lavender-purple rays. Then, towering over Giant-of-the-Valley came the sun, a huge bursting ball of flaming gold!

All around and beneath us great waves of soapy low-lying clouds lapped against Marcy's peak, completely hiding all other heights. We were "cleaving the sky." Gradually Skylight, Redfield, the McIntyres and Haystack came above the cloud waves like submerged rocks on a wave-tossed sea. And, as we watched Gray Peak appear, we saw on the rose-tinted clouds over it the shadow of Marcy. One such phenomenal view is ample reward of a lifetime of mountain hiking!

The winter of '39 some of us decided Marcy should be climbed on snowshoes. We had done it in spring, summer and fall. We had climbed it at dusk and before dawn. Some of us had even slept on its summit.

Only a winter ascent remained. Equipped with a key to the Winter Camp on Johns Brook, supplies and crampons, we snow-shoed in one evening. Undaunted by the mess the mice had made in the stovepipe, cupboards and beds, we cleaned up, ate a good meal and went to bed early only to arise before we had slept an hour, or so it seemed.

The snow was so deep we made our own trail through the woods, occasionally walking on treetops. Markers were out of sight. At one point we found and dug the junction sign from the snow and relaxed around it long enough to take a picture. By the time we reached the ridge leading from Haystack to Marcy (we had gone up Slant Rock Trail) it was 4:30 PM. Marcy glistened in the sun, cold and inviting. It was breathtakingly lovely and we wanted to go on more than anything else in the world. I shall never forget how Dad's words kept coming back to me, "It is not important whether you reach the top…but how you make the climb."

We turned our backs on Marcy and returned to Winter Camp, greatly fatigued, as it turned out, but in high spirits. Marcy would be there for another time.

There have been many notable ascents of the High Peak of Essex in my life. Each one was different and each one marked taking someone new to the summit and sharing with him that "heaven uph'isted" feeling which Old Mountain Phelps spoke of.

Outstanding among Marcy trips are the "random scoot" from Gray Peak at dusk, the October first climb with travel editors from other states, and the late summer overnight jaunts during which two young nephews, as well as certain members of the Troy Ministerial Association, were introduced to the grand old mountain.

Last fall, as we relaxed at Indian Falls before our ascent of Tabletop, we ran into a group from the Outing Club of the University of Vermont. "Climbing Marcy?" they inquired confidently. "No," we replied, "Table-top." They were stupefied.

We tried to explain why Tabletop, but of course, it didn't register. How could they know we knew the challenge of the highest, or that we could see Marcy, glittering with early frost in the late morning sun as we pushed up the trails of Tabletop? How could they know we still kept tryst with "The Cloud Splitter," whether we stood on its summit or saw it from Algonquin or the rock ledges of Phelps or the tree-covered summit of Redfield or scrambling up the Panther Gorge side of Haystack!

Climbers will always aspire to Marcy. Why? "Because it's there" and it's the highest in the area. "How" will they "make the climb"? Again and again, we hope, to capture some new mood of the High Peak of Essex, Mount Marcy, Cleaver of the Sky—the rooftop of the Empire State. ■

A VISIT TO ADIRONDACK COUNTRY

By Samuel Irenaeus Prime, *York State Tradition*, Winter 1967
An excerpt from *Under the Trees*, published in 1874

Halleck's Hill was not in our way, but we rode some miles around to cross it, for the sake of the view from its summit. The plain, as well watered as any Moses saw from Pisgah, stretches away and away to the St. Lawrence; frequent church spires and villages shone in the distance, and a world of wealth, prosperity, and contentment appeared to be reposing in this vast Vega.

Some years ago a Baptist minister in this quarter gave his whole mind to horseshoe nails, and when a man gives his whole mind to anything, something comes. So in this case. If the good man failed to make good points in his sermons, he made points to nails; and the wisest of preachers said that good words are like nails fastened by the masters of assemblies. Perhaps this analogy led him to invent his machine to point horseshoe nails; and, having perfected it, he has retired from preaching, and derives a large income from the royalty paid him by the company that uses his patent. The village of Keeseville, on the Au Sable River, flourishes with numerous manufacturing establishments. Besides its twine and wire works, the horseshoe nail factory presents a wonderful specimen of power and beauty in mechanical labor. In this thriving and beautiful village of Keeseville I spent the night, enjoying the hospitalities of H. N. Hewitt, Esq.

The stage called at six o'clock in the morning for me at the door. It was cool and exhilarating, and the ride to the Point of Rocks was exciting and delightful. Some of the views on the Au Sable River were picturesque and exceedingly beautiful.

We rode pleasantly on, and came to Ausable Forks, where some sportsmen halted from the stages, with rods and guns and dogs, to spend a day or two in the woods and streams. Here and at Black Brook village beyond we found the vast iron works of J. & J. Rogers, whose mines are mines of untold wealth; and the mountain on our right, as we ride on, is honeycombed by the miners' toil, taking out the bowels of the hills and bringing them down to be roasted and tortured into the thousand uses of man.

High on the hills the charcoal burners pursue their carbonic work, and we frequently meet their long, black, huge vans, dragged along toward the furnaces, loaded with coal. By the roadside kilns are built, to which the wood is drawn and carbonized, and in one place we pass an extensive manufactory of creosote.

All the industries of the country are such as relate to lumber and minerals. These are apparently inexhaustible. The pressure of demand will gradually compel better ways, for now we are riding over the ruins of a plank road, and worse going can hardly be found, unless the corduroy patent is worse on which Governor Marcy met with that accident to one of his garments for which he brought the State of New York into his debt to the amount of fifty cents.

The rough plank road became rougher as we proceeded. Nothing on it was kept in repair but the toll-gates. Jolting on, pitching about, turning out to get by a bad place, we picked our way through the woods, until at last we reached Franklin Falls, where we were to stop for dinner. This over, and the horses being rested or exchanged, we resumed our seats. We crept on, gradually rising, the scenery more and more wild and weird and gloomy.

At Bloomingdale I left the stage, which had thus far brought me on. Mounted upon the high seat in the front of the stage that bore upon it the name of Paul Smith, I rode a couple of hours from Bloomingdale right into the woods; now and then a clearing improved by culture met the eye, but it was plain that we were passing away from civilization and plunging into the wilderness.

Suddenly we emerged from the dense forest on the margin of a lovely lake, and a short turn in the road brought us in front of a large, handsome hotel. Its broad piazza was filled with genteel guests, ladies and children, apparently at home; and yet we are now in the lake country of the Adirondacks. The name of this place is Paul Smith. That is the name of the house—also of the proprietor and landlord. He was named Apollos Smith, and submitted to that name until he was long and widely known as Pol Smith, and then the heathen name gave place to the Christian, and Pol became Paul.

As Paul Smith, he began to keep a little tavern on this lake, to give shelter and liquor to travelers; but my good friend, Thomas H. Faile, Esq., encouraged him to drop the liquor, and the loss proved a great gain. He began to flourish forthwith. His tavern grew larger and larger every year. He built anew wings and raised the roof, and stretched the verandas, until now his house is by far the greatest and best in this whole region, and Paul Smith does more business than all the rest of the hotels together. His house is on the margin of the lower St. Regis Lake, bright mirror of the St. Regis Mountain that stands in full view of the hotel, and within easy reach by boat.

There is glory up here. There is one glory of the woods, and another glory of the lakes, and another of the mountains. And the heavens cover the wilderness with their glory. And nature is untutored, wild, luxuriant, free, jubilant. The Great Spirit is here dwelling in the forest temples, riding upon the circle of the heavens, speaking in the wind and thunder. ◤

❄ THE SKY WAS TOO BLUE—A TRUE TALE OF THE GREAT BLIZZARD OF 1888

By Cynthia Smith, *North Country Life*, Winter 1948

> *Of all the tales about the North Country's great blizzard of
> 1888, perhaps none have been retold more often than this one.
> Mrs. Smith, who has recorded the story here, recalls having
> seen often as a child the characters of the story ride past her
> home and having heard the tale many times. Though the story
> is said to be true, the author—much to the regret of folklorists,
> no doubt—has used fictitious names in this account.*

Rosie LaMere stood in the doorway of her little log house and watched the doctor take the blanket from his horse and then settle himself comfortably under the fur robes of his cutter.

"An' you sure you can pull dat leg out de way you say?" she asked anxiously.

The doctor's laugh was pleasant and reassuring, "Joe will be all right, Mrs. LaMere. It will be just as I explained to you. As I said before, if I had known it was a dislocation I would have brought the necessary help and equipment, but when they said it was a break—"

The doctor gathered up his reins and continued, "Don't worry, keep Joe quiet, give him those tablets every four hours and I will see him first thing in the morning."

For a few minutes Rosie stood at the door listening to the jingle of the sleigh bells and then she gave her whole attention to the weather.

There had been brilliant sunshine all the forenoon with the sky a deep metallic blue—"too blue" she had told Joe. Now it was overcast and great flakes of snow were floating lazily down through mild, still air.

Rosie walked to the corner of the house and held up her hand as if to feel the air. Even as she stood there the house door slammed shut in a sudden gust of cold wind that seemed to come from no direction in particular.

Rosie hurried back into the house and went into instant action.

She was a huge woman, about 65 years of age, but she moved about silently and swiftly, putting on coat, cap and overshoes. Then, seizing two water buckets and a milk pail, she beat her way to the barn against the rising storm.

Here she worked quickly. Feeding, watering and finally milking, and then with her pail of milk in one hand and a pail of water in the other, she went out once more into the storm.

Pausing in the kitchen only long enough to put down her heavy pails, Rosie went to the woodshed and carried in armful after armful of dry, fragrant stove wood and piled it near the kitchen range.

Then she removed her outer garments and shook the snow from them.

Meanwhile the wind was increasing with every moment. Rosie opened the door and looked out. A wall of fiercely driving snowflakes filled the fast-gathering darkness. She closed the door and went to the range. Lifting a griddle with great care so as to make as little noise as possible, she filled the fire box with wood and, replacing the griddle, walked softly to the bedroom door and listened.

Joe was sleeping and Rosie turned back to her work. She lighted the spotlessly clean kerosene lamp in the oil bowl of which shone a piece of bright red wool, making a cheery spot of color in the room.

The little two-room log house had been literally hewn out of the wilderness nearly fifty years before, when Joe and Rosie crossed the border from Canada to make a home for themselves in the North Country.

The land had been cleared with Rosie doing the lion's share of the work, for Joe had always been small and "pindley" and now, as Rosie moved back and forth in the freshly scrubbed kitchen, preparing their simple meal of corn meal mush and milk, her mind went back over those toil-filled years. Often she brushed away the hot tears as she thought how easily she had carried poor Joe into the house when he had fallen in the barn.

She paused by the table as she caught sight of the saucer in which the doctor had placed four tiny white tablets. Rosie looked long at the pills. What good could anything so small do for a dislocated hip? She picked them up—poked them around in the dish for awhile, then marched to the stove, lifted the griddle and tossed them into the fire. A bowl of corn meal mush would be of far more benefit to Joe, and Rosie knew it.

That night was a night of agony for Rosie as well as for Joe. He had wakened during the evening in great pain, and Rosie had to stand helplessly by and watch him suffer. The idea that the tablets might have helped never entered her mind.

All night the storm roared around the little house. The snow pelted against the outside windows, and Rosie knew the drifts were piling higher and higher. It might be several days before the road could be opened. As Joe's moaning grew weaker, Rosie grew more desperate.

The afternoon saw no abatement of the storm. Joe, completely exhausted, had fallen into a doze. Rosie quietly filled the stove once more and sat down by the open oven door to think. A few minutes later she was up and moving about the kitchen with swift, quiet steps, preparing to go out.

When she was dressed, she went to the woodshed and returned with the clothes line. She tied one end of this to her arm and the other to the outside iron handle of the door latch and, pulling the woolen cap down over her eyes, plunged into the storm in the direction of the barn.

Although the barn was but a short distance from the house, it was a good half hour before Rosie, with the rope as a guide, fought her way back to the door.

It was another half hour before she had disposed of the snow that covered her and the accumulation of ropes and harness straps that she had dragged from the barn.

Meanwhile Joe had awakened and was moaning once more.

"W'at you doin', Rosie?" he called feebly.

"You not ask me, Joe. Me, I make it a plan to help you."

She continued the process of taking the frost out of the rope.

Soon she dragged the rope into the bedroom and began fastening one end to a rafter overhead. Rosie was an expert with the block and tackle. No man in the whole country side could haul up a carcass at butchering time as quickly and neatly as Rosie LaMere.

A wild fear came into Joe's eyes.

"Tell me, Rosie, w'at you goin' do? Tell me, Rosie!"

Rosie paused a moment by the bed and looked down at him. Her face was set with the grim determined expression that Joe had come to understand long before.

Her voice was firm: "Joe, I'm goin' fix dat leg lak-a-ways de doctor, he say. It be two, mebbe t'ree day 'fore he can come. You be dead by den. Me, I can do it. You see. Me, I use dese t'ings lotta time; you know how I do. You jus' trus' me, Joe. Me, I be easy like I can. You got be brave leetle w'ile more, Joe."

And then while old Joe alternately pleaded, threatened and cursed, Rosie worked steadily, tightening the straps that were to hold him firmly to the bed.

With gentle hands she wrapped his ankle in a piece of woolen blanket before fastening the rope, and then carefully and slowly she began taking up the slack. With the first upward movement of his leg Joe started screaming in agony—but Rosie, her face white but grim, pulled steadily, giving her whole attention to the leg that was being drawn slowly but surely away from that tortured body.

Then suddenly it was all over. With a soft little snap the leg as back in place.

Joe lay white and still, mercifully unconscious.

Rosie, with a sobbing little cry, eased the leg down onto the bed, and with tears rolling down her weather-beaten cheeks she rushed to the bed, wiped the cold sweat from Joe's face and hurried to loosen the straps.

Sometime near morning of the next day the wind died down and the snapping of nails told of the fast-falling mercury.

About noon a slowly moving line of men with shovels and horses hitched to heavy sleds started down the cross road toward Joe LaMere's place.

Rosie heard the shouts, and scraping the thick frost from a pane of glass in the upper part of the window, she looked out. A bright sun glittered on the snow-covered fields, where huge drifts were piled into fantastic shapes. A half mile down the road she saw the clouds of steam rise from the laboring horses and men, and inching along behind came the doctor's cutter with two fur-bundled figures in it.

She turned from the window and looked at Joe sleeping peacefully on the bed, and as she smiled, something of the beauty that had been hers as a young bride, came back into the face of Rosie LaMere. ◼

❄ ICE HARVEST, 1890

Author unknown, *York State Tradition*, Winter 1964
Reported in the *Utica Saturday Globe*, February 15, 1890

The failure of the ice crop along the Hudson River has created the greatest excitement in Northern New York, wherever there happens to be an ice-bound stream or lake of even moderate size.

Ten years ago when the ice crop on the Hudson failed, the New York dealers were first compelled to visit Lake Champlain. Several local speculators made money at that time. The lesson was not lost. The dealers and speculators in Northern New York have been watching the state of things down the river and now that their harvest has come, it has found them ready to reap the advantage.

One lesson learned by the southern dealers was not lost on them. At the time, they were charged the highest prices for everything. Owners of teams charged them double, the sawmills raised the price of lumber, and the owners of straw stacks, figuratively speaking, became millionaires. This year the southern dealers are making contracts with local men and realizing that they can do better than if they go to the expense of putting up ice themselves and shipping it to New York and other southern points.

At Whitehall the ice men are arriving on every train, and the fever of speculation is running high. All sorts of combinations are being made—capital is combining with labor. New Yorkers will have ice even if they have to pay big prices.

While the excitement extends from Plattsburgh to Glens Falls, Whitehall seems to be the main point. However, dealers are cutting ice on Ballston Lake, Round Lake, Saratoga Lake, Glen Lake, Round Pond, Lake George, and Lake Champlain. Contracts for nearly 300,000 tons have been made, and every day adds more contracts to the number. In this vicinity (Glens Falls) and along Lake Champlain the ice is of good quality—clear, bright water ice, from 10 to 16 inches thick.

The Mutual Benefit Ice Company of New York has staked off a claim on Lake Champlain 200 feet wide and over a mile long. It is alongside the Delaware & Hudson Canal Company's coal trestle. Slides have been built, upon which the huge cakes are hoisted directly into the cars. About thirty cars a day are being shipped by this company at present. Next week they will begin shipping twenty cars a day to Philadelphia and twenty cars to New York.

Two miles from Whitehall is South Bay. It is here that the greatest activity prevails. This bay is a great arm of Lake Champlain. There are no currents here and the ice does not go out until late in the spring. The bay is about five miles long and one mile wide. Its shores are dotted with piles of lumber and ice houses, and sheds are being put together as rapidly as hosts of carpenters can work. There is a great demand for lumber, and mills there cannot get it out fast enough. Labor is also in demand. Any man in want of work can get it. For hauling the ice in the channels, cutting, plowing, etc., the men are paid at the rate of $1.50 per day; for inside work in the cars, $1.75 per day…

A few dealers from the south are not making contracts, but are putting up ice on their own account. Shipments are being made by rail from Plattsburgh, Port Henry, Putnam, Dresden, Crown Point, Whitehall and other points…Ex-Congressman H. G. Burleigh, of Whitehall, and Smith M. Weed, of Plattsburgh, will put up 100,000 tons near the same place where Mr. Burleigh owns a large amount of real estate. They will erect an elevator and have the latest improved machinery.

The ice men are flocking up to Lake Champlain, but some way or other seem to give Lake George the go-by. Here is this charming sheet of water closer by many miles to New York than is Lake Champlain, and yet to date but very few tons of ice have been cut there. ◾

Saturday October 25, 1924. The mountains, the forest, the dirt roads all turned wild in the eyes and voices of these touring campers from their running board outlook.

Courtesy The Town of Webb Historical Society

♛ LAKE PLACID CHILDHOOD

By Leila M. Wells, *York State Tradition*, Spring 1972

ake Placid was my home until the spring of 1889. I still remember my grief when we moved to Keene Valley. I resolved that as soon as I was old enough, I would return. I never did return, however, except for occasional visits with relatives.

One of my earliest memories is of the brook between our house and Hank Summer's blacksmith shop. I remember trying to follow my brother down a slanting rock to the water's edge. He was barefooted, but I had teased my mother to let me wear my Sunday shoes all day. They weren't "Sunday shoes" after that. I slipped into the brook and then walked home in the dusty road. Mother dried them on a brick on the back of the kitchen stove. My brother was older than I and I was a tomboy, so I got into many similar scrapes.

John Brown's grave site. *A Seneca Ray Stoddard photo. Courtesy Maitland DeSormo Collection*

We lived in a frame story-and-a-half house built in the spring and summer of 1882. My parents moved into it just before my sister was born in early September. To one side of the house were the well and the vegetable garden. On the street corner were my mother's flowers. She was really the first florist in Lake Placid. Every summer her flowers were in great demand. When President and Mrs. Grover Cleveland came to the Grand View on their honeymoon, my mother sent them a box of flowers—sweet peas, nasturtiums, and double poppies. They wore them at the Grand Ball that night. A third bouquet was for Mrs. Cleveland's mother, who was with them. The next day they came to thank Mother personally for her thoughtfulness.

My first memory of church services must be of a time when I was nearly six years old. I must have attended before, but one Sunday stands out clearly. My father carried my sister on his shoulders, and my brother and I trudged along behind him and my mother. It was a long walk from our house to the White Church, which is now the Grange Hall. I have no memory of the minister, but the choir is distinct. The only Negro family left in the town of North Elba composed the whole choir.

When I first started to go to school, I had to walk to the Red Schoolhouse, which has since disappeared, like so many buildings of my childhood in Lake Placid. One teacher taught all the grades from the "big boys" down to the "beginners." A Mr. Bruce was my first teacher, and I was afraid of him. The next year, Mrs. May Stickney opened a "select school" on the second floor of a large boathouse on the shore of Mirror Lake. We had to go over a "bridge" to reach the school door. I was happier here.

The next year a new school was built almost across the road from my home. It was a one-room school, though my father had urged at least a two-room building, for he knew that Lake Placid was growing. This school had "bought" desks, though they had to use several handmade ones to accommodate the large number of pupils.

Nearly every child in Lake Placid had whooping cough and measles that winter, but school wasn't closed. When one started coughing, he left the room until it was over. Sometimes nearly a dozen would be coughing at the same time. Measles were different. We couldn't go to school, and nearly everyone had them. There were six at our house, four children and my mother's two brothers, all in bed at the same time.

I was born in the John Brown farmhouse on October 29, 1880, during a heavy snowstorm. I've always had a sentimental feeling for the Abolitionist. I think it must be because of my birthplace. I learned some of my letters by tracing the letters forming his name, which is chiseled into the big rock near his grave. Although my parents moved from the farm before I was two years old, I went back often, for my uncle and aunt owned it. Souvenir hunters nearly ruined the headstone on John Brown's grave until my uncle made a wooden case with a glass front to fasten over the stone. One of my cousins and I used to go down to the brook and gather pebbles to scatter over the grave for the tourists to carry away as souvenirs. Some had them polished and set in rings or brooches, proudly explaining, "The stone comes from John Brown's grave."

As children we were gum chewers like the children of today, but our gum grew on spruce trees. During the winter my father used to go "gumming." This meant traveling in the spruce woods usually on snowshoes with a canvas sack or pack basket on his back and a "spud." This was a funnel-shaped container with a long handle and a sharp edge. The gum oozes out of the bark and hardens, and when pried off the tree and cleaned makes delicious chewing. A "chew" of gum wasn't thrown away after one chewing. It was carefully hoarded, for it was hard to come by. Sometimes during the summer, when our supply of gum was low, we would go down to the sawmill and dig the gum off the logs on the skid-ways there.

My sister and I hoarded our pennies all one summer so we could have a "boughten" sled. It had a blue box with a little girl painted on it, and we always called that sled Marjorie Daw. Mostly, we slid downhill on "skippers." These were barrel staves with a post nailed on a small board nailed on that for a seat. The skippers were wonderful when there was a crust.

Older people had "double runners," which consisted of two sleds held together by a plank on which several could ride. We also had toboggans. The double runners and toboggans were mostly for the grown-ups. They

Three old so-called military roads and early coach highways crossed the Adirondack region from wide-ranging points. This Stoddard photograph shows a stagecoach going up Blue Mountain. *Courtesy Special Collections, Feinberg Library, SUNY College at Plattsburgh*

use to have sliding parties on moonlit nights and slide down Steven's Hill out on to Mirror Lake. If there wasn't much snow on the lake, they would go nearly all the way across.

My childhood memories wouldn't be complete if I didn't mention the dancing bears. Some time each summer two men with a large brown or black bear would come through Lake Placid. At first, I used to run for my mother, for I was afraid, but before they had passed too far, curiosity would draw me from my hiding place and I would be following along with other children "to see the bear climb the telegraph pole." That was part of the song the men sang to the bear to make him stand up and dance. The last traveling bear I saw was in 1906.

The tin peddler, like the traveling bear, has vanished. Sometimes the peddler had an enclosed box on his wagon and sometimes just a rack with tin ware hung on the frame or stacked inside. He could be heard quite a distance away because of the rattle of his wares. Some of the more prosperous ones were really traveling stores and were always welcomed, for they usually had something different from the local stores.

"Old Blind Foster" was the broom peddler. I never knew where his home was, but he used to come every spring or summer, selling the brooms that he had made during the winter. Twenty-five cents was the usual price for the best broom.

"The tally-ho is coming!" Everyone who heard the horn rushed out to see it pass. I didn't know much about transportation in those days, but I knew that the "city people" always came by tally-ho—as the large stage coachers were called—or by the three-seated mail stage, which came every other day from the railroad station at Westport. Sometimes they would stay overnight in Elizabethtown. The stagecoaches, usually drawn by four horses, came along much like the western stagecoaches in today's movies. There were almost always people on top, and someone with a large horn announced their coming in a more or less musical manner. A heavy wagon usually followed, miles behind, piled high with trunks and valises and other baggage.

I remember the morning that Mirror Lake House burned. There was only a bucket brigade. Men threw the water on the burning sides and dodged back to escape the steam and falling hot water. Many suffered burns because they couldn't move fast enough to escape.

I think the first pageant held on Mirror Lake was during the summer of 1888. It was a sight long to be remembered. Nearly everyone who owned a boat or a canoe was on the lake that night. The boats were beautifully decorated and lighted. Japanese lanterns were used extensively every-where—along the shore, on the boats, and wherever there was a chance to hang one. It was a beautiful sight. The reflections in the lake made it a fairyland of beauty. ▰

A LOG CABIN SPEAKS

By Marjorie L. Porter, *North Country Life*, Fall 1955

The story of the Adsit Cabin near Willsboro and the pioneer family who built it.

Sometimes people say, "That cabin has a comfortable look." And why not? Nobody can set in one spot for 177 years and not have some kind of a special look, even if it's just a sort of "I belong here" one. And I was raised of big pines that've been around here a sight longer than that. You shoulda been here then!

Maybe it's a good thing I like this piece of land so much and the things I see when I look out over the lake to New England, where my folks came from, or when I look down on Ligonier Point and across Perue Bay, lifting my eyes to the hills.

"Twas a young couple, newly married, as made me their first home, right in the wilderness, too. They were named Samuel and Phebe Purdy

Logs were a common building material throughout the Adirondacks. Ben Stickney's cabin on the north shore of First Lake, Fulton Chain. *Courtesy Town of Webb Historical Society*

Adsit, and my, my, but she was pretty—and smart, and strong, besides. I heard them say as how his grandfather John had sailed across from England just one hundred years before we had the year without no summer, 1816. He struck his country where the Connecticut River hits into the ocean and made himself and his family a home up near Stamford, Connecticut. Lots of things happened in the American colonies before his son Samuel had growed up (he was borned in this country in 1719). Guess they liked the name Samuel, 'cause there was a second Sam—the one that wed Phebe. Sometimes seems if Providence arranged to have a new batch of upstanding young fellers ready for fighting the wars that come along. Sam had to say goodbye to Phebe soon he got me fixed up for living in and go off to fight in Peter Van Ness's regiment in the Revolution. Guess he woulda been kinda discouraged if he'd known his grandson was going to help in the militia at the Battle of Plattsburgh in 1814 and his great grandson had to fight in the War of Rebellion.

I never knew just how it come that Samuel the second (he was born at Stamford in 1757) took up land on Willsboro Point, but of course he and Phebe didn't want to live with the old folks after they were married. Maybe they had found out that the 3,000 acres granted to John Montressor, Francis Mee, and Robert Wallace on what they called Ligonier Point was an English patent of June 6, 1765, and was open to settlement as long as the Colony of New York didn't take any stock in English grants. The three men who first held the land also owned the Four Brothers Islands, which had been named by the French, "Des Isles des Quatres Vents," and an island called Schuyler not far to the north. Anyhow, Samuel the second and pretty Phebe were the ones who picked out a sightly spot to set me on—and here I be!

'Twant long before Sam went off with his regiment, so Phebe went back to her folks for a while. Her son Jacob was born at Stamford in 1780. She had two other sons named Samuel and Keziah. Perhaps they were born right here—I can't seem to recollect that part. Anyhow, one of their boys, Samuel the third, lived right north of here with his wife, Olive Green Adsit, and Jacob took me over for his family—and a big one it was, as he had two wives. He and Hannah Hale Adsit had two babies here, Jacob and Julia. Then he and Sally Moore Adsit (they became man and wife about 1806) had fourteen young 'uns—and I took care of them all, and they was snug come hail or high water.

They was a mess o' children for Sally to cook and sew for, and no easy ways to do it, neither. Her spinning wheel did a rack of turning and her loom like to banged through the puncheon floor, what with her throwing the beater over. Better take a look at my fireplaces and ponder on how Sally managed to boil and stew and bake for such a crowd.

She was mothering Jacob's first two and had three of her own when he had to march to Plattsburgh with the militia to protect the frontier and then take a hand in the Battle of Plattsburgh. He could have been one of them who held up the Britishers to keep them from crossing the "bloody Saranac." I recollect one of the boys having words with Sally about going through the woods alone to find out what had happened during the battle. The booming of the cannon had stopped. He went, too! And best of all, he brung back tidin's of victory for Macomb and Macdonough.

Well, things were different after the War of 1812. Men folks hereabouts didn't have to be ready to leave home any minute to march north to the border with their "journey cake" and their old muzzleloaders. They could set their minds to clearing the land and rafting timbers to the St. Lawrence, and making potash to sell for good hard cash, and raising wheat for whiskey, and cutting staddles and making ploughed fields. You should of seen the plow Jacob used, all wood with just an iron point. It jerked this way and that when the oxen pulled it over crooked roots around pine stumps.

But 'twant all work and no play, sir, for in them days Joe Call, the Lewis giant, was rassling champions what come from fur off to challenge him and showing his power at some raisings of mills and barns. He could raise a big ridgepole timber across his shoulders and put it in place, when nine or ten men together had a time doing it. They was rasslin' matches and the ring o' rassle hereabouts and camp meetings, too. Ever hear of Lorenzo Dow, the preacher? Crazy Dow, they called him. He had lodging with folks around here when he was holding meetings up this way. And every wedding was a time for jollification, eating and dancing, and passing the fug around—maybe a day or two of celebration!

Jacob and Sally's children were growing up and getting some schooling in the neighborhood, for they was a number of settlers on the Point by then—the Hoskins family, the Strouds, Bacons, Pattersons, and Barneys—all God-fearing folks. They held Sunday service in the schoolhouse before they was a church in the settlement on the Boquet. My! My! Brings back old times!

They was the awful setbacks of 1800 and freeze to death, when scarce any crops was raised. Snow fell every month and drought kept up till late October. Seed was hard to come by them days. But Jacob and Sally were good managers. I recall as how Jacob was always a figuring, figuring. Seemed to hanker to puzzle out sums and do problems nobody else would tackle, not even his boys.

Well, I don't want to weary you with my remembering, so I'll get on. Harvey, the youngest but two of Sally's fourteen, was the one to call me home, after that. His good wife died here in 1900, and one o' her daughters, Mary E.—she was Mrs. Fowler—looked out of my windows near 40 years before she went across the lake to Burlington to live. It was Mary's youngest brother Horace's daughter Laura who was the last baby borned here, and I don't like to think of no more young 'uns growing up here with my walls around them. I recollect one of Mary's sons, Zell, I think they call him, dressed up in the wedding suit worn by Phebe's Sammy way back in Revolutionary days, and had his picture took, hat and all, a-standing by a cheer given to a bride in the family back in 1796. She had six of them cheers and they were good ones, too.

Bad times come to me after Harvey Adsit's wife died. Bad times had already come to the Point, in a way of thinking, for they had stopped cutting stone at the limestone quarries, Bird's Eye, they was called, and the neighborhood, where they was a post office, telegraph office, three or four boarding houses, a general store, and one of the finest wharfs on Lake Champlain, had sort of gone to pieces. Even the old Oakes Ames docked out here in her palmy days. They were about 300 men a-working at the quarries along in the 1860's and '70's. Looked like I was a going to be forgotten, too, for I was covered up with clapboards and my chimbly went to pieces and fool building was done on to me. Even it hadn't been for a stranger to these parts, a Dr. Van Derwerker from New York City, you might never of known about me.

Just so happened that the doctor bought this place, about 60 acres at that time, in 1927. Investigation, he was surprised to find me a good sound dwelling of hewed logs under them clapboards, and he was glad and made up his mind to something. He got real set on having me look as nice as I was a hundred years or more ago, so that folks could see me and think about how the Adsits and other pioneers lived. And the doctor got to feeling kinda as if I had belonged to his people and he was real fond of me. You can see what a good chimbly he had made for me and everything. He took pictures of me, front and back, too, to show visitors who had never been on Willsboro Point, and he come to set great store by me.

Now, other folks take care of me, seeing how their new house is just next-door. They had an idea just lately to put back in the old room where so many babies was borned some of the same kind of fixings as was used when I was a young feller. They aim to have the old log cabin look somewhat as 'twas when Sally and Jacob lived here, and they'd like for you to look around and imagine you're visiting me in them times.

If I could talk your way, I'd tell you about some of the arguing I heard inside my walls when come time for the men folk to go to war, Samuel the second in 1778, Jacob in 1814, and Harvey in Civil War days. Their women folk didn't like fighting any more an' you do. One of the boys went west, too, and that made a lot of talk. And being on the lake meant some drowning and narrow escapes on sloops and schooners way back.

But as I see it, changing times don't always mean better folks. My folks, men, women, and children was the salt of the earth and I recall a piece that says what I'm feeling: "For there is room enough for spring's return, for lilac evenings and rising moon, and time enough for autumn's idle days, when soul is ripe for immorality. And there when winter comes with smoldering dusk to kindle rosy flames upon the hearth, and hang his starry belt upon the night, one firelight room is large enough for heaven, for all we know of wisdom and of love, and the eternal welfare of the heart." ▰

T.R.'S MIDNIGHT RIDE

By C. R. Roseberry, *York State Tradition*, Winter 1969

The Adirondack Museum recently acquired the buckboard sur-
rey, which in 1901 carried Theodore Roosevelt over the last lap
of his 35-mile dash out of the Adirondack wilderness to a train
at North Creek waiting to carry him to Buffalo in an attempt
to reach the bedside of President McKinley while he was still
alive. Since that famous ride, the surrey has been kept as a
prized possession of the family of Michael J. "Mike" Cronin,
who drove the last lap, sixteen miles from his Aiden Lair Lodge
to North Creek.

"Cronin became a sort of national hero," wrote Alfred L. Donald-
son in his History of the Adirondacks. *"He was written to and*
interviewed about it until gradually evolved a recital of the
adventure that connected some thrilling detail with every bump
and turn in the road. He also gave away more souvenir horse
shoes than his team of blacks could have worn in a lifetime."

Following is the full story of the dramatic incident in Adirondack
history and the events leading up to it as it was told (with some
abridgement and a few minor alterations) by C. R. Roseberry
in the Buffalo Evening News *in June, 1958.*

Two revolver shots broke into the Bach counterpoint that was being played softly on the pipe organ in the ornate Temple of Music. President William McKinley—portly, pious, and handsome—stiffened, stared in blank amazement at the young man with whom he had expected to shake hands, then slumped into the arms of those nearest him.

It was President's Day at Buffalo's Pan-American Exposition: Friday, September 6, 1901. McKinley had insisted upon going through a brief hand shaking reception for the public. Leon Czolgosz had taken his place in line, wrapped his right hand in a handkerchief and cocked a .32 revolver beneath the fake bandage, under the very noses of the guards.

The wounded president was given emergency surgery and taken to the home of John G. Milburn, head of the Exposition, at 1168 Delaware Avenue, where he and Mrs. McKinley were guests.

As in every case where a president's life is in danger, the urgent question was: "Where is the vice-president?"

Vice-President Theodore Roosevelt was as near the Canadian border at the opposite corner of the state as McKinley was at this. He was on Isle LaMotte at the north end of Lake Champlain. He had gone there to address the Fish and Game League, with Nelson W. Fisk, ex-governor of Vermont, as host at his summer home. When TR finished his address, he mopped his brow, flashed his famous grin, and went into the house for a change of clothes and a brief rest. While he was freshening up, Fisk summoned him to the telephone. Long distance from Buffalo, he said.

As Roosevelt listened, his jaw muscles tightened and his eyes filled with tears. When he hung up, he clapped his hands to his head and exploded two words: "My God!"

That evening the private yacht, which had brought TR up the lake from Burlington, Vermont, took him back. A special train was waiting on the Rutland Railroad. It took him to Buffalo around the north end of Lake Champlain and down through Malone and Watertown, then switched to the New York Central. He arrived in Buffalo on Saturday, September 7, shortly before 1 PM, and then went directly to McKinley's bedside.

The Vice-President remained in Buffalo until Tuesday night, a guest at the Delaware Avenue home of Ansley Wilcox. McKinley's condition gave every appearance of steady improvement. That day, upon emerging from the sick room, TR told reporters: "The President's recovery is assured."

He said he had decided to leave Buffalo that night and hinted that he might go to Oyster Bay to wait out McKinley's recovery. He had no such intention, however. He headed straight for the Adirondacks.

The invitation to speak at Isle LaMotte had fitted neatly into his vacation plans. James MacNaughton, with whom he had become friendly while governor, had invited the Roosevelt family to spend September in a cottage he owned at the Tahawus Club in the heart of the Adirondack high peak area. Mrs. Roosevelt and the six children went on ahead, and he was to join them there after the Lake Champlain detour.

The Tahawus Club was 35 miles from the North Creek railhead and was reachable only by horse-drawn rigs over the most primitive mountain roads.

Traveling only with his secretary, William Loeb, Roosevelt boarded a train late that Tuesday night at Buffalo and got off at Albany on Wednesday at 5:15 AM. He had breakfast in the Union Station. Then he boarded a 7 AM train on the Delaware and Hudson for North Creek, leaving Loeb in Albany as an anchor to windward. At North Creek he hired a rig and driver for the long, rough jaunt up to the Tahawus Club, arriving in the evening.

Roosevelt wanted to climb Mt. Marcy, the state's highest mountain. He had climbed the Matterhorn during his first honeymoon with ill-fated Alice Lee.

On Thursday, September 12, the headlines said: "McKinley Out of Danger." And at the Tahawus Club, a hiking party set off up the Calamity Brook trail bound for Lake Colden, a picturesque lake, which snuggles against the steep avalanche-scarred wall of Mt. Colden. It was a distance of six miles. Mrs. Roosevelt went along, as did some of the older Roosevelt children. There were two guides—Noah La Casse and Ed Dimick.

They camped overnight on the shore of Lake Colden. During the night it began to rain.

Friday, September 13. A typical Adirondack drizzle persisted at Lake Colden. Roosevelt said to La Case: "Noah, I hate to ask a guide to pull out in this kind of weather, but I would like to go as far as U.S. Grant went, if I go no farther." (At timberline on the way up Marcy is Grant's Rock, to which General Grant is reputed to have climbed before turning back.)

La Casse said he was game. At 9:30 AM, Mrs. Roosevelt and the children set off on the return hike to the Tahawus Club, with Dimick as their guide. The rest of the men branched off up the steep Marcy trail, which follows up the brawling Opalescent River. TR and his party climbed rapidly despite the rain and mud, reaching the summit in three hours.

The climbers had left their duffle behind on the margin of tiny Lake Tear-of-the-Clouds for the final assault on the pinnacle of Marcy. Roosevelt and his companions scrambled back down that far for lunch.

While they were eating, they saw a man laboring up the trail toward them. "Why, it's Harrison Hall," said La Cassee. "What could he want?"

Hall, a Tahawus Club guide, joined them silently and handed Roosevelt two pieces of paper, urgent messages from Buffalo. President McKinley had taken a turn for the worse.

The party started down the mountain almost at once. They covered the 12 miles back to the clubhouse in three hours and 15 minutes.

Finding no further news, Roosevelt decided to wait until morning before starting for Buffalo. His secretary, Loeb, had chartered a special D. & H. train at Albany and had it waiting, steam up, at the station in North Creek.

At 10 PM another telegram was relayed to the clubhouse saying that McKinley was dying.

With that, Roosevelt bolted a quick lunch, took a single bag with him, and began the midnight ride that became so famous. When his family and friends tried to dissuade him from trying to make the trip over the hazardous road in the dark, he is reported to have said he would go on foot if no rig were supplied.

Will Loeb, arriving at North Creek with the special train, had arranged for a relay system of three separate carriages and drivers to rush the Vice-President from the Tahawus Club to North Creek. David Hunter, the quiet and efficient superintendent of the Tahawus Club, took the first relay— ten miles over a rutty, soupy road down to the Tahawus "Lower Works." He harnessed the only available horse, a hefty bay workhorse, and hitched him to a buggy. They started down the road at 10:30 PM. It took two hours to cover that first ten miles.

It was one of the inkiest black nights the Adirondacks had ever seen. There was a drizzling, misty rain most of the way. It was "an utterly reckless dash through the darkness—a race with death in more senses than one," wrote Alfred L. Donaldson. "That the nation did not lose two presidents that night was little short of miraculous."

At Tahawus, Orrin Kellogg was waiting with a team hitched up to a two-seated surrey. Kellogg was a regular driver for the Club. Roosevelt paused ten minutes at Tahawus, long enough to drink a cup of coffee and make a phone call to North Creek. Then Roosevelt got in the back seat, and Kellogg let him take an old raincoat of his to protect him from the spattering mud.

This relay, from Tahawus to Aiden Lair, a distance of nine miles, consumed two hours and 20 minutes, during which time (at 2:15 AM) President McKinley died. Today a bronze tablet in a roadside boulder on Route 28-N marks the approximate place where Theodore Roosevelt actually became president.

But Roosevelt did not know that McKinley had died. Although the news was promptly telephoned to Aiden Lair, nobody there told him while he was changing vehicles.

Michael Cronin was a gregarious, handsome Irishman, who was proprietor of the big summer hotel known as Aiden Lair—all there was to the community. TR had stopped there frequently on Adirondack trips while governor, and the two were good friends. Mike elected to do the driving himself on the last lap.

Cronin owned a fine pair of black Morgan carriage horses. Both he and the horses knew the sixteen-mile stretch of dirt road from there to North Creek like a book.

Orrin Kellogg drove his passenger up to Aiden Lair at 3 AM. The hotel guests were all gathered around to witness the historic occasion. No time was wasted at this stop, Roosevelt merely transferring from one carriage to the other. They were off at 3:05.

Mike Cronin decided not to tell Roosevelt that McKinley was already dead, figuring that his state of mind was already agitated enough.

Cronin kept his horses going at a rapid clip. Despite the darkness and rain, he made a record for the sixteen miles that never was equaled by another horse-drawn vehicle—one hour and 41 minutes. Occasionally he would turn and ask TR if he should slow up. TR would reply, "Keep up the pace," or "Hurry up! Go faster!"

The carriage came careening down the main street of North Creek at 4:45 AM, the black horses steaming and mud-bespattered. At almost one leap, Roosevelt vaulted from the surrey to the steps of the railroad car, the private coach of a vice-president of the D. & H. Only then was he handed the telegram, signed by John Hay, Secretary of State, reading: "The President died at 2:15 this morning."

The abbreviated train made a fast run down out of the mountains to Albany. At the lower levels it was extremely foggy. On one straight-away stretch, the locomotive ran down a handcar being pumped by two section men. The men jumped to safety and the handcar was knocked into the ditch. The train was held up fifteen minutes while its crew went back to investigate.

At Albany there was a six-minute stop—long enough for the coach to be uncoupled and switched to New York Central rails, where it was hitched to a fast locomotive. The blinds were kept tightly closed on the coach, and Roosevelt did not show himself, although a large crowd of citizenry was on hand.

The special was given clear blocks all across the state, and Roosevelt remained hidden behind drawn blinds past city after city. It covered a mile in 42 seconds on one stretch west of Oneida. It passed through Rochester at 12:15 PM and pulled into Buffalo shortly after 1 o'clock.

At the Delaware Avenue home of Ansley Wilcox, at 3:35 PM on Saturday, September 14, TR ended his bad week by taking the oath of office. And Mark Hanna, the Republican national chairman, commented wryly: "Now look, that damned cowboy is President of the U.S." ◼

President Cleveland fishing. *Reprinted from "Frank Leslie's Illustrated Newspaper"*

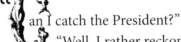 # PRESIDENT CLEVELAND IN THE ADIRONDACKS

Author unknown, *York State Tradition*, Summer 1968
Reprinted from *Frank Leslie's Illustrated Newspaper* for August 22 and August 29, 1885

"Can I catch the President?"

"Well, I rather reckon you kin, if I drive you."

The eager querist was an artist for *Frank Leslie's Illustrated Newspaper*. The man who "rather reckoned" he could, was no less a personage than Jake Cone, the celebrated driver, agent, guide, and general factotum of the Adirondacks. The place was the Plattsburgh railway station, where the drivers of mountain stages congregate to contend for and divide among themselves each installment of newly-arrived passengers, bearing their captives away to distant lairs and undiscovered lakes among the hills.

It was a bright August morning—the morning that President Cleveland went into the woodsy Adirondacks for a well-earned and sensible vacation. He had but one companion—Dr. Ward, of Albany—and traveled at a speed which baffled the newspapermen and hand-shakers. In fact, it was evident that, through the past few months' experience with office seekers, the President had attained a degree of skill in eluding visitors, which made the task of finding him very much like a chase after the traditional will-o'-the wisp.

The artist, however, still pursued him. Bent upon stalking the President, our representative enlisted the services of the redoubtable Jake Cone immediately upon arriving in Plattsburgh.

Plattsburgh is connected with Ausable Station by a little railroad, on which semi-occasional trains run at the dizzy speed of twenty miles in an hour and a half.

The drivers, leaving their stages at Ausable, come down to Plattsburgh to meet passengers, where temporarily they are "agents," wearing official caps, smoking cigars, and giving themselves airs of great importance. Jake Cone was an interesting type of this class. He was a shred-faced Vermonter, who at one period of his life had driven stage in California, and had been a "pard" of the famous Hank Monk, who drove Horace Greeley over the Sierra Nevada at the imminent risk of his vertebrae. It was easy to see that Jake was no ordinary person, from the colossal cluster of diamonds attached to a brass chain, which he wore on his expansive shirtfront. At Ausable he underwent a complete metamorphosis from agent into driver, as he mounted his stage, and, with a grand flourish, started his horses on a gallop up the winding road, headed for the mountains.

No trace of the President yet! He had got half an hour's start at Ausable, where "buckboard" travel began, and was long since out of sight. Relays of horses awaited him at stations along the route, so that the chances of Jake Cone's overtaking him before nightfall were not great. However, Jake's nags scudded along at an exhilarating pace, and the scenery was superb.

"Grench's," which nestles at the foot of the great White Face Mountain, with the bald, isolated Mount Catamount just opposite, was a particularly notable mountain nook about midway between Ausable and Prospect Lake. Great blue hills loomed up ahead, towering further and further into the clouds, which clung to their wooded summits like fleece.

Like to these vanishing clouds of mist, so vanished many of the artist's pet superstitions concerning the Adirondacks. For instance, he had loaded himself down with wraps, having heard much of the crisp, bracing air of the region. Well, at ten o'clock in the forenoon the thermometer stood at 86 degrees in the shade; by eleven it had crept up to 90; and before the day was over it came so near 100 that "there was no funning tit." And then, the wild animals—the deer, bear, elk, catamount, et cetera—where were they? From tales told in the city, the artist had innocently imagined that these untamed creatures of the forest were to be met with in droves in every glade, filling the mountains with their peculiar cries. As a matter of fact, the only wild animal seen during the whole journey was a curious one-horned beast, which, upon nearer approach, proved to be a pig in a poke!

At every log-cabined hamlet along the road the entire population turned out to meet the stage. The warm personal interest which these people manifested in the artist was surprising. At each place, he would be surrounded by twenty or thirty bold mountaineers, every one eager to become his guide, philosopher and friend. Everywhere he was followed and stared at in a manner which seemed to him unaccountable. Finally, it transpired that Jake Cone, who had been secretly disappointed at not securing the President himself for a passenger, had been passing off our artist upon the confiding villagers as the Secretary of State.

Further and further into the mountains wound the picturesque road. "Now for genuine backwoods scenes and types of character," said the artist to himself. In a romantic wood appeared a luxurious tent, with a carpeted floor, mirrors, feather beds, and other appurtenances of an effete civilization. Near this tent sat a lanquid swell, in knickerbockers and patent leather shoes, sipping iced wine from a crystal goblet, precisely as if he had been at Delmonico's or on the roof of the Casino. He was a type of summer backwoodsman of the Adirondacks.

The novice in this region is known by his elaborate sporting outfit and his five or six Saratoga trunks. Some of these amateur mountaineers actually wear dead-leaf colored suits of clothes, in order, as they allege, that they may get closer to the deer when stalking. It is needless to say that these sportsmen do not play great havoc amongst the game. The experienced camper-out brings little more than a gripsack.

The stage ride lasted all day and covered forty-six miles. The President was not overtaken on the road; but at sundown, by the sylvan shores of Prospect Lake, he was discovered taking his ease at his inn. Here, in one of the inmost valleys of the Adirondacks, appears, as if by enchantment, a fully equipped and fashionable summer hotel, quite Saratoga-like with its gray parlors and verandas thronged with promenaders in the correct toilets of town. Only the supper menu, on which jerked beef, beefsteak, hot biscuits and huckleberries figured most prominently, suggested the mountains. Evidently there is more than one way of "camping out in the Adirondacks," and the President has chosen the most comfortable for his short period of rest and recreation. Without undue intrusion upon this pleasant temporary retirement from the public gaze, our artist has faithfully pictured the novel sights and adventures of his enterprising journey. ▰

THREE LITERARY GREATS ON AMPERSAND BAY

By Lee Knight, *York State Tradition*, Spring 1963

One of the most scenic lakes in the Adirondacks is Lower Saranac Lake, located about a mile from Saranac Lake village. At the northeastern terminus of the lake is Ampersand Bay, which like the rest of the lake has an interesting history.

The lake is a product of the glacial age, the Lower Saranac Lake basin having been dammed by sand deposits, which form the shore of Ampersand Bay. For many years, the lake was important for transportation, being part of a system of lakes and rivers used to carry people to various parts of the Adirondacks. It was first used by the Indians who visited the region for hunting purposes, and who called Lower Saranac, "The Lake of the Clustered Stars." Although there are some Indian legends concerning Lower Saranac, apparently the Indians never did more than travel through the lake.

The Indians were followed by the famed Adirondack guides with their parties, and the loggers. For many years before roads were built, stagecoaches would bring visitors to Martin's Hotel on Ampersand Bay, and from there, the guides would transport the visitors in their guide boats up the lake and through the system of rivers and lakes, however far into the wilderness the party might wish to travel. Later, roads were built, and Lower Saranac, while no longer so important for transportation, remains a popular source of recreation.

Among the many visitors to Ampersand Bay on the Lower Saranac were three popular writers: Ralph Waldo Emerson, Robert Louis Stevenson, and Mark Twain. The three writers either quartered or visited at three different points on Ampersand Bay.

The first of the three to visit Ampersand Bay was Ralph Waldo Emerson, the writer-philosopher-poet-lecturer from Cambridge, Massachusetts. Emerson came to this region as part of a group of distinguished men from Cambridge, brought here by the painter, William James Stillman, who had previously spent a good deal of time in the Adirondacks painting. The group also included James Russell Lowell, the poet; Louis Agassiz, the botanist; and John Holmes, the brother of Oliver Wendell Holmes. Stillman tried to get the poet, Henry Wadsworth Longfellow, and Justice Oliver Wendell Holmes to come, but neither of them cared to make the trip. The group traveled to Keenseville by train, and from there took the stagecoach to Martin's Hotel on Ampersand Bay, which was the terminus of the stagecoach route. After spending the night, the group prepared to begin their trip. Emerson described the beginning in his poem, "The Adirondacks."

"At Martin's beach/We chose our boats; each man a boat and guide, /Ten men, ten guides, our company all told.

"Next morn, we swept with oars the Saranac, /With skies of benediction, to Round Lake,/Where all the sacred mountains drew around us,/Tahawus, Seward, MacIntyre, Baldhead,/And other titans without muse or name."[1]

The group continued on to Folensby Pond, where they set up camp and remained for about a month before returning to Cambridge. In his writings, Stillman wrote of Emerson's reaction to the Adirondacks, "To Emerson, as to most men who are receptive to Nature's message, the forest was the overpowering fact."[2] Stillman also wrote:

"But among the memories which are the only realities left to it, this image of Emerson claiming his kinship with the forest stands out alone, and I feel as if I had stood for a moment on a mount of transfiguration, and seen, as if in a vision, the typical American, the noblest in the idealization of all the race."[3]

One can find Emerson's reaction in reading his complete poem, "The Adirondacks," and an enjoyable first-hand account of the Philosopher's Camp can be found in Stillman's work, *The Autobiography of a Journalist.*

On October 3, 1887, Robert Louis Stevenson arrived in Saranac Lake to spend the winter. He and his wife had been planning to spend the winter in Colorado, but fearing that the long trip might affect his health, and that the altitude of Colorado Springs might affect Mrs. Stevenson's health, they decided to winter at Saranac Lake. In 1887, the Trudeau Sanitarium had been open only for three or four years, and it was only during Stevenson's stay that the railroad was completed to Saranac Lake.

It is commonly thought that Stevenson did not enjoy the Adirondacks. He thought the area was barren and cold, and described his residence, the Baker Cottage as "The house in the eye of many winds," for he found it to be quite drafty. But he did find the mountain air to be invigorating. At one point he remarked, "The hill air is inimitably fine," and on another occasion he wrote, "On such a fine frosty night, with no wind and the thermometer below zero, the brain works with much vivacity."[4]

During his stay in Saranac Lake, Stevenson was very active, taking daily walks and skating frequently. Stevenson did not socialize much while in the Adirondacks, but he did enjoy visiting Mr. and Mrs. Louis Ehrich at their camp on Ampersand Bay. This camp was located on the northern side of the bay where the present "Pinehurst" camp is located. Stevenson enjoyed the Ehrichs because of their informality.

After leaving Saranac Lake in the middle of April, the Stevensons returned to New York City for a short stay. While in New York, Stevenson spent an afternoon visiting on a park bench in Washington Square with the American writer, Mark Twain, who was soon to visit Ampersand Bay himself.

While Stevenson was in the Adirondacks during the winter months and wrote of the coldness and bleakness, Mark Twain only spent summer months there and wrote of the cool climate and beautiful surroundings. During the summer of 1901, Twain resided at a two-story camp close to the water's edge on the south side of Ampersand Bay. He named the camp "The Lair," and in a letter to friends he wrote, "Everybody knows what a lair is, and it is a good and unworn name. Lairs do generally contain dangerous animals, but I bring tame ones to this one."[5]

In a letter to his friend, Rev. Joseph Twitchell, Twain described his life on Ampersand Bay.

"I am on the front porch (lower one, main deck) of our little bijou of a dwelling house. The lake edge is so nearly under me that I can't see the shore, but only the water smallpoxed with rain splashes—for there is a heavy downpour. It is charmingly like sitting snuggled up on a ship's deck with the stretching sea all around—but very much more satisfactory, for at sea a rain storm is depressing, while here of course the effect engendered is just a deep sense of comfort and content. The heavy forest shuts us in on three sides—there are no neighbors.

"There are beautiful little tan-colored impudent squirrels about. They take tea, 5 PM (not invited) at the table in the woods where Jean does my typewriting, and one of them has been brave enough to sit upon Jean's knee with his tail curved over his back and munch his food. They come to dinner, 7 PM, on the front porch (not invited). They all have one name—Blennerhasset, from Burr's friend, and none of them answers to it except when hungry.

"We have been here since June 21st. For a little while we had some warm days, according to the family's estimate: I was hardly discommoded myself. Otherwise the weather has been of the sort you are familiar with in these regions: cool days and cool nights. We have heard of the hot wave every Wednesday, per the weekly paper—we allow no dailies to intrude. Last week through visitors also—the only ones we have had—Dr. Root and John Howells.

"We have the daily lake-swim; all the tribe, servants included (but not I), do a good deal of boating, sometimes with the guide, sometimes without him—Jean and Clara are competent with the oars. If we live another year, I hope we shall spend its summer in this house."[6]

Later in the summer, Walter H. Larom paddled across the bay to visit Twain. Larom no sooner got to the Lair when Twain began extolling the "beauty of the lakes and the mountains, the lights and shadows and the wonderful, life-giving air of the Adirondacks."[7] He then engaged Larom in conversation about the many canoe trips that it is possible to make over the many lakes and streams of the Adirondacks, and mentioned that he might like to make a canoe trip at some time. As Larom paddled away after completing his visit, Twain called out, "I see you do all the work in the bow and stern; well if I were going along, I'd take the middle seat."[8]

In the middle of September, it came time for Twain to leave the Adirondacks, and in a farewell note to his friends, the Duryeas, written on September 19, 1901, Twain wrote:

"Hail and farewell! It has been a paradise to us all summer. One doesn't need to go to the Swiss Lakes to find that condition."[9]

Of the three residences visited by Emerson, Stevenson, and Twain, only the Twain camp remains similar to what it was when Twain was there. Martin's Hotel has long been gone, and its grounds are now occupied by a beach, a field and private residence. The Ehrich camp has been extensively redone and added to. Ampersand Bay today is surrounded by homes and boat marinas, yet it is still the entrance to one of the most beautiful of Adirondack lakes, Lower Saranac, surrounded by the forests and mountains of the Adirondacks. The poet, Thomas Bailey Aldrich, who lived in Saranac Lake for three years, wrote to James Russel Lowell, "When all is said, there is a charm in the place. There is something in the air to heal the heart of sorrow."[10]

THE PHILOSOPHER'S CAMP

By Lee Knight, *York State Tradition*, Fall 1972

The Philosophers' Camp was adventure in outdoor living deep in the wilderness of the Adirondack Mountains. It was an outgrowth of what came to be known as "The Saturday Club," started in 1855 by a group of Boston and Cambridge poets, scholars, statesmen, scientists, artists, lawyers, and other distinguished men. These men met once a month at a dinner in Boston to exchange thoughts and ideas. Among them were Henry Wadsworth Longfellow, Nathaniel Hawthorne, John Greenleaf Whittler, Oliver Wendell Holmes, Ralph Waldo Emerson, James Russell Lowell, Charles Summer, William J. Stillman, and Louis Agassiz.

William J. Stillman was largely responsible for the expedition which led to the Philosophers' Camp. He was an artist and a traveler who specialized in landscapes and was therefore a lover of nature and the natural. He became acquainted with the Adirondacks through another painter, S. R. Griffin, who had visited the Saranac Lakes. He visited the region in 1856 and fell in love with the woods. That winter in Cambridge

Following the death of her grandfather, Marilyn Breakey returned to the site of her Adirondack roots. Breakey, like Cole's contributing writers, hankered to record history— for history's sake. *Courtesy Marilyn Breakey*

he interested some others in visiting the Adirondacks in the summer of 1857. This party consisted of Stillman, Lowell, Lowell's two nephews, Charles and James, Dr. Estes Howe, Lowell's brother-in-law, and John Holmes, the brother of Oliver Wendell Holmes. The party made a quick trip through the three Saranac Lakes, the Raquette River and Tupper Lake. Then the party returned to the village of Saranac Lake, and all except Stillman returned to Boston. Stillman went back to Raquette Lake, where he built a camp and spent the rest of the summer painting.

In the summer of 1858, the Philosophers' Camp, consisting of ten men from the Saturday Club plus their guides, spent most of the month of August deep in the wilds of the Adirondacks. The ten from Boston included the poets Emerson and Lowell, the scientist Louis Agassiz, Judge Ebenezer

Hoar, Professor Jefferies Wyman, John Holmes, Horatio Woodman, Dr. Binney, Dr. Estes Howe, and William Stillman.

Stillman tried to get Longfellow to go. Longfellow asked if Emerson was going to take a gun, and when told that Emerson was, he replied, "Then somebody will be shot."[1] Stillman felt, however, that the real reason behind Longfellow's refusal was that Longfellow and Emerson were of "antagonistic intellectuality."[2] Longfellow was refined, courteous, and cultured, with much self-control. Emerson was serene, but quite capable of antagonism and indignation, and was rigidly devoted to truth. Stillman wrote, "He brushed away contemptuously the beauties on which Longfellow spent the tenderness of his character."[3] In any event, Longfellow chose not to go with the group.

Stillman also tried to get Oliver Wendell Holmes to go, but Holmes loved Boston too much and was too involved with what was going on there to leave it for such a length of time.

Stillman was in charge of arranging the details for the party and therefore preceded them into the mountains. He reports an amusing incident, which he did not witness but heard about from other members of the party concerning their arrival in the Adirondacks. The rumor of the party's coming had preceded them, and at the village of Keeseville, a reception was held. The guest of honor was not Emerson or Lowell, but the botanist Louis Agassiz. It seems that Agassiz had turned down an offer from the French emperor to be keeper of the "Jardin des Plantes" and a senatorship, if he would live in Paris. The people of the small Adirondack community admired his desire to remain in America. They picked him out by comparing him with an engraved portrait they had, and all lined up to greet him, virtually ignoring the others in the party.

In the meantime, Stillman had gone into the wilderness and had chosen the site for the camp. It was on Follensbee Pond, named after a philosopher and hermit who had lived on its shores many years before. Though near the Raquette River, the pond was isolated from the Raquette by a swamp several miles wide and surrounded on three sides by hills covered with forests. It was forty miles from the nearest civilization, which was Martin's Hotel on Lower Saranac Lake. Stillman described the region as "a virgin forest, where the cracks of our rifles reached no other human ear."[4] There, with his guide, Stillman built a landing place and a bark camp and then returned to Martin's Hotel to meet the rest of the party.

The next day the party went up the lakes to the camp. Stillman had to wait for a new boat to be finished and thus did not leave till the afternoon. In his writings, he expresses his regret at not being able to see Emerson's first reactions to the wilderness.

After their arrival and settling in at the camp, their activities were varied. Stillman wrote, "In the main, our occupations were those of a vacation, to kill time and escape from the daily groove."[5] Some of the members would go off exploring, either hiking the region surrounding the camp or going off in a guide boat with a guide. Some went hunting and fishing, venison and fish being the staple food of the camp. Agassiz and Wyman were interested in the ecology and botany of the region. They examined soil samples, water samples and swamp samples. They dissected the animals that were caught or killed. Some members would go swimming. Most afternoons the group engaged in long discussions and talks about many varied subjects.

Emerson was fascinated by the Adirondack wilderness and appears to have enjoyed his visits there. Stillman apparently watched Emerson closely while in the woods, for his writings concerning the Philosophers' Camp are filled with comment and reflections concerning Emerson. Stillman wrote, "The rest of us were always at the surface of things—even the naturalists were only engaged with their anatomy; but Emerson in the forest or looking at the sunset from the lake seemed to be looking through the phenomena, studying them by their reflections on an inner speculum."[6]

During his stay in the Adirondacks, Emerson never fired his gun. Thus, Longfellow's prophecy did not come true. At first Emerson never even carried a gun. He neither hunted nor fished. He loved animals and did not want to harm them personally although he recognized the need to kill them for food for the camp. But as time went on, Emerson developed the desire to hunt and shoot a deer. Stillman went hunting with him and they came across two deer, but Emerson could not see either of them and they got away. Emerson never did get another chance to hunt and thus never did get a deer, a fact which he was no doubt later glad of.

Towards the end of August the members of the Philosophers' Camp came out of the woods and returned to their homes. During their meetings back in Cambridge in the fall, they decided to buy a tract of land in the Adirondacks, as isolated as possible. There they should build a permanent clubhouse. Stillman was selected to go back to Saranac Lake and make the purchase.

In Saranac Lake, Stillman asked the guides of the region for their suggestions. Some of them had been involved in making the official survey of the region and knew of just the place. It was a region known as Ampersand Pond. The land had just been forfeited to the State for failure to pay taxes and was therefore available. After examining the region in the snow, Stillman bought it. The Club thus obtained 22,500 acres for the sum of $600.

The following summer, Stillman brought a party of friends in and built a camp for the club. In his writings, he reports that the club meeting that summer was successful, but gives no details. None of the others who attended that summer left any record of it in their writings either. In the summer of 1859 there was a notable decline in interest, possibly because Stillman did not attend. He had gone to live in Europe. Again, no record of this meeting is available.

The Civil War brought about an end to the meetings at the Philosophers' Camp. Most of the members were very much involved in the affairs of the world. Their attention was largely centered on the war. The club ceased to exist, and the land was soon claimed by the State for non-payment of taxes.

Twenty-five years later, Stillman returned to the Adirondacks for a visit. He found that few people knew much about the Philosophers' Camp and that almost no one knew where it was. He wrote, "Like Troy, its site is unknown to all the subsequent generations of guides, and I doubt if in all the Adirondack country there is a man, except my old guide, Steve Martin, who could point out the place where it stood."[7] He was referring to the site at Follansbee Pond, which he considered to be the site of the camp.

He went with his guide to revisit it. In his writings, he reports that he could not recognize the place. The forest and been cut and reforested, and the fires of the lumber camps had burned through the region. A dam had been built on the Raquette River, which had flooded much of the land. Pike had been placed in the stream and had killed of much of the trout. For Stillman, the place had lost its charm. The Philosophers' Camp had passed on, and all that remained was the memory of this aspect. ▰

AN 1842 FISHING TRIP TO MOOSE RIVER

Unknown author, *York State Tradition*, Spring 1963

This account came from an unsigned manuscript given to Fort Stanwix Museum in the 1960s.

Early one morning in August, in the year '42, I was awakened by a queer noise at my chamber window, which at first I took for a tree whipping against the sash, but when I got my eyes partly opened and had collected my scattered senses, I recollected having agreed with four other young blades like myself to go on a fishing excursion about twelve miles from this place. The place we had chosen was Moose River, which raises somewhere up in this country and empties itself in the Black River at High Falls.

I went to the window and raised the sash and put my head out, but no sooner was it out than it was hit over the skull cap with a fishing rod, and a suppressed voice from below exclaimed, "Come, Charlie, put on them trousers of yours middling quick. It's after two o'clock, and we sha'n't get to the river before noon."

I told him I was on hand, and after some more conversation he departed to serve the rest of the company the same kind of sauce; in the course of half an hour we were on our way.

We sang a parting hymn as we left the village. On we went with hearts as light as our heads; each with a pack and pole and a good set of tackling. We arrived at our destination a little before noon, after wading in muck and mire, through brush and brake, over bush, rocks and fallen trees. We sat down to rest our weary limbs, and with keenly whetted appetites dispatched a part of the contents of our packs, to which was added a few handsome trout, caught in the river. Little did they think when they were snatching at the delicious bait that they were to be burnt at the stake to appease the craving appetites of a lot of harem scarum—but I am digressing.

As we were pushing up the river, we passed the hut of an Indian hermit. Some of the company had some marvelous tales to relate of him.

As near as I can recollect, this was his history. He had been there but a short time, as the newness of the hut showed, and no one knew whence

Guide George Abner Blakeman and Henry Nelson on their way to fish the south branch of the Moose River in today's Moose River Recreation Area, ca. 1900s. *Courtesy George Blakeman*

he came or the reason for his leaving his tribe and removing into the heart of a wilderness to lead the life of a hermit. He had been known, when fishermen applied to him for a night's lodging, to leave his hut and wander about the forest and perform many peculiar antics. He would raise his eyes towards heaven, and with his arms elevated would cry incoherently at intervals and then seem to settle down into a state of sorrow and despondency. He had never been known to enter into any rational conversation with anyone. He would be seen no more that night, nor would he make his appearance till after sunrise the next morning.

But we were not disposed to trouble the old man. When the sun hid his red face behind the trees, we were about two miles farther up the river, each with an accumulated load. We had passed several little shanties and we began to think we had passed them all when we saw one, about eight by ten, situated at the foot of a long bank that extended along the north side of the river, covered with a heavy growth of birch, hemlock, and spruce. The shanty's construction was even simpler than those belonging to the origins of our country. Two crotches were driven into the ground about eight feet apart and five feet high. A pole was placed across these, and from this to the ground was laid long strips of bark peeled from young spruce trees.

We gathered some hemlock boughs to make us a bed for the night; we built a log heap in front of the shanty and set fire to it. After having dressed our game and collected more wood, we laid ourselves on our bed of hemlock to enjoy the sweets of a night's rest in the woods.

Just as we had got nicely to snoozing, we were aroused by a horrid yell, followed by a noise somewhat resembling the laugh of a red-nosed baboon. I thought my time had come. I pictured to myself a long, slim, sly, ferocious panther (there have been many caught in these woods) stealing towards us with sharpened fangs and claws, and eyes gleaming fire, intent on the death of one or more of us. Then one of the companies, more experienced than the remainder of us, gave a hoot to answer the noise just heard. We asked him who was the father of such a screech as that. "Why," says he, "it's an owl."

Our fright being over, and there being one among us who was a good singer, we prevailed upon him to tune up his pipes and give us the best of his store. All joining in the chorus, we "made the rocks and hills of the dim woods ring with our songs of lofty cheer."

At last we were sound asleep. We had forgotten our fright, our songs and our toils; we had given ourselves up to that sleep god Morpheus, the true friend to beggar and king.

When we awoke, the cool and fragrant breeze of our August morning was fanning the light ashes into our faces. On attempting to move, we found our joints had lost their power, but after a deal of hard tugging they began to work, but they squeaked like the joints of a loom. After limping about a while, we got them in motion. We cooked our breakfast and went to our sport again.

We camped in our old quarters the second night, and then started for home. On nearing the hut of the old hermit, we saw him a few rods from his door. We quickened our pace and reached the door before him. On approaching his door—if it could be called by such a name, for it was only three loose boards set up in the doorway—he came up and closed it, but we had a glimpse of the contents of his habitation. There was a bedstead with a tick of straw and a few ragged bedclothes. A kettle hung over the fire in a fireplace made of limestone. The chimney of it was built of sticks and clay. There were no chairs of any kind. There were a couple of shelves on which were about half a dozen teacups, plates and spoons.

On being asked if he ever received visitors, he replied in very good English, "Yes, I have company sometimes," and pointing to an old and blasted hemlock that stretched out its crooked limbs, "Black man come and sit on that tree and wind his long tail round his leg and talk to me." To all our interrogatives he gave such wild distracted replies that we were not much at loss now to account for his leaving the haunts of rational beings.

After resting at the old man's hut about half an hour, we left him to his solitude and turned our noses towards home. When we had traveled about half the distance, we were threatened with a ducking. The distant thunder rolled. The edge of a black cloud appeared above the horizon, gradually increasing in length, breadth, thickness and blackness, gleaming forth streaks of lightning, and threatening a second submerging of our little world. In a short time the cloud had spread over one half of the heaven. The rain began to pour down like smoke and bulrushes. In five minutes we were soaked, but we trudged on with a determination not to halt till we found ourselves at our doorways.

But you perhaps will think the description of my travels rather long and dry. I admit it was long enough, but as to the dryness of it I would not say. Let time roll on, let new things turn to old and old things become new—I never shall forget my fishing excursion. ✖

THE MATTESONS AND THEIR SWEET MOUNTAIN HOME

By S. R. Leonard, Sr., *North Country Life*, Spring 1951

Stephen R. Leonard was born in the Oneida Community and always worked for Oneida Ltd., successor to Oneida Community when it changed from its social organization to a stock corporation in 1881. He served in positions of considerable responsibility in the company and for more than fifty years has been a member of its Board of Directors. Fishing, hunting, and camping have been his life-long hobbies.

David Beetle's book, "West Canada Creek," satisfied for me a long-felt wish to know better the history of the people along that stream. But also it stirred old memories and nostalgias, mostly about Morehouseville and the old Mountain Home in Hamilton County.

My first trip in to Morehouseville was in 1902, with Frank Primo, now long gone. We went by train to Prospect Station and by stage to Prospect, where we hired a rig. The 25-mile drive to Morehouseville was exciting for us, both office men just released for a two-weeks' fishing vacation in wilder country than we had known. We drove through Hinckley and Grant, where we heard that the State was surveying for a huge storage lake for the prospective barge canal and that the storage lake would nearly submerge Grant.

We went through the Ohio sandy stretch to the West Canada and across the bridge to Wilmurt, which had one or two houses, a store, and a post office. Next came Noblesboro, which had once been a busy little place but was then practically deserted. Fort Noble Mountain was impressive, boldly sitting between the north and south branches of the Creek. We crossed to the south branch, up the hill, past a few farms, dry and far apart, to Morehouseville and Henry Kreuzer's Hotel.

Morehouseville was a busy place, for Mr. Kreuzer was a lumberman and his hotel was full of lumberjacks. They were working a tract north of the river.

Primo and I were again at Kreuzer's the next summer (1903) when the terrible forest fires raged to the north. There was talk of drafting fire fighters from Morehouseville if the fires came any closer, and some of Kreuzer's men went anyway. Plenty of smoke came down our way.

That year I came to know a little of the Mountain Home, which seemed to be accommodating a great many fishermen. So, in 1907, when I was a little below par from an illness and my employer asked me where I would like to go for a month's vacation, I promptly said, "To the Mountain Home."

Early in May I packed my stuff in a blanket and by train and stage eventually arrived at the Mountain Home and received a hearty welcome from Joe and Mrs. Corriveau. Their name was then Caribou. It is probable that Joe didn't know the true spelling of it, for he could not read or write. It was still Caribou when I was there in 1922, but later it was understood to be Carriveau, and on his grave marker in Forest Hills Cemetery it is Corriveau.

The Mountain Home had been started by Frederick Becraft as early as 1850 and was first known as Becraft's Place. It was bought by Mr. and Mrs. O. B. Matteson of Utica about 1881. An addition was built on, and it became their summer home. The story of the Mountain Home and the Mattesons contains a great deal of gaiety, social life, romance, the open life of the Adirondack woods, and some tragedy. The leading character was a lively young lady, granddaughter of O. B. Matteson, who was Mrs. Joe Corriveau.

Mr. Matteson carried a resounding full name, Orasmus Benajah Matteson. Born in 1805 and admitted to the bar in 1828, he was the first Utica City Attorney and served four terms in Congress. He became very well-to-do and had a fine home at 294 Genesee Street, now the Catholic Women's Club. In all the old city directories his name appears in prominent type.

His daughter Mary fell in love with George Pomeroy, a son of Dr. Theodore Pomeroy, who had built the large house across the street (289 Genesee Street). Probably George was born there, and he and Mary Matteson were friends from childhood.

At the time of the Civil War, George enlisted in the army. He and Mary were married either when he left with his company or when he was home on a furlough. Their only child, Augusta Pomeroy (the above Mrs. Corriveau) was born in 1864, probably at Grandfather Matteson's house, and she grew up under his solicitous care. In turn she loved and cared for him until his death.

Her father stayed in the army after the close of the war and went west to the Indian frontier, his wife accompanying him, it is said, and leaving little Augusta in the care of Grandfather Matteson. George reached the grade of Lieutenant Colonel and died in Omaha in 1869, still a young man. Augusta perhaps never saw him. After his death, her mother returned to Utica and Mr. Matteson and Augusta.

About 1866, Mr. and Mrs. Matteson acquired about 3,000 acres of forest land in Hamilton County north of West Canada Creek, including Wilmurt Lake. Their partner in the enterprise was John French of New Hartford.

Under the direction of John French's son, Frank, a cottage was built on Wilmurt Lake, and Mrs. Matteson, an invalid, spent the summers there, enjoying the invigorating Adirondack air. And, of course, Augusta—or Gussie, as she was then called by everyone—was at Wilmurt with her grandparents, acquiring a passionate love for the woods life.

What Mr. Matteson yearned for was a large enough place to make a really sociable summer life for his many Utica friends. That was why he and Mrs. Matteson, in 1881, purchased Becraft's Place and its adjoining

100 acres. It was at the end of the trail, deep in the forest, yet accessible by horse and carriage.

To complete their ownership, they bought John French's interest in the 3,000 acres which included Wilmurt Lake. Then they enlarged the Becraft Place and called it Matteson's Mountain Home.

A Utica paper of May, 1882, contains a description of the interior improvements which the Mattesons made: "It was done in the handsomest style, with the best and most substantial furniture, costly carpets, rich and tasty wallpaper, fine painting and graining, fine linen and tableware, and the serving of food fit for a king."

The paper mentions also the presence of expert guides for the convenience and safety of their visitors. The names mentioned were those of the Freeley brothers, Milt Griffith, Mike Butler, and Theodore Remonda.

Life in the Mountain Home must have been gay. And Gussie Pomeroy enjoyed every bit of it. She was eighteen when it was opened and had already learned to enjoy outdoor life. The Utica paper of May, 1882, says the guides liked her because she was an apt pupil in learning to fish for trout and to handle a boat on the stream. Mr. Matteson was seventy-seven years old the summer of 1882. He must have leaned on Gussie to do much of the entertaining and running of the place.

Mr. Matteson died in 1889, and apparently Gussie either inherited the Mountain Home or was given charge of it by her grandmother.

The Grant-to-Hoffmeister stage in the late 80s was driven by a young man named Albert Wheeler, whose first wife had died in 1883. This stage was one of the connecting links with the railroad for those going to or from the Mountain Home, and probably Gussie had made that journey many times with Albert Wheeler. The Morehouseville neighbors say that one day in 1891, when Gussie was going out by the stage to Utica, Albert dared her to marry him. She said she never refused a dare, so they stopped at the next Justice of the Peace and were married. She was 27 and he was 30.

He gave up his job, took over the management of the Mountain Home, and opened it to the public. Their marriage was successful and the place did well under their management. Utica society, however, was extremely shocked when it heard of the marriage. Gussie never returned to her friends in Utica, though her mother and two grandmothers did not cast her off. In 1902, Albert was taken sick and died. After his death his son by his first wife stayed at the Mountain Home with Gussie for a year and a half.

About 1904, Joe Corriveau appeared in the story. He had a good team of horses and worked at drawing logs, probably for Kreuzer or his gang. He was a French Canadian, a strong, handsome man, just Gussie's age, not a literate man but one of good character. Joe and Gussie fell in love and were married.

Joe worked with his fine team of horses for the club of Buffalo men, who had bought Wilmurt Lake. They arrived in automobiles that summer, a valiant drive for autos in 1907, but it was utterly impossible to drive an auto up the mountain to the lake. Joe took the party up with his team. Joe was also tender for the Mountain Home stillwater dam on the creek close by. This little lake and the dam were a necessity for log driving down to Hinckley.

That summer in 1907, when I was there, I was lazy and didn't try to do much stream fishing. I just sat by the dam and bait-fished the deep water above it. It seemed as though all the trout in the lake came to me, for the four of us—Gussie, Joe, Len Hollenbeck, and I—ate trout without end.

Len Hollenbeck, the house painter, came from the village of Ohio, below Wilmurt, and had evidently worked at the Mountain Home before. I thought perhaps he had been one of Gussie's admirers, for he was very attentive to her. Still, he and Joe were good friends, and our family of four were frank and congenial.

The year 1907 was the year after the Grace Brown murder on Big Moose Lake, related in Dreiser's An American Tragedy. The trial and conviction of Chester Gillette had been held at Herkimer in the fall of 1906, and the woods folk had been deeply stirred. As many as could make it went to Herkimer to get a glimpse of the trial. Len had been down, and he recounted it to us at length.

The last time I saw Joe Corriveau and his wife was in 1922. They were living in the cottage near the Mountain Home. Joe was running the mail and stage by auto from Hoffmeister to the railroad. The Mountain Home had been opened under the management of L. J. Helmer, who had bought it from Gussie in 1916.

With a friend of mine, Jack Milnes, I stayed overnight in the Mountain Home, and in the morning Mrs. Corriveau invited us to the cottage for a breakfast of bacon, eggs, coffee, and flap-jacks.

As a side trip for trout, Mr. Helmer suggested that we try the brook entering the lake at its southeast corner. We followed his suggestion, and that forenoon, near the brook we ran into an almost unbelievable gathering of hummingbirds, feeding and buzzing over a quarter-acre patch of brilliant cardinal flowers. Jack, a good bird observer, estimated that the birds numbered at least 500.

The Mountain Home burned down in 1923, and Kreuzer's hotel in 1924. Gussie continued her very active life until one day, returning from Hoffmeister, she fell and broke her hip. Her hip mended, but she was lame and seemed never quite to recover her spirit. She died in 1931.

She is buried in her Grandfather Matteson's plot in Forest Hills Cemetery, Utica, between her two husbands. Her granite marker reads: Augusta Pomeroy Matteson, wife of Joseph George Corriveau.

Joe's end nearly three years later at the age of 69 was tragic. He was an honest man and was never one to break the law. But it is said that one day in November at a friend's request he carried out a deer without a tag. He couldn't read the game laws, and the tag business was new to him. The troopers questioned him in Poland.

Joe's pride was terribly hurt. A week later he was found dead in the cottage from a rifle bullet. Opinion of the neighbors is divided on the question of whether someone shot him or he shot himself.

A Rochester lady owns the cottage, now surrounded by reforested pine. The cellar walls of the old Mountain Home can hardly be seen for the weeds, and the dam has washed away. The road up the mountain to Wilmurt Lake is just as steep as ever, however, and the Buffalo Club is there yet.

Invaluable wisdom and instilling a lifelong passion and love for all things Adirondack was gained from old-time family. *Courtesy Marilyn Breakey*

A smaller but attractive Mountain Home has been built by Mr. and Mrs. Helmer a little further up the creek, and it is beautiful up there still.

★ ★ ★

For assistance in preparing this article, the author acknowledged his indebtedness to the following: David H. Beetle; Dr. T. Wood Clarke; Mrs. William Beecher Crouse; Miss Abigail Camp Dimon; Mrs. Elizabeth N. Farber; Henry C. Hart; Mr. and Mrs. L. J. Helmer; J. C. Jones; Mrs. Stella King; Earl Kreuzer; J. N. Milnes; Emil A. Ober; Fred Remonda; Mr. and Mrs. Lee Swift; and Mr. and Mrs. Ephraim Wheeler.

ICE FISHING IN THE ADIRONDACKS

By Gladys R. Brown, *North Country Life*, Winter 1958

Ice fishing is one of the oldest winter sports in the North Country. Long before the white man came to this continent, Native Americans were fishing through the ice with the crudest tackle imaginable. It still is a simple, relaxing and economical sport. It has a lure that continues to attract many new sportsmen each year. Yet very little is written about it.

From the Niagara Frontier, as far as Lake Champlain and the Adirondacks, thousands of fishermen are to be found each winter chipping holes in the ice of ponds, lakes and rivers. Lake Champlain, one of the largest fresh water lakes in the country to freeze completely over, and numerous waters of the Adirondacks are easily accessible and have some of the finest ice fishing to be found anywhere in the way of smelt, pike and perch.

Men have no monopoly on this air-conditioned form of recreation. Many women take to it, although to really enjoy it, one must have a certain zest for the rugged outdoors, as any expanse of ice is wide open to every uncongenial whim of the elements. Then, too, it often affords an added opportunity for the ski or snowshoe enthusiast. The flat snow covered stretches are excellent for either in reaching the fishing areas.

Little equipment is necessary for ice fishing. Dressing warmly and comfortably is the first essential. Finding the fish is the next consideration. Twenty feet one way or another can make an amazing difference in the catch.

With a sharp long handled chisel, holes 8 to 12 inches are cut in the ice, and fishing is done through these in water from 15–75 feet deep. Out of respect for the many ice chisels lying on lake bottoms as they slipped cutting through the last bit of ice, shot out of cold hands or slippery mittens, it is a good practice to have a rope or leather wrist strap attached to the top of the handle.

Because the line runs down through such a small area, there is a great restriction in the rod action, and therefore most tackle used for summer angling is useless. Rods should be short, and very diversified are those used by ice fishermen—a hunk of broom handle, the rung of a chair, or various types of handmade line winders.

Some out-in-the-open anglers use willow branches five to six feet long. These are placed so that its slender tip bends down directly over the water, and responds to the slightest nibble. The thick end of the whip is usually set down into the ice a bit, and when covered with snow, quickly freezes there, thus eliminating the necessity of continually holding the whip.

Silvery smelt that run to about eight inches long are a great delicacy, and in some places bring a fairly good income. Although generally regarded as salt-water fish, smelt have been caught in Lake Champlain as far back as there are records, and it is a native of other northern fresh waters. Where it is not a native, it has gotten in by some sly maneuver, so that many lakes now have them. It is a company loving fish and often congregates in vast numbers during a portion of the winter, hardly moving from the general area for days at a time. It can be caught with a simple hook and a bit of bait. When biting good, the lines are in constant motion, and it is not unusual for a good fisherman to catch 60–80 smelt in a day.

Favorite bait is a small pike of another smelt. Pork strips or bacon rind can be used to make a first catch. Many use a "jig" spoon between the line and tackle to attract the fish. It is a three or four inch piece of curved metal with a hole at either end. When pulled up and down a few feet, it twirls and flashes, attracting the smelt. A long-handled dipper-strainer is handy to carry along for scooping pieces of ice that form in the water. For any amount of out-in-the-open fishing, a snow fort serves adequately as a windbreaker.

There are many who enjoy this sport in the fairly comfortable shelter of little cabins, or shanties, as they are more commonly called. Some are cozy as a living room; colorful curtains at their windows, with little bucket stoves, smoke drifting lazily from their chimneys, and the added aroma from a coffee pot continually brewing atop the tiny stove. Whenever these shiny fish are biting best, veritable "boom towns" of little houses appear on the lakes. Some accommodate only two. Others are larger and include bunks and benches with sufficient holes through the floor and ice for four or more lines. The majority of them are built on runners, making them easier to be moved from place to place. Since no crafty fisherman stays long in an unproductive spot, the more eager anglers leave their shelter and start hitting and missing all over the lake until they run the fish down again. The shanty is then moved in that direction.

Occasionally they are used just as a place to eat and warm up, while its occupants set out and tend lines around the lake. This applies particularly to those who use "tip ups." Much could be written about the various kinds of tip ups, each with some small variation from others. In general it is a type of setline with triggered devices, which flash up and show a flag when a fish is caught on the hook. These can be made very simply by joining two sticks to form a T-shape. One portion of the signal lies across the hole, while the other part acts as the warning with a piece of cloth attached at one end and the line to the other end. Some actually ring a bell when a fish is on the hook. An interesting observation is that those who have experimented with black flags, rather than the usual bright red, claim the darker color can be seen better against the snow from a distance on the open lakes. The law varies in different sections on how many "tip-ups" are permitted to be used by each individual, and there are lakes where this method is entirely prohibited.

"When we were not snowshoeing we were ice fishing on Seventh Lake." —John Chamberlain
Courtesy John Chamberlain

Yellow perch, one of the lake's best-liked food fish, are enormously abundant in New York's smaller lakes, and it makes little difference about bait. These are one of the easier kinds to catch, although they usually travel in schools, to that stationary type of fishing is not the most productive.

Generally, the northern pike or pickerel is the top fish of the sport. They are active all winter. In addition, they are a big fish and put up a good fight, the sort that gives a fisherman a sense of accomplishment when catching one. They are rated high among flavorful fish, and make a delicious meal when taken from the icy waters. Small ones are best broiled or fried to a golden brown in hot butter, while the larger ones are usually better when baked in milked or stuffed, if you prefer.

Although there are possibly as many tricks, variations and methods of ice fishing, as there are fishermen, each usually lets the other fellow enjoy his own technique. There are many who maintain that artificial lures will get more pike, while others prefer live bait, confident that pike will eat practically anything that moves. Both methods are equally popular and effective.

Pike are what the whip fishermen mostly go after and are considered vicious strikers. There is a certain challenge when suddenly one of the slender whips comes to life and is pulled down almost into the water. When he is hooked and you continue to feel the strong tug a sizeable fish, he must be kept coming almost straight up or there will be trouble getting him through the small opening in the ice. It is always a tremendous satisfaction to see the leering head of great northern pike, with its savage jaw and glaring eyes, coming stubbornly to the surface and poking through the hole in the ice, then slithering and flipping over the snow, as if wound up by a spring. One catch like this can fill you with the sense of enthusiasm to do more ice fishing.

At any rate, after a full day at this sport of emulating the Eskimo, when you crawl with a contented sigh under the blankets at night, you can be sure you will not need to be rocked to sleep.

Many improvements in this sport have evolved since Ms. Brown wrote this article. ▰

Winter stagecoach. *Courtesy Maitland DeSormo Collection. A Seneca Ray Stoddard photo*

I REMEMBER
By William J. O'Hern

It seemed that the whole forest began to smell like balsam as soon as I saw the brown wooden sign along Route 28 just north of Woodgate Corners, announcing in large letters that travelers were entering the Adirondack Park. I remember sitting in cramped backseat quarters and my father announcing "Deadman's Curve" as he slowed the car to safely negotiate the sharp ninety-degree bend in the road at White Lake corners.

I remember the Chevy sedan was loaded with camping gear that first year of family camping. The trunk was stuffed. The roof rack was loaded to capacity. Packed between, around and in the foot wells on each side of the center hump below our feet were blankets, pillows, clothing, groceries and a few toys. As tucked-in as we were, however, I don't remember being a bit uncomfortable.

The summer of 1950 proved to be an adventure that sparked within me the attachment to a place that has helped to keep inches off my waistline and put years into my physical bank for over sixty years and counting.

Realizing the need for summer recreational activity for their two children, my

PART ONE
Culture, Lifestyles and Mountain Air

COLLECTION ONE
Points in Time

➡ COLLECTION TWO
Adirondack Land

COLLECTION THREE
An Adirondack Past

COLLECTION FOUR
Adirondack School Days

Courtesy Meredith Ferlage

parents invested in some basic tenting equipment, used gear from my grandparents' camp, and borrowed items and headed out over the Boonville foothills toward the central Adirondack lake country. We passed White Lake, went through Otter Lake, crossed the Moose River at McKeever, went on through Thendara, Old Forge and Inlet, and arrived at Eighth Lake State Campground.

Eighth Lake is the last of the Fulton Chain of Lakes—headwaters of the middle branch of the Moose River. My mother remembers the day use camping fee "was fifty cents. We didn't have any money in those days for any other kind of vacation." The campground was enjoyed by a good quality of people. All displayed good sportsmanship. It was a simple, restful, clean and healthful vacation.

It took a few years to learn the art and secrets of temporary outdoor living. Our camp shelter consisted of an eight-by-eight-foot waxed canvas duck green umbrella-style tent that leaked every place the canvas was touched on the inside. Thus my parents' warning: "Don't touch the tent when it rains." There were no modern conveniences unless the smelly pit toilet counted as one.

The campground's ideal location offered (and still does) an abundance of hiking, nature study, fishing and camp craft opportunities, like climbing Rocky Peak, Bald and Black Bear Mountains, and 3,760-foot Blue Mountain. On the summit of Blue Mountain, we drank Kool-Aid the fire tower observer made from rain water he collected off his cabin roof. We hiked to Eagle's Nest and Bug Lakes, and followed the old Uncas wagon road. I remember pretending to drive the abandoned Marion River locomotive, riding in the mail boat around Fourth Lake, driving through the Moose River Plains' deep forest and listening to car tires hum as they passed over the hemlock plank joints of a covered bridge in Jay when we vacationed in the Wilmington area to visit the North Pole, the home of Santa's Workshop. There was swimming, fishing off the Seventh Lake dock, exploring campground woodlands, and paddling to Eighth Lake Island, where I always tried to recreate in my mind how hermit Alvah Dunning lived on that tiny slice of ground. The variety of activities at

Eighth Lake, the wholesome association of young and old campers, and the campground's family atmosphere provided experiences which contributed to both my physical growth and my character development.

The Adirondack Mountains linger long in the memory of all who come under their spell. Taking you back to my early Adirondack camping life gives you a brief glimpse of the strange thing that took hold of me during my childhood. I have been lucky to live in the midst of the most scenic and historic countryside in the Empire State while thousands of tourists travel great distances from every state in the Union to enjoy the sights I find so close to my back door.

For some still-unexplained reason, I came to prefer the low road—the drowsy mountain side roads and exploring North Country foot trails that lead to the Adirondacks' romantic past or to scenes of riveting beauty.

I have often wondered why I have been so gripped with the Adirondack land, and I think there is a strong tie to those first family camping experiences. I was fortunate to be raised by parents who tried to offer many life experiences. I was born during World War II. Dad never forgot his wartime experiences. When I was old enough to strike out on my own, I remember him saying he had "had enough wartime experiences of carrying a backpack and 'camping'" and [backpacking] didn't appeal to him. And yet, his Army experiences never dampened his spirit for family camping. Our outdoor dealings were kept apart by personal interest and his interpretation that backpacking was "work, not pleasure." I understood where he was coming from. Sleeping in a foxhole, eating K-rations, lugging a heavy pack with ammo, and being shot at had stripped away any interest in "roughin' it" beyond two weeks of camping in a park campground.

So, each year from the time I was five until I graduated from high school, Mom and Dad were to share moments of tranquility on our camping trips in the moss-carpeted forest by some scenic lake.

The Adirondack Park seemed more wilderness-like when I was a youngster. The life in the small communities I was familiar with, such as Old Forge, Inlet, Blue Mountain Lake, and Indian Lake was totally unlike that in larger cities. Here you remembered "Buster" Bird, who operated a float plane on Sixth Lake, and Gordon Rudd, who operated a butcher shop in Inlet, and MaryLee Kahil, whose family operated Inlet's grocery and department store. In metropolitan areas you knew the names of the men who delivered the ice and milk bottles to your home, and the proprietors of the corner Mom and Pop store, but you were lucky if you knew the names of the owners of larger businesses.

It was this "homely" interest reflected in the small community life in which all took pride that brought me my first interviews with native Adirondackers when I began collecting primary source recollection. Those native Adirondackers were proud of their heritage. All reflected on the land where they lived, saying they "wouldn't live in a city, but it's nice to spend a few days there to make the rounds."

Adirondack property was affordable then. Taxes were lower and jobs were still plentiful. This was the very land that grandfathers passed down to sons and daughters— and they stayed, most often carrying on a family business or trade. The land's natural resources helped support their livelihoods while the more primitive surroundings enriched their sportsman's zeal. The land was home, home for well over a hundred years for many families through all of summer's tourists and winter's penetrating hostility.

This was where I began my interest in the Adirondacks' wilderness character and the charm of the Adirondack High Peaks area, where bears came to eat in the town dumps, deer quenched their thirst in creeks, beavers walloped their tails to warn of our approach, trout leaped for the may-fly, and ducks paddled the shoreline looking for bread handouts.

This Adirondack land has meant, and will continue to mean, many things to many people. My preference has always been its geological and social history as well as the trailless directions up-grade through dense cold forest or the rough and steep trails over jagged rocks, slippery ledges and sprawling roots leading me to the awesome scenery the mountains offer.

Each issue of *North Country Life* featured a multitude of veteran and novice writers who shared my historical interest about the Adirondack land, its natives and places. "Excerpts from the Editor's Mail" offered

After finding a high and dry site to pitch the tent, and setting up camp in an advantageous spot to be used for sightseeing and resting, we were ready to begin the vacation. *Courtesy Meredith Ferlage*

interesting bits of information about the region's history, folklore associated with it, and relatives' connections to the land.

The "North Country Poets" section must have been well-liked by Cole and popular with readers because it appeared as a standard in every issue. Marjorie Porter Paulus, of Salisbury Center, N.Y., waxed about a special dirt track in "Road Through the Woods." Marjorie's mother never understood why it took her daughter "so long to travel" this road.

It's nice just to remember
Back when you were a kid
And to think of all the fun you had
And all the things you did.

We used to go, from Grandpa's farm,
Way back up on the hill,
To visit Uncle Wilson
Through the years I see it still.

We'd walk the mile between the farms,
And the road that wound between
Was filled with wonders we could see
And a million things unseen.

Great bank of lacy maidenhair,
A chipmunk in a tree,
And monsters, big as bears, we felt,
But these we couldn't see...
    North Country Life, Summer 1954

Marion S. Fresn's geological and historical account of the Lyon Mountain region in "The Lion Couchant," *North Country Life*, Winter 1954, stands as an example of the kind of lore and history one learned from the magazines' stories. She explains the coincidence of pioneer Nathaniel Lyon moving to Lion Mountain, which then became known as Lyon Mountain. Information like that has always added interest to me; I enjoy learning about areas I frequent.

Mrs. R. L. Foot wrote to Glyndon Cole after receiving *North Country Life's* Summer 1950 issue, pledging she was "ever grateful to my friend for acquainting me with" the magazine.

I...was much pleased with the article on Dannatburg. The pictures I had never seen but heard so much about them that they were doubly interesting. And Christ Church, Sackets Harbor, being my home church, looked so good to me. "Father's Last Decoration Day" [article] was so true for those times. Having spent my childhood in a military town, [it] brought back many memories of parades and celebrations.

J. Elet Milton of Brewerton, N.Y., felt equally gratified that he had "made a real discovery in making [his] acquaintance. It covers so much that is mightily interesting, the story of navigation on the Black River alone being worth many times what the magazine has cost me. Keep up the good work and more luck to you in every way."

And so the notes continued, asking for stories of particular topics, providing supplementary information, telling how a predecessor came to the Adirondacks, explaining the whereabouts of a disremembered place—which Cole found attention-grabbing enough to begin a periodic "Forgotten Things" column, sharing an adventure that was spurred by an earlier article:

> *"...I have been climbing to the caves on Norton's Peak and showing them to others for years. They are known as the Bats Caves, and Tanager Lodge, a camp run by Fay Welch, is responsible for the trail leading to them. For years they could only be found by locating a large pine from the summit of Norton's.*

> *"...I have spent many hours exploring the caves and believe that I have been further down into the cave than your son...."*
> —Jane Kelting, *York State Tradition*, Summer 1973

The reactions over the years of grateful readers of *North Country Life* and *York State Tradition* greatly satisfied Glyndon Cole. Their genuine interest and from-the-heart letters encouraged him to forge on year after year even though he only broke even most years. Some readers liked stories of yesterday, others favored tales of tourist attractions, while others looked for frontiersmen yarns and Revolutionary War and War of 1812 accounts. Some liked climbing and canoe adventures or learning about nifty out-of-the-way places or trendy theme parks. *North Country Life* and *York State Tradition* beamed in on these interests, truly offering "something for everyone."

As time passed and material came forward, Cole developed a pattern to please the wide range of interest of his readership. Because it seemed logical to follow his lead, I used a similar format, following a natural progression of collections to achieve a sense of Cole's magazine's continuity.

The book became *Adirondack Kaleidoscope*, for each of the collections chosen was exactly that, viewpoints of experience—a pattern of many styles, shapes, figures and profiles. I chose them for the most part for their information and interest, but some for myself, knowing that they are the only way readers will ever be able to know about the Adirondacks of an earlier era. The history within the land carries the same sense of human relationship and reassurance that has brought me back time and again for that pungent balsam reward.

Collection II, Adirondack Land, contains selections about those who traveled the wilds from when it was truly a "dismal" wilderness up to the creation of the Adirondack Park. ✄

High Peaks in Essex County, 1940. *Courtesy Fred Studer*

ᚔ ADIRONDACKS

Ragged, serrated peaks of mountains rise
In lofty grandeur 'ainst my northern skies
Mantled about with robes of living green
Crowned with gray stone, enduring and serene.

Low hills or rolling prairies may be fine;
Or beating sea and winds that taste of brine;
But forest aisles and rising slopes alone
Comfort the ache that calls me to come home.

—Julia Simmons, *North Country Life*, Spring 1948

"IT ALL BELONGS TO ME"

By Marjorie L. Porter, *North Country Life*, Fall 1948

High and far off on the hills the pipes of autumn call. Faintly heard, the magic tune sets vagabonds wandering, willy-nilly, High Adventure at their heels.

Across the wide fields, serene in valleys where "seven-mile still waters" give no hint of their upland tumblings, buckwheat stubble lays a rosy carpet—corn in the shock stands sturdily, row on row, punctuated with bright pumpkin periods—hay stacks testify to summer's largesse, the farmer's bulwark against a season of snows—crows caw-caw-caw, flapping black wings against a clear blue sky, and crickets madly tune their fiddles. The essence of all bonfires, heady, exciting, pervades the human heart, and color everywhere is a delight beyond expression.

This is a symphony of scarlet maples—russet beeches—birches glowing yellow—huge oaks in wintered ceremonial dress—flaunting vermilion and orange banners, berry laden—bright splashes of sumach along grey ledges. Up and down self-sufficient village streets—close huddled in silent farmyards beside uptilted roads that fight a losing battle with alder and witch hazel for the right of way—marking for their own with gay strands, fields embraced tiredly by stone walls and split rail fences—carrying on their October orgy at the very edges of cathedral aisles, evergreen pillared, and far up precipitous mountainsides, rainbow hued, they are the music of the Adirondack autumn.

The young six-foot philosopher and his companion climbed higher and yet higher, drinking deeply of that strong potion offered by Mother Nature in a forest "gone berserk."

The summit of a windswept peak was gained at last and survey, seemingly of the whole earth, begun. The philosopher spread a State Conservation Department map on the bare rock beside "Trails to Marcy."

"Remember James Whitcomb Riley's worm and the worm's remark when he crawled out of his hole? 'It all belongs to me.'"

"Pleasant viewpoint," his companion replied casually.

"Well, it's true." The student, practical conservationist, forester, suddenly not at all casual, was "off." His companion, enjoying what Old Mountain Phelps, former veteran guide of Keene Valley, described as a sensation of "uph'istedness," a sensation experienced only on mountain peaks of the "first class," listened and—agreed.

"Public domain," he said, and waved his arms to indicate lesser peaks, deep wooded valleys, streams and plains far below. "Nearly three million acres, yours 'n mine, where we can camp, hunt, fish, and walk over hundreds of miles of forest trails, marked for our guidance. Our parks, our campsites, our fish hatcheries, our game farms and refuges, our trout streams, our timber lands. So what?"

"Why, I've heard my grandfather tell of the fight that men of his day put up to save these lands from spoilage. Sure, they wanted hunting and fishing for themselves, but that wasn't all—not by a long shot. They were looking ahead, they wanted all that," and the conservationist waved his arms again, "for their children and for their grandchildren, like me.

"I'm willing to bet that if all those people who use our public parks and campsites and trails could sit right here and see what we're looking at, they'd feel just as I do. They'd fight, not only to keep the public domain intact by cooperating with the state departments they support, but to make it bigger and better for their own children and grandchildren. They'd really appreciate the fact that every boulder and tree, every pond and stream, every ranger's cabin and fire observer's tower, belongs to them. We've invested in a pretty big thing. I'd like to see my children get the same kind of dividends from our domain that I have, and so help me—I'll never have any part in destroying it—whether that means thoughtlessly dropping a lighted match—cutting trees where they shouldn't be cut—taking game out of season—polluting rivers and brooks—or permitting legislation that will make it possible for greedy men to invade and exploit lands controlled for the benefit of people like you and me."

He paused for breath and gazed out across great spaces where seas of clouds hid other seas of Adirondack peaks. The clouds drifted, separated to reveal steep wooded slopes beneath, and changed to blue and purple mistiness that softly veiled the earth, blending all in a colorful tapestry.

"It all belongs to me," he added dreamily. ▰

OUR FOREST PRESERVE…A RICH INHERITANCE

By Ralph S. Hosmer, *North Country Life*, Spring 1947
Condensed from the *Bulletin to the Schools*

In the Forest Preserve the people of New York State have a unique possession. Few localities anywhere in the world can offer a happier combination of satisfying mountains, beautiful lakes and streams, and places of scenic and historic interest, all set in a forest of a character that lends itself to the unusual degree to human enjoyment. And all this is within only a few hours travel from the greatest centers of population on this continent. The best part of it all is that both divisions of the preserve—the Adirondacks and the Catskills—a gross area of over 2,400,000 acres, belong to the people and are set apart for their use and enjoyment.

Such a holding is not created and set up overnight. Behind the Adirondack Preserve stretches back an extensive history, the record of a long line of active and preserving men.

In the 18th century the Adirondack region was indeed a wild and forbidding place. It was a hunting ground for various Indian tribes. It was, as well, the frontier between the Algonquins of Canada and the Iroquois of Central New York. Because of the constant warfare between these tribes, the region was known as the "dark and bloody ground."

It is said that the present name of this region comes from the term which the Mohawks applied in derision to the Canadian Indians— "Adirondack," meaning "tree eaters." Today the name Adirondacks includes all that great block of land, roughly 80 miles north and south by 100 miles east and west, which lies north of the Mohawk River and south of the St. Lawrence Valley, and stretches from the Black River on the west to Lake Champlain on the east. The boundary of the "park" is the famous "Blue Line." The lands owned by the State within the Blue Line constitute the bulk of the Adirondack Forest Preserve. Privately owned lands within the Blue Line are not parts of the Forest Preserve.

One of the methods by which what is now Northern New York State was subdivided for settlement was by means of land grants, or patents, made out originally in the name of the Crown; or later, after the Revolution, by the State of New York.

The practice by the State of selling its "wilderness land" was by no means confined to the earlier decades of the past century. The custom continued into the 1870s, or even later. In many instances virgin forest land was sold at prices which today seem ridiculously low, many tracts having gone for only a few cents an acre. There were individuals, however, who dissented from this practice and policy, and who were courageous enough to say so.

One outstanding public man of the first quarter of the 19th century was Governor DeWitt Clinton. Thought of first today, perhaps, as the instigator of the original Erie Canal, Governor Clinton deserves remembrance on other grounds as well. He also looked beyond, to larger benefits for the people. In his opening message to the legislature on January 2, 1822, are these significant statements:

"Our forests are falling rapidly before the progress of settlement, and a scarcity of wood for fuel, ship and house building, and other useful purposes is already felt in the increasing prices of that indispensable article. No system of plantations for the production of trees and no system of economy for their preservation has been adopted. Probably none will be until severe privations are experienced.

"It is certainly expedient for the Legislature, on all great occasions, but especially in relation to future internal improvements, to cherish a prospective spirit and to provide in season for the exigencies of future times. The creation of a general board of public improvements would be a wise and patriotic arrangement. This board…would be enabled, by a judicious application of the public resources, to conduct us to an elevation of unparalleled prosperity."

The northern wilderness is not specifically mentioned in those paragraphs, but Governor Clinton's ideas about the use of public resources could well have been considered by the commission to study the Adirondack situation which was set up by the New York Legislature just fifty years later.

The Adirondack region, being for the most part high in elevation and having a short growing season, was not thought to be well adapted for agriculture. The region was for this reason settled but slowly.

Alfred L. Donaldson in *A History of the Adirondacks* tells entertainingly of the early settlers, the hunters and trappers, and explains how these men later became the guides of those who wished to explore the wilderness. Pioneers of another sort were the technically educated men who first visited the Adirondacks in the interests of scientific work. In this group belongs Professor Ebenezer Emmons, who in 1836 was appointed to the geological Survey of New York. He it was who in 1838 proposed the name "Adirondack Group" for "the cluster of mountains in the neighborhood of the upper Hudson and Ausable rivers." Emmons was the first to climb Mount March, the highest Adirondack peak, 5344 feet, and to give to it and others of the neighboring peaks the names they have since held.

Another scientifically-minded lover of the Adirondacks was Dr. Franklin B. Hough, who in 1876 was appointed the first Special Agent in Forestry in the United States Department of Agriculture. Doctor Hough's writings, based on his intimate personal acquaintance with the Adirondacks, gave to many persons their first accurate information about this portion of New York State.

The man, however, who probably did more to introduce the Adirondacks to an ever-expanding audience was Verplanck Colvin, for over a quarter of a century, 1872 to 1900, superintendent of the Adirondack Survey of New York State, and for seven years prior to that active in private surveying work which led him to all parts of the northern wilderness.

As superintendent of the Adirondack Survey he designated and was responsible for the basic triangulation system which located with precision all the important peaks and other essential landmarks, and then by instrumental leveling, carried up to the highest mountain tops, determined with mathematical accuracy the exact elevation above sea level of each point.

Verplanck Colvin had a pleasant style as a writer and was a ready speaker. When describing some new "find" of scenic interest or discussing the bearing of newly made scientific observations, the text of his reports is anything but the dry pages which one might expect from the field notes of a survey. Besides maps, charts and tables, some of the Survey reports carry plates, drawn by Colvin, which outline ranges of mountain peaks or sketch chains of lakes amid their surrounding forest-clad hills. It is no wonder that tourists soon began to search out spots in the wilderness to which their attention had been so persuasively drawn and that it was not long before camps, and then hotels, were required to accommodate the increasing summer tourist trade.

Three items of especial interest are to be recalled in connection with Verplanck Colvin. First, he was the discoverer of Lake Tear-of-the-Clouds, that little pool, which, nestling high on the upper slopes of Mount March, is the true source of the Hudson River. Second, he emphasized the suggestion of what may at some time become a necessity, that it is possible to divert water from the Raquette River watershed over to streams tributary to the Hudson, and so augment the flow which may someday be required to supply water to the cities and towns that will ultimately line both banks of the Hudson River. Third, he was proud to claim that he had been the first to recommend that the Adirondack region should be set apart and maintained as a great forest park for the people of New York State.

Both Hough and Colvin were on the State Park Commission, of which Governor Horatio Seymour was chairman and which was set up in 1872 to report upon the feasibility of creating a Forest Reservation in the Adirondacks. Hough advocated a rounded program of management for the forest that envisaged economic use as well as esthetic enjoyment. Colvin, on the other hand, was ever the vigorous proponent of the park idea, holding that in the public use of the Adirondacks recreation should have first place.

No action was taken by the Legislature on the report of the State Park Commission. For more than ten years it lay unregarded in a pigeonhole. But the ideas back of the commission's suggestions had too much merit to be entirely forgotten. In the hands of another committee, in 1884, these earlier recommendations helped give direction to the report which led to the Forest Preserve Law of 1885, the organic forest act of New York State.

The year 1885 marks the beginning of present-day forest policy in New York. From that year to this there has been unbroken continuity in the administration of our Forest Preserves. They are now safe and well cared for under our efficient Conservation Department.

We of today have good reason to be grateful to those pioneers of around a century ago. The rights and privileges which we enjoy in our Forest Preserves we owe to their foresight and determination. It is a rich inheritance that has come down to us. Those who gave it must not be forgotten. ◼

❧ THE FIRST ADIRONDACKERS
By W. H. Burger, *North Country Life*, Spring 1953

"Adirondack" in Native-American means "tree eater." That's what the Iroquois called the Algonquins, some of whom lurked in the Great North Woods. It isn't a very complimentary nickname. But the Iroquois were the Nazis of Northeastern North America and had all sorts of silly ideas about national superiority. Anyway, the tree eaters were the first Adirondackers of whom we have record, and they ate buds, bark, and even wood only when there wasn't anything else.

The first white Adirondacker was Samuel Champlain, who discovered the lake which bears his name in July of 1609. His journal shows how profoundly he was impressed by the massive peaks to the west. Another fine Frenchman, Father Joques, traveled the same waterway in 1642, but under far different circumstances. He was a prisoner of the Mohawks and was to suffer torture and martyrdom because Champlain had shot a couple tribal chiefs thirty-three years before.

Three hundred years after, a sweet young thing is easing a Cadillac convertible through Cascade Pass at sixty miles per hour. A swift glance up the gorge to the top of Cascade Mountain gives a glimpse of the waterfalls. She murmurs, "pretty," to her companion and says, "Let's stop in Placid for cocktails." She, too, is an Adirondacker.

In between are an amazingly varied and colorful lot of people, and along the eastern edge of the 5,000,000 acre stage on which they play their parts the political destinies of a continent were fought out in a half century of conflict between France and England.

Our Native American predecessors were summer guests, as are many of us. Adirondack winters and birthday clothes didn't mix then any better than they do now. Even in summer the Saranacs or other possible Native American groups didn't linger anywhere long enough to leave much trace. Indian Carry, between Upper Saranac Lake and Spectacle Ponds and the Raquette River, is about the only place that Donaldson, outstanding Adirondack historian, regards as a permanent camping site.

While English colonists undoubtedly hunted and fished along the fringes of the Adirondacks, the first trek through the heart of the wilderness by white men was made by Sir John Johnson of Johnson Hall at Johnstown. In May of 1776, after the outbreak of the Revolution, he and a number of Tory friends and retainers fled north to Canada. Their course lay through the Raquette and Long Lake country to the St. Lawrence and Montreal. Because there was snow in the woods, they started on snowshoes, but had to discard the "raquettes" (French for snowshoes) at Raquette Lake and continue from there by birch bark canoe. They piled the snowshoes in a great heap on the shore of South

Inlet, and some people have thought that this incident gave the lake and river their names.

The Johnson party experienced nineteen days of intense hardship and suffering on their trip to Montreal. One of the portages they had to make was around Raquette Falls on the Raquette River between Long Lake and Tupper Lake. It is very possible that they found a dim Indian trail here. If they had to break one it must have been a tough mile and a quarter, as thousands of later Adirondack voyagers on the famous Old Forge-Saranac canoe route can testify, although the latter have an old carry road to follow. Two cannon which were found many years later, one near the outlet of Long Lake and the other two miles from the foot of Big Tupper Lake, are thought to have been abandoned there by the Johnson party. Think of the labor of packing or dragging 14-pounders with their ammunition on snowshoes or in birch bark canoes. It just goes to show what really scared people can do. ◾

Typical touring car and camping outfit in the early days of Adirondack camping.
Courtesy Special Collections, Feinberg Library, SUNY College at Plattsburgh

★ ADIRONDACKER FUNDAMENTALS

By John G. Broughton, *North Country Life*, Spring 1949

Deep in the heartland of each of the continents is an old and resistant area of bedrock known as a "shield." Each has served as the foundation on which the continent has been built up over the ages of geologic time. Over large parts of the continents the shields are deeply buried by more recent rocks. Only where the rock cover has been thin or where the forces of erosion have toiled mightily can these ancient basement rocks be seen. Such an area is the Canadian Shield, the heart land of North America, where two million square miles of foundation rock have been stripped bare.

Adirondack carpenters built around rock outcrops and huge boulders. Shown is The Saranac Club, renamed Bartlett's. *A Seneca Ray Stoddard photo. Courtesy Maitland DeSormo Collection*

New York has a stake in this area, for we have the Adirondacks, isolated in a sea of younger rocks and connected with the Canadian Shield by a narrow isthmus made up of the stepping stones of the Thousand Islands.

It is easy to use the phrase "ages of geologic time" and then pass on to more specific phases of Adirondack geology. However, scientific work, recently completed, allows us to be specific, for the first time, as to the actual age of the Adirondacks. In a quarry near Gouverneur, once worked for feldspar, a student of minerals has found a few small dull black cubes, each about as large as a half-carat diamond. These are crystals of uraninite, the oxide of uranium. Uraninite has the disconcerting habit of slowly disintegrating, by radioactivity, into lead (of a special sort) and helium. Moreover, this slow decay goes on at a very steady rate, unaffected by heat or cold, by earth pressures or by erosion. This rate of decay has been determined and can be used to compute the length of elapsed time since the mineral was first formed.

In the case of the Gouverneur uraninite, the uranium lead ratio was determined by chemical analysis, the ratio was inserted in the rate formula and the result, after a trip through the mathematical mill, was the age of the rock: 1,100 million years. Here then is justification for the phrase "ages of geologic time." And remember, the rock which contained the uraninite cuts across layers of other older rocks—a fact which pushes the Adirondack beginnings further back into the haze.

All of these rocks, hoary with age, are intricately mixed into some of the most complex geology in the world. Oldest are the ancient "Greenville" sedimentary rocks, long since changed by tremendous earth pressures into marbles, quartzites, and "gneisses," the streaked, layered, and nasty-appearing rocks so typical of the lower Adirondack peaks. These have been engulfed and indented by younger granite rocks and to a lesser extent by gabbro, a coarse grained, dark colored rock, much like the Palisades in chemical makeup, though not in appearance.

One rock type, anorthosite, is of particular interest since it underlies 1,500 square miles of high Adirondack country and is the buttress for Marcy,

Giant, Whiteface, etc. Anorthosite is slow to yield to erosion and its resistance is in large part responsible for the location of the high peaks.

The Adirondack rocks have suffered much. They have been heated, squeezed, broken, eroded, and uplifted. There have been times when Alp-like peaks characterized these mountains. At other times, they have been worn down to nubbin—a low featureless island in the midst of a vast inland sea. The latter was more often the case than not when the sedimentary rocks which underlie the rest of New York State were being laid down. At times these seas lapped far inland on the Adirondack Island, a bit of geologic history proved by the presence of sandstones and limestones well into the upland area.

The most profound rock breaking, or faulting, in mountains has resulted in a rectilinear pattern of mountains and valleys which is best illustrated by the shape of Lake Placid or by the Elizabethtown topographic quadrangle. It is very difficult to determine the amount of movement along these faults, but minor ones near one of the iron mines of the eastern Adirondacks have a vertical displacement of 200 feet. At any rate, they have created zones of rock weakness, which have forced a trellis pattern of stream drainage so beautiful that it is used as a textbook example.

The most recent indignity, to which Nature subjected the Adirondack peaks, both high and low, was complete burial in a shroud of ice—the Labradorian ice sheet of the last glacial period. Beginning about a million years ago, this great glacier crept down over the Adirondack area, grinding away the soft weathered rock debris of previous ages, polishing the hard rock and diverting the course of pre-glacial stream drainage. Complete burial is shown by the glacial grooving found on the highest peaks and by the boulders of "foreign" rock left there when the ice melted.

Probably the highest areas were deglaciated soon after the ice reached its farthest extent in southern New York and Pennsylvania, and these areas steadily enlarged as the ice melted. But it was late in the glacial period before the ice had left the lowland areas of the Black, St. Lawrence, and Champlain valleys. Glacial lakes, dammed up by the ice, left the great deposits of lake clay and of delta sand and gravel, which characterize these valleys today.

There has been little time, in the 25,000 years since the glacier left, for any great changes to be wrought in the mountains. Rocks are slowly weathering to soil; streams are carrying away rock debris and deepening their channels. Sometimes the land springs suddenly back, still shrugging off the weight of the foreign ice – then New York State experiences an earthquake and much ado is made over what is only a minor readjustment in the long geological history of the Adirondacks.

The story is there, easily read in some rocks, only faintly discernible in others. It has been pieced together by careful observation and reasoning, mental processes that are free for all. Try them on your next Adirondack hike and see if every attempt to interpret the rocks and scenery won't add to the sum total of your enjoyment. ◄

VERPLANCK COLVIN AND THE GREAT LAND SURVEY

By Roland B. Miller, *North Country Life*, Fall 1950
Reprinted from the New York State *Conservationist*

Verplanck Colvin was an amateur artist, a professional surveyor, and in varying degrees a topographical engineer, geologist, biologist, geodesist, historian and writer. He is best known, however as Superintendent of the Adirondack and State Land Surveys, and in that capacity he left a deeper and more enduring mark upon the North Woods than any man before or since. That mark can still be found in the copper bolts, set in the oldest stone in the world—Adirondack granite—and in the old blazes which are still prime reference points in discovering and rediscovering Adirondack property lines.

The earliest map to show the Adirondack region was one drawn by Abraham Oretlius, geographer for Phillip II of Spain, in the year 1570. Northern New York was then called "Avacal;" the lack of knowledge about this region was evident in the cartographer's work. Then came a

Adirondack survey camp near Long Lake in 1888. *Photo: S.R. Stoddard. Courtesy Special Collections, Feinberg Library, SUNY College at Plattsburgh*

map of New Netherland, dated 1616, which gave to the area the name of "Irocoisen," changed in later editions to "Iroquoisia." Then in 1771 appeared a map ordered by Governor Tryon, but this did not indicate any lake or mountain in the Adirondacks—only an unknown wilderness. Next in 1776, a map of the British colonies reported that the vast tract to the north was called "Couchsachrage," one of the four beaver hunting countries of the Six Nations and not yet surveyed. Finally, a map dated 1777 sketched in Tryon and Charlotte counties, also attempted to trace the Hudson River and to suggest the location of a few of the major peaks.

With such meager information at hand, colonial surveyors had little to work with. Nevertheless, they established the boundaries of the Totten and Crossfield Purchase—one of the first recorded surveys of the north country; the south line of Macomb's Purchase Great Tract No. 11; the south line of Great Tract No. 1; a resurvey of Township 11, Old Military Tract, and such other surveys as were required by the commisioners of the Land Office.

All of this was piecemeal work, and it was not until 1837 that a large scale geological survey was started by Professor Emmons, assisted by William C. Redfield and Ferdinand M. Benedict. That survey continued for four years, and during the course of it many of the major Adirondack peaks were named and measured, among them Whiteface, Marcy, Seward, Dix, McIntyre, Henderson and McMartin (later Colden). Although conspicuously inaccurate in many respects the reports of this survey summarized virtually all of the knowledge of the topographical and physical character of the region of the State up to that time, and for that matter, up to the year 1872 when Colvin embarked on his project. Between the Emmons survey and that of Colvin, there appeared only fragmentary and sketchy information, some of it reliable and some of it not, circulated by tourists, hunters, guides and miscellaneous authorities who visited the Adirondacks.

Suffice it to say that when Colvin began his land survey he had very little established and authentic material to work with. There was no reliable map; blazes and stakes and other boundary markers had in many cases disappeared. Lines delimiting state and private properties were often a matter of opinion or guess work, and there was nowhere in the records of the state a total picture, even approximately accurate, of the topography and geography of the region.

Colvin was convinced that to remedy this situation nothing would suffice but "A survey with theodolite or transit, entirely independent of the magnetic compass, the object in view being the discovery by trigonometrical measurement of the relative angular position of the mountain summits and other important landmarks for use in the preparation of a map of the wilderness." And he went on to say that "the vastness of such an undertaking necessitated the retraversing of so great an extent of wilderness, the ascending of numerous mountains several of which have a height of 5,000 feet, the labors and fatigues, the dangers of exploration in the great ocean of woods, of accident and of hunger, can only be appreciated by the surveyor who has passed through such an ordeal."

Even so, Colvin probably underestimated the difficulties of his job. Fieldwork began in the neighborhood of Lake Pleasant (Hamilton County) in late July, 1873, and right at the start appeared the difficulties which were to plague him throughout the survey. Some of these were of his own making, some were unavoidable.

The difficulties of his own making appear to have stemmed from the character of Colvin himself; he simply could not be bothered with many of the details necessary to the organization and administration of such a project. Therefore, he and his men often had nothing to eat but dry bread, no prepared camp to sleep in, no adequate provisions to take care of the delicate instruments required for the work, no definite schedule of activities nor any well-thought-out itinerary, no competent leader to take Colvin's place when he left the job and went back to Albany (which he frequently did), no overall objective which could be communicated to his men so that they might share his enthusiasm for the task.

On the other hand, many of the difficulties encountered by Colvin were the products either of his times or of the officials in Albany to whom he was responsible. His surveying instruments—although he insisted upon the best available and usually got them—were primitive according to present standards, and the support he received from the legislature was, to say the least, precarious. In more than one instance he had to resort to his own personal funds in order to pay his crews, and the completion of his survey was indefinitely postponed due to lack of appropriations by the Legislature. A combination of his own short-comings and those of the government for which he worked often resulted in poorly outfitted crews, unnecessary suffering, defection in the ranks, failure of instruments, false alarms and excursions, disease and hardship.

Furthermore, Colvin confronted many of the problems which beset surveyors in the same field today. There was a maze of trails and blazes made by hunters, trappers and lumbermen for their own mysterious purposes, and it was necessary for him to sort out the wheat from the chaff before establishing what he considered to be the true line. And to cap it all, there was the annual variation of the magnetic needle, as well as minor variations caused by ore deposits. Such mechanical difficulties were particularly trying to Colvin and were perhaps the cause of some of his major mistakes, since he had a profound respect for the lines established by previous surveyors and often stretched a point to prove them right.

In the course of gathering material for this article, we contacted two men who had worked for Colvin. One of these, Beecher Wilson of Deerland, helped Colvin to run the line between Townships 21 and 25. Significantly, he pointed out that the actual survey work was headed by Dan Lynch, since Colvin "wasn't there too much of the time. I helped find the old line trees," he said, "cut out sections of them, put them in a pack, carried them out. We were blocking out old blazes. Mr. Colvin had no idea of time, and no thought of comfort; he would lie right down on the ground and sleep just as well as he would in a feather bed."

We got the idea that when Mr. Wilson said he worked for Colvin, he meant to say that he really worked.

We also found James M. DeLong of Elizabethtown, who worked for Colvin during the summer of 1885. "I heard he wanted rodmen," Mr. DeLong said, "so I sent him a letter and he told me to come on. I acted

The hunters did not know how long they considered the honest, natural woodland, only that it was long enough to fall in love with the Adirondack Mountains.
Courtesy The Town of Webb Historical Society

as rodman some of the time, and chainman some too. Mr. Colvin was a very fine man, but he was a very obstinate man. I can't remember how many there were in our party, but anyway there was a head cook, camp man, two rodmen, three chainmen, and three or four axemen, in addition to the instrument men and their assistants. While our party was at Placid, Colvin was away a great deal of the time."

The remarks of these two men seem to confirm a rather general impression of Colvin's character; that he was highly volatile, or as one historian put it: "When the high mountains had been measured and the location of lakes and the sources of the major rivers determined, the glamour wore off and his reports lost most of their popular appeal." The critics over the years have found much of his work to be of uneven scientific value. Resurveys have proved many of his lines inaccurate (he tried so hard to prove old lines correct); his successors could do little with the great mass of material he accumulated for the simple reason that he had no organization or system for handling such material; his Albany office is said to have looked more like the dressing room of a sporting club than the office of a surveyor, what with its confusion of pack baskets, snowshoes, trophies and bric-a-brac.

Nevertheless, there seems to be general agreement that as a surveyor Colvin was tops. As Mr. Wilson of Deerland said, "Colvin was one of the greatest men I ever saw to locate a spot on a tree. He could locate one that you couldn't see any sign of—one that might be five, six or seven inches grown over. But he could see it, and we couldn't."

Colvin was born in Albany in 1847, was tutored at home, later attended Albany Academy, then studied law, then developed a taste for the sciences. First practical application of the latter was on the headwaters of the Sacandaga, where he made mining surveys, studied geology and in general interested himself in the physical aspects of his environment. He taught higher surveying, geodesy and topographical engineering at Hamilton College, published over 30 volumes of notes and records, and in 1920 died in an institution in Troy seriously crippled in mind and body. He had never married.

The bare facts about Colvin's life do not suggest the importance which he assumed in making and writing the history of the Adirondacks. During the course of his professional activities, he evidently did a great deal of constructive thinking about the future of our state and its citizens; he was one of the first, if not the first, to suggest the idea of the Forest Preserve, and in 1872 he became secretary of the State Park Commission appointed to investigate the possibilities of creating such a preserve. He did much of the work of this commission, and wrote its reports.

But when Colvin retired from the Adirondack survey, the dreamer in him supplanted the surveyor; he became president of the New York Canadian Pacific Railway, an organization that never progressed beyond the paper state, and when this failed he retired from public life to live and die in seclusion. ◣

CREATION OF THE ADIRONDACK PARK, PART ONE

By Michael J. Rushman, *York State Tradition*, Fall 1973

With the recent controversy over the master plan for both private and state land in the Adirondack Park, it is worth looking back to the park's birth. An understanding of the conditions and events which resulted in the park gives the New York resident some historical background with which to view the present situation.

The Adirondacks did not offer a very attractive picture to early settlers who had the option of moving to the rich lands of western New York and later to the Midwest and Far West. The mountainous terrain, rocky soil, and harsh climate combined to limit development. The topography dictated land use patterns; the valleys became avenues of settlement, with the rivers and lakes providing most transportation. Trapping and mining were the first economic incentives to prospective settlers, but the first real pressures for large-scale development came in the 1850s as the lumber supply in other parts of the state began to disappear. With the discovery of the pulp method for papermaking, any and all trees were coveted by the loggers, and the forces were set in motion that would eventually lead to the park.

So as 1872 approached, the Adirondacks were virtually unpopulated, and prospects for rapid settlement of the area were bleak. The conditions which later enhanced the area's recreational value—mountainous terrain, heavy annual snowfall, and inaccessibility—made it unattractive for settlement on a regular basis. An agricultural based economy was out of the question. What was present were mining operations, which required little land, and logging operations, which required an ever increasing amount of land, leaving it unusable in its wake. The recreation industry was in its infancy and played only a minor role in early efforts to create a park. It was the forestry and watershed question that gave rise to the park movement.

The formal legislative action began on March 15, 1872, when Thomas G. Alvord introduced in the Assembly an act creating a state park commission. It was to be charged with the task of inquiring "... into the expediency of providing for vesting in the State the title to the timbered regions lying within the counties of Lewis, Essex, Clinton, Franklin, St. Lawrence, Herkimer, and Hamilton, and converting the same into a public park"...[1] "While the immediate cause for such an action is not known, Charles Z. Lincoln and others suggest that the Federal action creating Yellowstone National Park only two weeks earlier provided Mr. Alvord with the idea. This act began the process of reacquiring woodlands that had been previously sold and regulating the harvest of timber. In addition, Verplanck Colvin was commissioned to undertake a topographical survey of the Adirondacks. Mr. Colvin is generally given credit for first proposing the creation of a park and was one of the first seven members of the park commission.

Their report was issued in 1873 and concluded: "We do not favor the creation of an expensive and exclusive park for mere purposes of recreation, but, condemning such suggestions, recommend the simple preservation of the timber as a measure of political economy."[2] It can be clearly seen that the commissioners decided to base the case for a preserve on economic considerations. This thinking surfaces later in the report when reasons for the preserve's formation are stated. In order of importance the commission listed the maintenance of the water supply to insure navigable rivers and ample water power, the Adirondack forest's impact on the climate of the state, the timber supply, and the use of the area as a resort.[3]

The report reviewed past state policies in relation to public lands, gave a brief history of the area, and set forth their recommendations. The first two sections allude to the vast land sales at ridiculously low prices and the natural conditions which stymied development, and the last section dealt with the forest question. A serious effort was made for the first time to convince legislators of the need to institute forest management principles. Although a new discipline to this country, as the commission pointed out, forest culture was an accepted practice in Europe. Unfortunately, no method of adding to the state lands was outlined, and considering the state controlled only 40,000 acres of the proposed area of 800,000 acres, this failure to suggest any program of land procurement was a serious weakness. The commission did propose the state should retain all land then under its control until a final remedy was decided upon.

Joel T. Headley, a figure who had done much to educate the public about the area, commented on the problem of acquiring land for the preserve: "Much has been said lately about turning this whole region into a state park. Without presenting the arguments so strongly urged, we would say that the obstacles in the way of such an enterprise are almost insurmountable, while the benefits sought for can be secured by a much easier mode. In the first place, this Adirondack Park would embrace over 4,000,000 of acres of which the State does not now own 40,000. These 4,000,000 of acres, with all their timber, water privileges, mineral beds, railroad, etc., would have to be purchased … The attempt to do so would lead to endless litigation and legislation."[4] Although Headley's figures were not totally accurate and he never outlined an alternative, he was correct in predicting legal and legislative problems.

Colvin's first survey report, entitled *Report on a Topographical Survey of the Adirondack Wilderness of New York*, appeared in 1873 and contained some valuable data and statistics. Colvin recommended protection of the forests and conservation of its water supply by the formation of a preserve. Neither report resulted in any legislative action, although Colvin continued to issue reports at irregular intervals until 1884.

In 1874, Governor John A. Dix made the first mention of the Adirondack problem in the governor's message. He reminded the legislature of the park commission's proposal and suggested some action be taken. The legislature failed to heed his words and no action was taken. In fact, not until 1882 would the park issue be raised again. Attention was focused on recovery from the Civil War and panic of 1873, expansion of business and industry, and the corruption that ran rampant during this period.

It was a governor, in the person of Alonzo B. Cornell, who brought the matter back into public light. In his annual message of 1882 he stated:

"By far the greater quantity of land within the Adirondacks wilderness proper belongs to the State. Individual ownership is now confined to a few hundred thousand acres. Heretofore it has been the practice of the State, with questionable policy, to sell its wild lands, at nominal price, to private parties, who having gone on in most cases, and cut off the marketable timber where accessible, and then abandoned to the State the clearings, worthless for agriculture generally, thereby escaping the payment of taxes. Forest fires have followed and raged with destructive fury, denuding the mountains and checking the flow of springs and streams that supply the navigable rivers to the north, and the Hudson River southward. Furthermore, many of the lakes, the natural reservoirs of the mountain courses, have been damaged by dams and overflows, so the shores of those lying within the working timber limits present the effects of irreparable injury. It has, therefore, become a question of serious import whether the State should any longer part with its title to land in this quarter, now held or may hereafter revert by the non-payment of taxes. It might be leased, perhaps, with safety, for certain purposes, but its uses should be carefully restricted.[5]

In just these few words, Cornell touched on almost every aspect of the forest problem which would plague state officials for the next ten years. His words indicate a remarkable grasp of the situation. No action was prompted by his remarks that year, but in 1883, Erastus Brooks, a metropolitan New York assemblyman, introduced a resolution asking "…that the committee on agriculture examine and report to the Assembly, at their earliest practical convenience, upon the subject of some positive legislation for the protection of the forests and trees of the State from destruction …"[6]

The resolution was adopted and the committee made its report one month later. They recommended the passage of a bill proposed by George Smith, of Herkimer, which would have created a three-man commission to study the entire matter. It was felt, perhaps a bit optimistically, that once a clear picture of the scope and location of state lands emerged, some suitable course of action could be agreed upon. The report argued emotionally:

"… the grand and picturesque Hudson, the magnetic and silvery Mohawk, the musical and restless Genesee, the busy wandering Chenango, the solemn and abrupt Oswego, the dark and dreary Black, and the impetuous, rushing Racket (sic) are still, thank heaven, preserved, still whispering tales out of the heart of the old forests whence they flow, and may God keep them fair and free as the guardians of our soil. But if a craven fain should raise his arm to fell the forests, then breathe no weak word of scorn or shame, but crush the villain where he stands."[7]

Despite such stirring prose, the measure was not passed. A substitute bill was passed, and it provided that "… no sales shall be made of lands belonging to the state situated in the counties of Clinton, Essex, Franklin, Fulton, Hamilton, Herkimer, Lewis, Saratoga, St. Lawrence and Warren."[8] This helped correct the unhappy tax sale problem. As is often the case with governmental policy, loopholes remained and had the effect of removing the state's title to a good deal of land it had acquired. There were two methods by which an owner could reclaim his land if he acted within two years after a tax sale. Redemption allowed him or any other interested party to pay the back taxes and gain title; cancellation allowed the former owner to regain title if there were any legal irregularities involved in the assessment, sale, or taxation of the land.[9]

A resolution by the Senate shortly afterwards, while not important operationally, was a precursor of land procurement methods. It provided that state land suitable for farming and villages, but not forests, be catalogued, and that privately-held woodlands adjacent to state land be catalogued and priced. An appropriation of $10,000 was made for the purchase of such lands in which the state was presently a joint owner. Finally, Mr. Colvin was commissioned to make a second survey to find and determine the boundaries of all state land in the Adirondacks.

In 1883, private organizations also became involved in the fight to preserve the forests. The New York City Chamber of Commerce appointed a forestry commission under the chairmanship of Morris K. Jesup to spearhead its efforts and invited other public organizations to join the cause. This call was answered by the Brooklyn Constitution Club and the New York Board of Trade and Transportation. In the years to come, these bodies were to play an important role in the park's formation.

Yet another governor felt it necessary to include the Adirondack preserve in his annual message in 1884. Although Grover Cleveland agreed that preservation of the forests was essential, he did criticize the expenditures for land surveys. It is worth noting that timber was not considered the prime reason for preservation. Instead it was the value of the Adirondacks as a watershed that was of prime concern. The state still depended heavily on its system of canals and rivers to move goods and produce. Everyone by this time realized the connection between a sufficient water level in the waterways and a healthy watershed protected by its covering of trees. The water situation had rapidly deteriorated as Charles S. Sargent indicates, "Not more than two-thirds, and in many cases not one-half, as much water now flows during the summer months in the streams issuing from the Adirondack regions as was seen in those streams a quarter of a century ago." [10] Besides the wasteful expenditures on surveys and the bureaucracy they had spawned, Cleveland was opposed to any state purchase of land, except for tax sales, until every other means of regulation had been tried.

The Special Committee on State Lands which had been appointed by the Senate in the previous year made its report in early 1884. A series of public hearings had been held, and the members became the first committeemen to visit the area as part of their investigation. It was found

Captured in time. Remembering how much fun it was to dress up for a train trip to the big city. *Courtesy Marilyn Breakey*

that most natives wanted the State to sell its land. It is somewhat unexpected that pressures for protection originated in the city, while local residents were in favor of a laissez-faire policy development.

The committee was the first to deal with the huge private estates that had been carved out of the wilderness. They rejected proposals that would have granted tax-free status for private land in return for restrictions on its use. They noted state land now totaled 750,000 acres as compared to 40,000 acres only ten years before. The committee felt that state lands were much more valuable than previously imagined, and protection was imperative. To this end they proposed a permanent three-member commission to deal with the preserve question. The legislature instead authorized the Comptroller to set up yet another commission to propose a system of forest preservation.

The year 1885 marked a crucial period in the three-stage process which resulted in the Adirondack Park. The Committee, appointed by Comptroller Chapin, is known by the name of its chairman, Charles S. Sargent. Its report was the most far-reaching and constructive of the seemingly endless series of such reports. For the first time the Catskills were included in the discussion and the infant recreation industry's dependence on the presence of the forest was acknowledged. Perceptively, the committee recognized the area's economy would be based on tourism in the future. While many lists of reasons for protection had been advanced, for the first time a list of the destructive influences was offered. In order, the committee placed the blame on artificial reservoirs, the manufacture of charcoal, lumbering, and forest fires.

Because of the difficulties in implementation, the committee stopped short of advocating state purchase of privately-held lands, and instead submitted three bills which contained their recommendations. The first would create a three-member commission, the second bill dealt with fire protection, and the third provided for taxation of state lands in the area and prohibited lumbering upon lands on which taxes are due.

Now that the ice had been broken, everyone suddenly had his own legislative program to solve the problem. The Sargent bills became stalled in committee, and here the New York Board of Trade and Transportation and the Brooklyn Constitution Club re-enter the story. One should not assume they had been inactive in the interim. Their joint committee under the chairmanship of Edmund Philo Martin had recently issued a report strongly urging state land purchases. To revive fading interest, Mr. Martin, with the help of Frank S. Gardner, drafted a single bill encompassing the Sargent proposals, state purchase of privately-held land, and the creation of a 2,500,000-acre forest preserve. It was approved and signed into law on May 15, 1885. Following are the two most important provisions of the law:

Section 7. All the lands now owned or which may hereafter be acquired by the state of New York, within the counties of Clinton, excepting the towns of Altona and Dannemora, Essex, Franklin, Fulton, Hamilton, Herkimer, Lewis, Saratoga, St. Lawrence, Warren, Washington, Greene, Ulster, and Sullivan, shall constitute and be known as the forest preserve.

Section 8. The lands now or hereafter constituting the forest preserve shall be forever kept as wild forest lands. They shall not be sold, nor shall they be leased or taken by any person or corporation, public or private.[11]

So ends the first period in the creation of the Adirondack Park. ▰

CREATION OF THE ADIRONDACK PARK, PART TWO

By Michael J. Rushman, *York State Tradition*, Winter 1974

The creation of the preserve did not end all problems it was intended to solve. To begin with, the $1,000,000 request for land requisition was not granted. Instead, the Forest Commission received an appropriation of $15,000 to cover administrative expenses. The commission issued annual reports, and in 1886 it recommended granting itself the authority to lease state land for limited uses. The legislature refused permission in 1886 and again in 1887. The report for 1891 contained a map outlining the proposed park area in blue, hence the term "blue-line."

In this period from 1886 to 1892, a new reason for a park was advanced—the recreation boom. The Sargent Committee had foreseen this development, but even they did not foresee the immediacy of its impact. Tourism was well on its way to becoming a big business in the North Country, and as visitors to the preserve increased each year, the idea of creating a park made more sense. The park owed its existence to worries concerning the protection of the watershed and the supply of lumber. These concerns were not forgotten, but supporters of the park felt it would exist side by side with the preserve. Again the fight was led by a downstate group, the Adirondack Park Association, organized by some of New York City's leading citizens. Their aim was "the preservation of the Adirondack forests, and by practical means the establishment of a state forest park therein."[1]

The movement for a park was helped by the mismanagement of the forest preserve. Gurth Whipple states, "Between 1885 and 1893 the State lost title to 123,980 acres through cancellations and redemptions granted by the Comptroller."[2] The legislature attempted to clarify the situation, but the entire matter remained confused until 1895, when the U.S. Supreme Court upheld New York statutes which ended any claims after a four-year grace period. The concept of a multi-headed commission was inefficient, and most of the work was done by the executive secretary. Another abuse was the sale of timber on state land, since the land itself could not be sold. Also timber stealing, title juggling, and the construction of illegal dams were commonplace.

This was the situation in 1890, when Governor David B. Hill made the first specific proposal for a park in his annual message. The governor suggested defining the park as a 50–70 square mile area, selling state land outside the park to obtain funds for buying land within the park, and leasing small parcels for specified purposes. All of this could be done for a relatively small sum when compared to the good that would result. To accomplish these goals, he called for the creation of a new park commission to draw up a workable plan for the creation of an Adirondack park.

The Senate committee which dealt with this matter agreed with the governor's conclusion that a park should be established. Serious difference of opinion arose over the estimated cost, and the senators felt there was no need for a new commission. So a concurrent resolution passed on April 4, 1890, ordered the existing Forest Commission to submit a report by the next session which would cover the governor's proposals.

In January of the following year the report was issued, and it noted "Public opinion, so far as it could be ascertained, has been from the first as a whole, strongly in favor of the park."[3] A good deal of the report deals with the size of the park and the future of the system of forest preservation. The size could range from 1,000,000 to 3,136,000 acres. It was felt that 2,250,000 acres would encompass the governor's suggested regions. The minimum area would neither protect enough forest land, protect the watershed, provide climatic controls, nor contain some of the wildest sections of the Adirondacks. The state controlled 760,000 acres at this time. The commission worried that unless boundaries of the park coincided with the existing preserve, the latter would be endangered. They felt the preserve should be retained in any event. To secure these ends the commission submitted a bill calling for immediate creation of a park, efforts to acquire all woodland in the park area at a cost not exceeding $3,500,000, and continued forest preservation efforts.

Again a private group offered a counter measure: this time it was the Adirondack Park Association that submitted a bill proposing a park and preserve of 2,238,000 acres of private land be created immediately. The land could be purchased for $7,000,000 outright; or for $3,000,000 if owners were allowed timber rights for 15 years. No action was taken on either measure in 1891.

In 1892 the legislature, cognizant of public desire for a park, passed an act which provided that:

"Section 1. There shall be a state park established within the counties of Hamilton, Herkimer, St. Lawrence, Franklin, Essex and Warren, which shall be known as the Adirondack park, and which shall, subject to the provisions of this act, be forever reserved, maintained and cared for as ground open for the free use of all the people for their health or pleasure, and as forest lands necessary to the preservation of the head-waters of the chief rivers of the state, and a future timber supply."[4]

In addition the Forest Committee was empowered to purchase lands in specified townships, sell lands in the preserve not needed for the park or preserve, lease five-acre campsites to individuals for not longer than five years, and allow private land owners to remove trees above a certain diameter for ten years after the sale of his land to the state. So ended the second stage in the park's development.

The actions of Governor Roswell P. Flower, the legislature, and the Forest Commission in 1893 triggered the call for a constitutional amendment. The year began with Governor Flower making lengthy remarks about the park in his annual message. He suggested that instead of buying land in the park zone and running the risk of scandal, the state should grant tax exemptions and limited lumbering privileges to private land-owners in return for promises that the land would not be despoiled. He went on to call for reorganization of the commission. Its new function would be temporary, consisting only of setting up the park. Routine operation and administrative matters would then be carried out by a forest bureau in the department of agriculture.

The governor's speech did result in legislative action, though not entirely to his liking. The commission's membership was increased to five, with all new members being appointed. The definition of the park was changed slightly, but the action most debated was granting the Forest Commission the power to sell timber of a certain size. The New York Board of Trade and Transportation and the Brooklyn Constitution Club opposed the change strenuously, but to no avail. This widening of the commission's powers was contrary to the public's wishes and clearly illustrates the legislature's ability to mold forest policy to meet the needs of the lumber industry in the face of public opposition. Frank S. Gardner, secretary of the New York Board of Trade and Transportation, commented after Flower's signing of the new legislation, "I am convinced the forests will never be made safe until they are put into the State Constitution."[5] Born of repeated frustrations, this remark became the rallying cry for the third stage in the park's development.

Once again downstate groups came to the fore. The Special Forestry Committee, chaired by Edmund Philo Martin, and the Special Committee on Constitutional Amendments, chaired by Simon Sterne were formed by the two New York City groups we have already encountered. The already-planned constitutional convention for 1894 greatly facilitated their efforts since the legislature, which had already shown their susceptibility to lumber interests' lobbying efforts, could be bypassed. Ratification of the convention's work would depend on the electorate at large.

The convention was convened on May 8, but it was not until late July that the proposed amendment, drawn up by the two special committees previously mentioned, was forwarded to Albany. There it was introduced by David McClure, a Democrat, on July 31. In a private meeting shortly before with the convention's leaders, Joseph H. Choate, convention president, said, "You have brought the most important question before this assembly. In fact it is the only question that warrants the existence of the Convention."[6] This was said despite the absence of any mention of the park in Choate's opening remarks or the existence of any committee to draft an amendment.

On August 1, McClure argued for the proposal in a speech that was favorably received by all. His request for a group to study the matter was approved on August 2, 1894. Despite his status as a Democrat in the face of a Republican majority of 99-60, McClure was appointed chairman of the five-member body. On August 23, their report was issued and on September 7 debate began. The amendment was kept short in contrast to the very lengthy proposals of the private groups, because it was felt that once the safety of the forests was assured, the legislature could be trusted to provide for enforcement and operational details.

It is worthwhile to follow the amendment's course in the convention and the changes offered by various delegates. William P. Goodelle, from Syracuse, suggested changing "sold or removed" to "sold, removed, or destroyed." This would eliminate any dams and reservoirs which caused destruction of woodlands. Nicoll Floyed put forth additions supporting the exchange of state lands outside the preserve for land within the preserve, use of park wood for fuel for area residents, and the continuation of leasing practices then in force. Frances Forbes and Henry R. Durfee offered amendments that would require the legislature to enact laws insuring the protection of the park and provide tax credits for any agricultural land kept in a forested state. The only speech in opposition was made by Thomas W. MacArthur, who implied the proposed amendment did not go far enough. He not offer an alternative, nor as we shall see, did he vote against the measure.

McClure opposed all changes except for Mr. Goodelle's suggestion, and he went on to suggest adding "leased" to the phrase "sold or exchanged." Surprisingly his advice was heeded, and all other amendments were defeated. The amendment as finally passed read:

"The lands of the State, now owned or hereafter acquired, constituting the forest preserve as now fixed by law, shall be forever kept as wild forest lands. They shall not be leased, sold, or exchanged, or be taken by any corporation, public or private, nor shall the timber thereon be sold, removed, or destroyed."[7]

The vote was 122-0, with 37 delegates absent, a victory quite amazing considering the years of bickering and divided opinion. It is perhaps more understandable when one discovers the vote came up late the evening of September 13, only two days before the planned adjournment. Darwin Benedict tried to make an argument that the vote did not reflect the true feelings about the amendment in light of the limited debate (two hours), absence of nearly 25% of the delegates, and Mr. Forbes' remarks that many were trying to ram through the measure so they could adjourn for the evening and get on to more important business the next day. I agree the unanimous vote overstates the support; however, a majority of delegates agreed something had to be done and the amendment seemed to be the only alternative to continued despoilment of the land. This final victory was summed up in the following day's *New York Tribune* as follows: "The convention took up the forestry amendment late in the evening. After some discussion it was passed as follows, receiving 122 votes …"[8]

The convention's work was presented to the voters in three separate packages. The first included all measures dealing with apportionment, the second listed all dealing with canal improvements, and the third lumped together all others including the forestry amendment. Elihu Root was responsible for this division, despite his feeling that each of the 33 amendments should be voted on separately. The practicality of such a division was precluded by the existing election laws.

The apportionment section was approved 404,335 to 350,625; the canal section was approved 442,998 to 327,645; and the remainder, including Article VII, Section 7, was approved 410,697 to 327,402. On January 1, 1895, the new Constitution became effective.

In looking back at the twenty-two-year struggle, it is interesting to note the main participants—the governors, the legislature, lumbering interests, the commissions, and public interest groups—and the role each played. Nearly every governor made mention of the park in at least one of his annual messages. For the most part they argued in favor of state controls over the area, but not state ownership of the land. Governors did not act out of concern for the forests, but in response to public outrage at the atrocities being committed against the land. That they did at least react was commendable.

The legislature's role in the whole matter is less commendable. They did pass a lengthy list of restrictive measures from 1885–1893 and authorize an even lengthier list of commissions. While a few legislators were genuinely concerned about the forests, the legislature enacted protective measures only grudgingly and then filled them with loopholes. The true feelings of the body are revealed by measures which permitted land leasing, sale of timber, tax exemptions, construction of dams, and questionable land transfers.

Lumbering interests should have been the group most opposed, yet no spokesman for their viewpoint emerged. This can be explained for a number of reasons. First, they undoubtedly had certain legislators on the payroll and left the defense of lumber interests to them. Secondly, they did not realize the resolve of those who were determined to protect the forests. Thirdly, and most importantly, they did not obey forest protection measures, including for some time Article VII, Section 7.

The commissions were generally comprised of responsible and knowledgeable individuals who did much to educate the public about forest conservation. They also compiled a great amount of information which provided a firm foundation for the arguments of park proponents. While the commissions did perform a necessary function, there was a tendency to overstudy the problem.

Finally there were the private organizations which could be considered forerunners of Nader's public-interest research groups. They argued endlessly for broadened forest protection, and although their motives may have been selfish, their results were positive. Their carefully-planned strategy kept the issues before the public at all times, and they persevered until the safety of the Adirondack forest was assured beyond any doubt.

Even this brief look at the park's creation shows us that the Adirondacks' present condition is not the result of a policy of benign neglect, but is the result of the conscious effort by many citizens who recognized the value of such a forest to the state of New York. ▪

⚡INFERNO IN THE ADIRONDACKS

By Harry W. Hicks, *North Country Life*, Fall 1948
Reprinted from the New York State *Conservationist*

In the year 1903, forest fires burned over approximately 600,000 acres of land in the Adirondacks. This was the worst holocaust of its kind in the history of the State.

Cinders fell in Albany, 150 miles away from the chief fire center of Lake Placid. It has been reported that smoke from the Adirondacks caused concern in Washington, D.C. Darkness like that of an eclipse of the sun fell on Northern New York, and consternation and panic seized upon the populations of many villages and isolated communities in the mountains.

In many places every able-bodied man was repeatedly called into firefighting service. A few population centers were completely surrounded by conflagrations threatening home and hearth, and many families, carrying what they could, fled before the inferno. In the main, however, each community organized for self-preservation and fought it out with the elements in long and bitter battle.

The unpopulated areas? Like tinder, these unprotected forest zones became unchecked roaring infernos of flame and smoke until there was nothing left to burn or until, in early June, Nature came to the rescue with long-deferred rains.

Modern fire towers, constructed throughout the mountains, were the first line of defense against forest fires. Climbers, like these gals on Goodnow Mountain in the 1930s, often used the lookouts as a background in their Adirondack vacation photo albums.
Courtesy George Shaughnessy

North to south, fires burned from Malone to Mayville; east to west, they burned from Elizabethtown to Carthage. Passengers arriving in Lake Placid via the Delaware and Hudson Railroad reported that the whole country to the north, from Dannemora to Saranac Lake, was in flames.

The fire zone was not limited to one area. Fires raged in widely separated sections. The Webb estate on the south was hard hit, as were the Rockefeller and Whitney holdings. The region of Tupper Lake in the west, and all intervening sections almost to the shores of Lake Champlain and Lake George, were likewise affected. In the vicinity of Keene Valley, a fierce battle was fought that swept northward from North Hudson, burning all of the peak of Noonmark enroute.

Adirondack Lodge, Heart Lake, was built in the winter of 1878–79. It burned on September 3, 1903. *A Seneca Ray Stoddard photo. Courtesy Maitland DeSormo Collection*

This blaze threatened Keene Heights (now called St. Huberts). Keene and Keene Valley were also in the danger zone, and the people of these towns fought for the lives of their beautiful communities. On May 8 *The Adirondack Record* (published in Ausable Forks) listed fires as burning in Lake Placid, Saranac Lake, Bloomingdale, Blue Ridge, Lewis, Clintonville, Ausable Forks, Port Henry, Olmsteadville, Newcomb, and Schroon Lake. And on May 29 *The Record* carried an article which began: "Our country people are beginning to wonder for what particular sins of theirs they are being punished at the present time. They are studying up Bible history to find which of the plagues of Egypt they may expect next."

The Lake Placid area was one of the hottest centers of the 1903 fires. Charles Wood, then cruiser for the J. & J. Rogers Company, gives the facts. Starting at Tableland Farm, fires raged southward about five miles to Heart Lake, and southeast to South Meadows, and on and on up into the Klondyke. In this last remote region, a cache of dynamite had been stored for lumbering purposes. Proof of the southeast boundary of this particular fire is that this dynamite exploded on June 3, the culminating day of the battle.

Both Mr. Wood and Mr. Walter Goff, of Cascadeville, confirm the reports that the turning point came on June 3. They also testify that it was on this day that the fire swept from Keene through Cascade Pass, and on past Cascadeville to the west. Here it merged with another fire that roared down from Scott Mountain (now named Van Hoevenberg), and with still another that burned from Tableland Farm south to Mt. Jo and Heart Lake. This fire ended in the destruction of Adirondack Lodge, resort home of Henry Van Hoevenberg and the largest and most beautiful log structure in America.

At Adirondack Lodge, so they say, Henry Van Hoevenberg was so frantic at the prospect of losing his building that he drew up a chair in front of the fireplace in the great living room, pistol in hand and rifle across his knees, and declared that rather than leave, he would go down with his house of logs. His chief aide tried to argue him into a state of normal reason, but at first failed. Then he announced that if Van Hoevenberg would not flee to safety, neither would he, and so a second chair was drawn up to the fireplace.

This action is said to have brought Van Hovenberg to his senses. Taking his latest patents constructed of metal, along with his silverware and other valuable possessions, he submerged them in Heart Lake, and then he and his aide fled along the shore of the lake toward Indian Pass. Several hours later they heard the crash of the high tower of the Lodge as it fell in flames.

Walter Goff, 15, drove a team in the very nick of time to Cascade Lakes Hotel to rescue Mrs. Weston and her daughters. Happily the fire swept around the clearing on which the hotel was built, but it raged over the southern slopes of Pitchoff (properly called Keene Mt.), and burned all of Cascade Mt. and large sections of Porter Mt.

Mr. Goff tells how he fought the fires. His father ordered out 300 sap buckets from their sugar bush, filled them with water, and distributed them around his farm. Thus every newly started fire was within easy distance of at least a bucketful of water. Walter recounts how large cinders, or flaming pieces of birch bark, leaving trails of fire and smoke behind them, sailed through the air like rockets, each capable of starting a new fire.

All eyewitnesses, including Henry Willis, Henry Lacy, Frank Randall, Jesse Martin, Perry and Joe Call, Morton Peacock, Dr. Godfrey Dewey, and Katherine Jones, speak of the terrifying noise created by the raging wind and fire, especially when it jumped from one treetop to another. Many witnesses reported that the roads in the vicinity of Lake Placid were filled with rabbits, porcupines, and deer, seeking refuge.

The manager of the Webb estate was reported in the June 12 issue of *The Adirondack Record* as having invited Carl E. Meyers to bring his "explosive balloon" to that area, to attempt artificial precipitation of rain. There was no report that Mr. Meyers accommodated the manager. *The Record* also tells a story of a man named Washington Chase, whose marriage was scheduled to take place at the Caughnawaga Club Camp. The groom, however, was out on fire-fighting duty. The bride and minister sent word that they were ready for the ceremony and that he should report forthwith,

Goodnow Mountain fire tower, 1932. Fire wardens from tall lookouts were once the first line of defense against forest fires. *Courtesy George Shaughnessy*

but Chase sent back the message: "No time to be botherin' with wimmin folk." A providential rain shower, however, relieved the groom of his fire-fighting duties, and he finally appeared for the wedding.

Walter Goff kept a diary in which his first record of fire fighting assignment appeared on April 27. Similar entries throughout May and well into June show that in the Lake Placid area fires burned during a period of about six weeks. This is confirmed by Dr. Godfrey Dewey on the basis of facts given him by Henry Van Hoevenberg. Two hundred fifty men dug a trench completely around St. Huberts, and 300 more were called out to save the town of Lake Placid. Charles Wood states that for years before the Cascade fire, a pair of fish hawks had nested and reared their young near the Lower Lake. They were favorites with the patrons of the Cascade House. During the great fire the hawks circled over the lake with loud and protesting cries and then disappeared, never to return.

How did the fires start? It must not be forgotten that for 72 days there had been no rain, the last moisture having been provided by the disappearing snows in late March. In 1903, as now, the period of spring preceding the fresh green growth of ground cover was highly dangerous, because of the layer of dry vegetation remaining from the previous autumn. Conditions were "made to order" for forest fires.

One of the many individual fires was caused by the carelessness of the foreman of a crew which was burning stumps on Tableland Farm. Others were no doubt the result of unextinguished campfires. Many more were attributed to sparks spread by railroad locomotives, and it is stated by some persons who were consulted in the preparation of this article that fires were sometimes started deliberately so as to induce employment— at two dollars a day—to fight them.

In 1903 the system of fire prevention was relatively undeveloped as compared with present protective measures. Nevertheless, the experience of that year may well serve as a text on which to base an appeal to all users of the forested areas of New York: Be careful with fire!

A few years ago the late Jim Hopkins, District Ranger of the Conservation Department located in Saranac Lake, stated that in fourteen days,

93 forest fires were extinguished, of which more than 80 were on the roadside. This simply spells the guilt of the smoker who flips his unextinguished stub out the window as he drives along.

No torment meted out in hottest Hades is too awful a punishment for the careless smoker, camper, hunter, fisherman, lumberman, or motorist who takes chances with fire. We have learned much as a result of what happened in 1903; since then our fire detection and fire fighting organizations have been modernized and greatly expanded. But no matter how effective these organizations, we can never afford to be careless with fire.

What happened in 1903 *could* happen again. We must see that it doesn't. ▰

PART ONE

Culture, Lifestyles and Mountain Air

COLLECTION ONE
Points in Time

COLLECTION TWO
Adirondack Land

➡ **COLLECTION THREE**
An Adirondack Past

COLLECTION FOUR
Adirondack School Days

Deer hunters at "Jock's Lake," 1880s. This transparent body of water was named after Jonathan Wright, a famous hunter-trapper-guide who roamed the Adirondacks. The Adiondack League Club changed the name to Honnedaga Lake. *Courtesy Peter Costello*

A DELIGHTFUL MIX OF STYLES AND "VOICES"

By William J. O'Hern

Readers were the backbone of *North Country Life* magazine. Every month publisher Cole received dozens upon dozens of letters, but rarely had space to devote to a regular column of "Excerpts from the Editor's Mail."

Readers' letters included complimentary feedback, reactions to articles that were of particular interest, commentary and additional insight, shared eyewitness descriptions, family history and interesting source material, as evidenced in Clara Louise Spenser's 1952 letter that provided personal historical background that is rarely found in history books.

Spenser wrote, "…our family bought land from the original patentee in 1795, cleared off the timber, and began farming, paying off their debt as they could…in the Yankee project of 'getting ahead.'

"…my grandfather Thomas, born in 1809 lived all his life overlooking the rolling foothills of the Adirondacks. He…devoted his life to farming and fruit raising, though he did teach school of a time…"

Every now and then Cole would encourage a writer with especially exceptional memories to put them down on paper, saying the recollection would make "a notable

Many old timers remember attending Rev. Byron-Curtiss' lakeside Sunday services held at St. Catherine's Chapel built in a woodsy grove at the shore of North Lake. "My mother, Galen Glasgow Hoxie," Meredith Ferlage said, "is in the foreground at the left (in white). Byron-Curtiss is behind the second boy." *Photo by George Hoxie. Courtesy Meredith Ferlage*

contribution" to the lore of the North Country as well as entertain magazine readers. Some readers were born in the Adirondacks. Others arrived from other places. Many resided in the mountains until their deaths, while others physically vacated the mountains for far-away places but left their hearts back in their Adirondack homeland.

Frederick H. Cowles was one such magazine subscriber. By 1950 he had moved to California, but his correspondence revealed glimpses into his memory's treasure chest. It was obvious he could turn time backward in its flight.

He might have had no interest in leaving the present, even for a moment, lest he miss some exciting adventure or opportunity of the time in which he lived—but he also did not want to lay aside his earlier Adirondack experiences.

In the end he was satisfied to leave behind the years of satisfied hopes and events, enjoyed in contentment "near the summit of life's expectancy." There, he maintained, one could face whatever the day offered with complacency.

His "Recollections of the Adirondacks" is a personal glimpse back to moments of rare pleasure, much as one might glance back for another look at an appreciated picture in a gallery of art treasures. ◼

◪ RENDEZVOUS WITH BEAUTY

I have a rendezvous with Beauty
When Spring comes back upon the hills;
I have a thousand new enchantments
To fill my eyes and ears with thrills:
I'll hear the meadow larks and bluebirds
And listen to a laughing stream
Set free from winter's gloomy prison,
Sparkling in the sun's warm gleam.

I have a rendezvous with Beauty,
A dream to hold through ice and snow,
That waits my ever-eager longing
Spring's wonders freely to bestow.
I hear Pan's footsteps gaily dancing
Round some greening bush to me,
As the fairy-folk peek slyly,
Wondering if my human eyes can see.

I have a rendezvous with Beauty
That's waiting for me one day in Spring
A poet's soul to stir and strengthen,
And so in faith my heart can sing.
Will you who love the fresh, rare glory
On hill and meadow, flower and tree,
Come apart in awe and rapture,
To keep that rendezvous with me?

—Edna Greene Hines, *North Country Life*, Spring 1947 ◼

Chazy Lake, ca. 1900. *Photo by N. L. Burdick. Courtesy Special Collections, SUNY College at Plattsburgh*

RECOLLECTIONS OF THE ADRIONDACKS—PART ONE

By Frederick H. Cowles, *North Country Life*, Fall 1952

With some thought of the younger generation, I will refer to the Survey of the Adirondack Region which began in 1872 "with the smallest appropriation" when surveyors stood for the first time on the little lake, "Tear of the Clouds," described by them as a "mossy springlet lake by the mountain domes of Marcy, Skylight, and the Gray Peak, this lovely pool lifted on its granite pedestal toward heaven, the loftiest water mirror of the stars."

If this description seems flamboyant, it must be borne in mind that these surveyors were hampered in their work by the reluctance of the State Legislature in securing sufficient funds for even the publication of the annual report, during the years of 1874, '75, '76, and '77. Only the financial report, with bills of items and vouchers, were rendered to the comptroller.

Existing maps and imperfect surveys had been marked by what was described as "monstrous" errors, and up to 1872 a geodetic survey of the

Adirondack region did not exist. The appropriation made by the 1874 legislature "for salary for '72, and '73," amounting to five thousand dollars, had never been paid, and according to the Report of the Topographical Survey, there was actually a reduction in the appropriations, which did not exceed some five thousand dollars. Comparing means of transportation available to the surveying party late in 1875, September to be exact, when Ticonderoga was reached by the new railroad then being constructed down the western shore of Lake Champlain, with comparative luxury of transportation over the Delaware and Hudson Railroad of sixteen years later, the time of my first venture into "the wilderness," it is not surprising that those who left Albany on September 30th in '75 were moved by the wild and beautiful landscape "new and unvisited" and had the vision of its priceless value to the inhabitants of cities to be along the Mohawk and Hudson Valleys. In these cities there was to be born a love for this wild region, with its life-giving and spiritual uplift of forest, lakes, ponds, streams, and mountains that in later years was to bring forth staunch defenders of the principal of a State Park set aside in perpetuity against the despoiling fate of Michigan and Minnesota, by fire and axe. Possibly Verplanck Colvin, surveyor, in his "bark shanty" shelter, near the sand beaches of Blue Mountain Lake, felt that it was necessary to arouse in the breasts of some of these legislators a kindred feeling for what was to become the Empire State's "summer home."

I have a copy of this Report which came into our family possession in 1883, and from which it is possible to trace the beginnings of the deep affection the writer has for the Adirondacks. The very names in the table of altitudes stimulate the imagination—at least they did mine. For instance— Ampersand Mountain and Pond, Ausable Lake and Forks, Chair Rock, Oswegatchie, Beaver Meadows (Spruce Lake), Big Moose, Black Creek, Bog River Falls, Bouquet Mt., Cedar River, Evergreen Pond, Hurricane Mt., Horse Shoe Pond, Hurricane Mt., Indian Pass, John Brown's Place, Mirror Lake, Lilly Pad Pond, Loon Lake, St. Regis, Sacandaga River, Tahawus, Owls Head Mt., Pitch Off Pass, Partridge Hill, Poke-a-Moonshine Mt., Red Horse Chain, Roaring Brook, Saranac, Wallface, Utawana, etc.

It was several years after The Colvin Survey was given to my Father that I came across the Report. Passing over the triangulation, barometric pressure figures, base lines, monuments and road surveys, I found enough in the text itself to stir the longing of any boy with a natural love for mystery and wild regions. In 1888, on page 163, I came across the following comment by Colvin:

"Crossing the inlet we reached the river. The ice of the river was not smooth and bare like that of windswept lakes, but covered with snow, yet not deep enough to render snowshoes necessary, and offered us an easy footpath through the forest. Here we came upon the trail of a huge wolf. The footprints were as large as those of a panther. Crossing the forest we reached at noon 'eighth lake', where we sought our camp of the preceding fall and lunched within its shelter."

Could any boy have resisted that, I ask? Came a summer when my parents decided to go abroad. My brother and I, left in the care of my grandmother, were told we were to spend the summer at a place in the Adirondacks called Loon Lake and to that spot in the "North Woods," as it was called, we were routed over the now active "D. and H. R. R." on the night sleeper from the Grand Central Station in New York City.

Had I only realized that this was opening a new and priceless experience in my life, one whose memories were never to be effaced during a lifetime, I would have been less fretful that hot June night when, perched in an upper berth I listened to the click of the rails, sniffed at the heavy oily odors of the sleeping car corridor and wished for morning. I had a vague idea we were to travel along the west side of historic Lake Champlain. Determined to awaken early in the morning, I could not sleep at all, so excited I was to see Champlain, which I understood was very long and very broad. I tossed around in the berth uncomfortably, conscious of the stuffy air of the car, and exchanged whispered comments with my brother. Somehow I became aware that we had passed a small place called Whitehall and were beyond another called Crown Point. That awakened recollections of Ticonderoga and Ethan Allen, the "Great Jehova and the Continental Congress" of my school examinations, but brought little comfort.

Not long after, a thunder shower, probably fresh from its growling journey over the Adirondack forests, along whose edge we were winding, announced itself by frequent flashes of lightning, visible through the ventilators. Soon the rain fell in torrents. The roar of the rain on the metal roof of the car appeared to intensify the feeling of stuffiness and the heat. Altogether I began to feel miserable. Within half an hour the storm moved, muttering away to the east and, had I been able to look out of the windows of the car, I would have been able to see its forked outline over the Green Mountains of Vermont across the lake. As it was, I saw only the dim yellow light cast by the lamps and prayed for daylight. And then it stole into the car, a heaven-sent, cool, sweet breath of the passing storm, laden with something unfamiliar, growing things, balsam fir, a perfume-laden welcome to the forest barrier we were skirting, as if it were saying, "This is the gateway entrance of the years to come, little boy." And then I slept. ▰

Early-days North Country home. Descendants of native Adirondack pioneers were prime contributors to *North Country Life* magazine. *Courtesy of Clifford Gill*

⚑RECOLLECTIONS OF THE ADRIONDACKS—PART TWO

By Frederick H. Cowles, *North Country Life*, Fall 1953

The old *New York Sun* once carried in its "Letters from Subscribers" a prolonged discussion as to whether mountain lions, catamounts, panthers or varmints screamed while roaming the North Woods.

I recall being taken with a group of other small boys, years before, to the zoo in New York City, where with open mouths we remained during feeding time while the zoo attendants shoved huge chunks of meat between the bars of cages to lions, tigers, leopards and other meat-eating specimens of the cat family, including the "varmints." These last, excited by the snarls and roars of the other beasts, paced nervously back and forth in their cages, rubbing their heads against the bars like big pussycats, and emitting screams similar to those of a woman in hysterics. At the time I had never heard a woman in hysterics, but later I remember a red-headed cook, employed by our family, throwing a sort of fit, my brother and I called it, and the janitor threw a bucket of water on her. The cook stopped her kicking and screaming and disappeared through a door and never had another attack that I can remember. No one threw water at the pumas in the park, and they continued to give forth blood-curdling sounds—whether because of captivity or their natural way I was not to know for many years.

Around 1908, while stopping at a hotel owned by the Day family at Blue Mountain, I arranged an overnight fishing trip with a guide, Ira Weller by name. The Day property of several hundred acres adjoined the William G. Rockefeller "preserve," through which the West Branch of the St. Regis River flows. It was understood that the State of New York had secured a legal opinion that if the owner of a piece of land posted his property, everyone was thereby forbidden to enter the land to fish from the banks of a stream or even to wade such a stream. If, however, the stream were navigable, it became legal to fish from a boat. What the status is now I do not know.

On starting out on our trip, Ira and I headed for a small log cabin several miles from Blue Mountain and just outside the Rockefeller preserve, taking with us enough supplies for a day or two, intending to fish the St. Regis River inside the private property—but also inside of the boat. The river there teemed with fine trout, and we soon had enough fish for our supper and breakfast.

In addition to the enjoyment of lively luck with the trout, it was interesting to watch the deer, seven or eight of them, as they browsed not far from us without fear, or waded in the shallows, apparently secure in their animal knowledge or instinct that they were protected by posted land and a closed season. In their red coats, with white flags twitching on account of the flies, they were a pretty sight. Two bucks among them carried antlers resembling Christmas trees, as the guides describe it, the horns being of course in the velvet.

But even the best of fishing loses out in time when hunger beckons. Up at camp, Ira started supper preparations, while I, following his directions, descended the path leading to the spring to fill the tin water pail.

The spring issued from the bank beside the river, and before filling the pail, I stood for a moment lost in the peace and hush of this lovely June evening. There was only the sound of a trout rising now and then with a soft "plup" to seize a white miller, and over in the forest across the quiet eddies of the St. Regis, the song of a thrush, bell-like on the evening air. Suddenly a scream issued from the darkening woods, and I glanced at the group of deer. Seven heads were up. Without shame I confess to an eerie feeling, a slight crawling of the skin.

Something in that sound took me back through the years, striking a familiar note. Through the silence and the cool breath of the forest my thoughts swept back through the years, and I was in Central Park Zoo once more.

Again that impatient scream. All doubt dispelled, I knew it for what it was. It seemed a good time to be going—the coffee and the trout were waiting.

I decided, between the river and the cabin, to be casual about this noise. On reaching the steps, I glanced at Ira, who stood listening and looking toward the Rockefeller boundary signs.

Merwin's Blue Mountain House, September 12, 1879. *A Seneca Ray Stoddard photo.*
Courtesy Maitland DeSormo Collection

"Mr. Cowles," he said, "did you hear anything while you were down at the spring?"

I replied that I had.

"Well," he said, "I haven't heard that sound for years in these here woods."

We both stood on the narrow porch, looking upstream to where the deer had been. But they had vanished. Something had disturbed them. ◼

RECOLLECTIONS OF THE ADRIONDACKS—PART THREE

By Frederick H. Cowles, *North Country Life*, Winter 1953

Around 1922, I built a camp at Cranberry Lake. As far as privacy was concerned, it was an ideal spot, surrounded, as it was, by State-owned lands; our only neighbor was a friend who had purchased the adjoining twenty-five acres together with an old camp of sturdy log construction.

Far across the lake was the school of forestry of a well-known university, and above us "flowed lands," difficult to navigate, unless one understood the devious winding of the channels. We hauled the logs, 27-inch spruce, down from Cranberry Lake Village, on the ice, peeled and varnished them, and made all snug, between the chinks, with oakum. A fine spring flowing, summer and winter, provided ample water supply, while some extra tents accommodated guests, who braved the indifferent road between Carthage and Wanakena. From the porch of the main building we watched the deer feeding across the lake on warm evenings, their far-away splashing punctuated by the chorus of scores of husky bullfrogs.

When the moon floated in the sky it shed a peaceful light over the forest, unbroken by human habitation or sound. In the neighbor's cabin, a huge fireplace was adorned with deer heads, several with magnificent antlers. On the ceiling of the large living room stretched half of a huge snakeskin. Attracted by the length of the anaconda, for that was the species, I took the trouble to measure the half nailed to the ceiling beams. To my astonishment, it proved to be nineteen feet from the top of the tail to the end half of the section, which was, undeniably, the widest part. A reptile measuring some thirty-eight feet was something so startling as to prompt inquiry as to the circumstance of its ownership and capture.

It appears that the previous owners had been boon companions and one of them in Florida, duck shooting, had strolled along the shore on the Gulf of Mexico side. Observing a tree floating near the shore, he also noticed that one of the limbs moved in waves. A second look revealed the unpleasant fact that it was no limb but a huge snake. Without ado, the hunter let go with both barrels of his shotgun and fled. When he returned later with curious but skeptical friends, they found to their astonishment a sure-enough anaconda—evidently washed across the Gulf by some hurricane sweeping the shores of Central America.

Its length made the trophy too large for display in the Adirondack cabin, and so the partners, we were informed, cut the skin right across the center, half-way of the length, where it may be seen to this day, if the cabin still stands.

Next to the anaconda stretched the skin of a nine-foot Texas rattler. Huge as this was, it was diminutive alongside of the other.

In July, 1878 the Colvin Survey party, in their search for the "true division line" of the Totten and Crossfield Purchase, marched forward "toward the great corner." On the 14th they reached Wolf Lake. It was their description of this body of water, described by Colvin as "strange," that was responsible for my becoming acquainted with the Cranberry Lake section of the Adirondacks. It was described as being the "outlet" for the Oswegatchie River. In their search for the lake, they speak of "a rapid above the marshy shores of the stream." It was the singular form of the lake in question, with its long sand ridge "separating two bays"—which proved to be two lakes instead—that influenced my decision to go over into this country. Here, too, a quicksand was described into which Verplanck Colvin waded and which nearly caused his death by drowning.

Early in August of the late nineties, Al Abbott, my guide and friend of many camping trips, met my afternoon train from New York at Remsen, a junction of the R.W. and O. and what was then called the Webb Road. He had come down from Paul Smiths bringing our boat and tents. The supplies we were to pick up at Carthage. From Carthage we proceeded via the Carthage and Adirondack Railroad to Benson Mines, at which point we engaged a team to haul us in to the Oswegatchie, several miles distant. Reaching that river at Sternbergs, our boat and supplies were unloaded, the teamster paid three dollars, and, with high hopes of adventure, we started upstream. Mosquitoes descended in swarms; the marshy shores described in the Survey twisted and turned and doubled back on themselves.

In five miles of paddling, wading, and cutting our way through fallen trees, we covered nearly sixteen miles of bucking the current. Near sundown we reached the rapid described by Colvin. A beautiful spot it proved to be. The marshlands were left behind and virgin forest surrounded us. Unfortunately, at this moment of appreciation, the rain descended in torrents.

For three days and nights, Al and I huddled in the tent. On the fourth day the sun arrived; so did one of the most interesting characters it has been my good fortune to meet in the North Woods. Down through the rapids he suddenly appeared, guiding his canoe with skill to the landing place out of the current.

Tall, rugged, all bone and sinew, he approached with out-stretched hand and a kindly smile of welcome. He had, he informed us, come down from the Plains several miles above our camp and where an ancient log cabin was occupied by a family who had settled there. Caretaker for the lumber company, on whose lands we had inadvertently located our camp, he tactfully made known that it was "customary" to pay a modest fee (one dollar) for which permission would be given to remain. We paid, and he receipted on a piece of brown wrapping paper. Not relishing a return trip by the river to Sternbergs, we inquired if he could suggest another route out. He then drew a rough map leading from "The Plains" to Long Lake West station, which he gave us nineteen miles to the east. He also produced a book of verses of which he was the author, the expense of which had been borne by "friends down in the St. Lawrence Valley." Before leaving, he suggested that we should be sure to visit Wolf Lake and, again, provided us with a rough map of that trail. This lake, he indicated, would require our "carrying" our boat through dense woods for a mile or two, but was worth seeing. As he prepared to depart after dinner in the still-damp tent, we ventured to inquire of his age. He informed us that he was ninety-three, a fact afterwards verified. He also solemnly insisted that the stream upon which we were camped was not to be called the "Oswegatchie" but that the correct Indian name was "Oswegatanie"—which meant "inflowing" into Cranberry Lake, and that

"Oswegatchie" meant "out flowing," also Indian. This correction of names appeared in his book of verses, one of which was dedicated to Bear Mt. in the Cranberry Lake district. The weather having cleared, our old friend took his departure, promising to see us when we came through the Plains on our way to Long Lake West. As he, with seeming ease, bucked the swift current up the rapids of the "Oswegatanie," we marveled at his strength and skill until, lost to view, he disappeared around a bend in the river. Taking advantage of the good weather, we lost no time setting forth the following day for Wolf Lake.

The trail—very difficult to trace—led up through a forest that apparently had never seen an ax. Carrying a ninety-pound Adirondack skiff proved a man-size job for both of us. It was with considerable profanity that the trip finally ended on a small outlet to the lake luring us into this wild country.

Colvin's description proved 100% accurate, with the added excitement of a huge animal ploughing its way across the far end of the seldom-visited body of water. Oars we had none; leaving them at camp, we had depended upon a paddle, owing to the rough carry. In vain we endeavored to head the animal off, until we discovered it to be a huge bear. On this discovery, speed did not appear so important and we drifted with diminished energy. The bear soon made a landing, upon which he stood on his hind legs and, Al swore, laughed at us. "The Survey" speaks of a deer lick made of potash, alumina and iron—"a natural lick." This may have accounted for Bruin's presence. In the wilds of New Brunswick, Canada, in moose country, I have seen such natural licks with deep-trodden trails from the four points of the compass, to which deer, moose, bear and smaller game wended their way. I have taken snapshots of partridge attracted to these licks. Before leaving Wolf Lake, we climbed to the top of the sand ridge along the southerly shore where, as far as the eye could reach and to the northeast tumbled forested mountains unbroken by human habitation.

The journey back to camp, downhill, was less arduous, and later, around a cheerful campfire, smoking our pipes, we went over the events of the day, thanking in our hearts the man and men whose explorations for the State had opened a new experience for us. A week later, we headed for the Plains, arriving in time for supper, leaving behind Wolf Lake with its "pine trees, its moss and whortleberry bushes, the beautiful waters, and strange sand dune."

The effort required to pole the boat up through the rapids enhanced the respect generated by the "old" caretaker. We saw him for the last time upstream where a warm welcome awaited us at the Plains—a small clearing surrounded by dense forest. Supper was ready, with venison, hot johnnycake, honey and flapjacks. We slept in a loft over the kitchen. This was reached by a rough ladder and had the advantage of heat from the kitchen stoves plus the aroma of coffee and bacon, a welcome reminder the next morning, when frost-covered pastures surrounded the cabin. Hospitable as it was, the owners refusing any remuneration, we reluctantly said our "good-bye," heading for an early start. We had nineteen rugged miles to go, relieved by a series of lakes and ponds lying between the Oswegatanie and the Webb Road. The Old Timer accompanied us far up the trail. As we came to the parting, we handed him another dollar, which we learned from our hosts was expected by him and in return for which he grasped our hands and solemnly recited:

> *"Farewell, dear friend,*
> *For we must part.*
> *Parting causes pain.*
> *Hope lives eternal*
> *In my heart*
> *That we may meet again."*

★ FATHER'S LAST DECORATION DAY

By E. Eugene Barker, *North Country Life*, Spring 1950

Having been conducted in essentially the same manner since it was first initiated eighty-one years ago, Crown Point's Memorial Day observance has become something of a folk custom. The author of this description of the custom is a native of Crown Point.

Memorial Day always meant a great deal to my father. He had served during the entire duration of the Civil War, having enlisted as a private at the age of nineteen. He rose to command his regiment in battle at the age of twenty-three and was brevetted lieutenant-colonel when he was mustered out of service at the close of the war.

His patriotism was sincere, and he had a deep loyalty to his comrades of that long conflict. Because he revered the noble emotions and fine qualities of human character, Memorial Day was, to him, a serious occasion. Even the baseball game that entertained the younger generation after all the exercises were over seemed to him, I am sure, out of keeping with the spirit of the day.

We always called it "Decoration Day," and truly it was just that. All the ceremonies of the observance were formed around the rite of decorating the graves of soldiers. In my boyhood these were almost entirely veterans of the Civil War. There were, however, several graves of men who had served in the Revolution and in the War of 1812. The Spanish-American War had recently been fought, but none of its veterans yet lay in our cemeteries. Now we have others—boys who fought in the two World Wars. These young men were known to all of us—they came from our own homes.

Decoration Day has always been an occasion that has drawn everybody from the remotest parts of our rural town. Even circus day and the county fair have never appealed so universally as has this, our own community day. It has grown up over the years since it was initiated eighty-one years ago, and there has never been a single lapse in its observance.

New modes of living have brought changes in the ways of life here, but the celebration remains essentially the same. Automobiles take one

Fouquet Hotel. Guests sat out in the gardens drinking tea, and imagined that
they could taste the sweetness, the coolness, and the refreshment of the mountains.
Courtesy Special Collections, Feinberg Library, SUNY College at Plattsburgh

whirling up the hills over surfaced roads in minutes instead of hours. The small local schools have long since been closed and consolidated into a central school. The school band members in smart uniforms ride in their school bus. These and other minor changes have come about with the passing years, but the spirit of the day is perennial.

I so well remember Father's last Decoration Day. He had aged and his health had been very poor for months. Yet his valiant spirit would not give up. He would not stay in bed and he scorned to let us provide him with a wheelchair. He would be dressed every day and would make his way about the house, supporting himself by the backs of chairs and a cane. He had several years previously turned over the active superintendence of the Decoration Day activities to a competent young man, the son of a veteran. Father remained a sort of Elder Statesman to be consulted.

As the day approached that meant so much to the old man, I wondered how he would be able to take it. Obviously he could not possibly stand the exertion and the excitement of the day in his customary active manner. Yet remaining at home on the hill above the village, seeing in his mind all the familiar activities, and hearing the band and the cheering at the baseball game would be heart-rending for the old war horse.

But he never had a thought of not participating. Came the morning of his last Decoration Day, he had us dress him in his dark blue uniform with felt hat and white gloves, his moustache neatly trimmed. Mother had passed on the year previous, so it fell to me to pin on his badges. I fear my fingers trembled, and I had difficulty seeing to make the badges hang straight.

He had his car brought across the lawn to the front steps and we assisted him into it. He sat up as erect as ever and looked around with the air of assurance that always distinguished him as a person to whom all turned with respect and love.

Father appeared better than he had for months past, and seemed to gain strength rather than to tire. At the first regular stop in the pilgrimage, he had me go into a thicket and cut a stout walking-stick, which he used the rest of the day. I still have a Kodak picture which shows him standing with that stick—he was not leaning on it—near the monument of his gallant commander and lifelong friend, General John Hammond. He made the rounds of the pilgrimage in his car without apparent fatigue, and at the end of the morning he ate a hearty dinner served by the ladies of the church. After dinner, he sat and talked with friends and watched the afternoon parade. Not until everything was over did he go home.

My recollections of Decoration Day go back to early childhood. Perhaps I was somewhat nearer to it than most other boys because Father was the prime mover of it all. He was for years Commander of the local Post, Grand Army of the Republic, the veterans' organization corresponding to our present American Legion and Veterans of Foreign Wars. He was, therefore, ex-officio chairman of the organized activities of the Day.

We always got up very early in the morning of the great Day. Of course, the farm animals had to be fed, the cows milked, the horses groomed even slicker than usual, and other chores done as on ordinary days before time for an early start at the real business of the day. I can now see Father in his dark blue uniform with broad-brimmed hat that had a brass wreath of leaves at the front of its band, and Mother, standing in front of him, pinning on his badges so that they would all hang straight. There was the one with the bronze insignia of the Grand Army, and there was his regimental badge, a yellow ribbon with various bars and symbols—the crossed sabers of the Cavalry at its top, the bar that designated his rank, and at the bottom the Grand Army star. Most beautiful of them all was the enameled star of the Loyal Legion, an order restricted to officers only. It hung on a lovely bit of folded red, white, and blue ribbon. Then he'd put on the white cotton gloves and would be ready to go.

Father told me that in the first years after the War the veterans all rode on horseback. It must have been a stirring sight, for there were many of them, all young men, of course. This feature had been abandoned long before my time, and the veterans, although still numerous, were old men to me, with white beards and graying or scant hair.

It had been a company of cavalry that originally went forth from Crown Point in the early months of the Rebellion (we had never heard the term "War Between the States"). They had provided themselves with the finest horses available locally and from the surrounding country. These were mostly Morgans, and were procured in the territory where that noble breed originated and was at the time at its best development. These horses were said to have been unexcelled by any others in the whole service, and I do not doubt this was so. Hence, it was natural that the veterans should go their way on horseback until this became impractical.

All the old soldiers and all others who wished to make the rounds met at the village at seven o'clock in the morning. The big flag had already been raised and hung at half-mast on the "liberty pole" at the village Four Corners. The Town Band assembled and climbed into their great chariot, as large and as flamboyant as a circus wagon. There were the great bass drum, the huge brass horn, and all the host of lesser but strident voices of the brasses. It took four stout horses to pull that ark with its men and metal up the hills.

The usual procedure was to make the rounds of all the various hamlets of the community. A stop was made wherever there was a cemetery where veterans were buried. Brief exercises were held at each place. The children of the locality met us, each carrying flowers, the little girls wearing new hair ribbons and fresh frocks, the little boys with large bow ties, their hair conquered for the moment, their faces clean and shining. Their school teacher put them in line, two abreast, and we all marched into the cemetery with more or less order. There were an invocation and brief remarks by a speaker. The band played and the children dispersed and threw their flowers rather indiscriminately on graves marked by small flags. These rites over, the cavalcade proceeded to the next place. The route was uphill, and because our conveyances were horse drawn, the pilgrimage was necessarily slow, consuming the entire morning.

When General John Hammond died in 1889, it was very appropriate to hold his funeral two days later on Decoration Day. It is said that "every able-bodied man" from the remotest parts of the town was present that day to pay last tribute to their revered fellow citizen. Persons who were present have told me about the impressive cortege in which, according to military custom, the General's Arabian saddle horse was led by its groom directly behind the hearse. The empty saddle had the General's boots reversed in the stirrups, and his saber with crepe hung at its side.

My thoughts go back to the parades I saw when I was a boy. In those times there were still many veterans of the Civil War, although they were getting old—very old, it seemed to my boyish eyes. There was no gaudy fire apparatus in those days, no silly drum majorettes prancing self-consciously down the middle of the village street. There was a long line of venerable men, two abreast, shambling along the dusty way in their faded uniforms, but what a spirit of gallantry and patriotic devotion seemed to enshroud their feeble forms!

The parade in those days broke up at the Brick Church, and the old veterans filed into the cool sanctuary and took their places in the pews reserved for them. I can so clearly see their white-gloved hands resting on the dark mahogany pew backs and the staff of the revered flag held erect in the end of the pew next to the aisle by a shaky old hand.

It was wrapped tight, this old flag, and was regarded by all with utmost respect. Safeguarded all the year in the vault of the bank, it was taken out only on such occasions as this. It had been made at Ironville by the ladies of that village in 1861 and presented by them to the first company of soldiers that was formed on May 1st of that year.

Chester Rhodes, the bearer of this flag, was born at Crown Point. His father and two uncles had been in the Battle of Plattsburgh in the War of 1812. Three of his brothers also served in the War of the Rebellion. It is recounted that:

"When the ladies of Crown Point made this flag, they placed it in the hands of Chester Rhodes as the Bearer. His mother stepped up to him, throwed (sic) her arms around his neck, and while the tears were rolling down her cheeks, she said, 'Chester, the ladies of Crown Point have placed great confidence in you, they have placed this banner in your hands. Go to the front, bear it aloft, and never turn from the enemy!' On the bloody battlefield of Antietam he obeyed the last command of a loving mother, turned and faced the whole Rebel army with the words, 'I will run no further!'—and was pierced with seven bullets."

His remains lie in the National Cemetery at Antietam. Another Color Sergeant, Charles B. Barton, took up the flag and was wounded the same day.

As today's parade breaks up, the watchers and the visiting groups of old friends turn to the village park. Here is a tall granite shaft that was given by the father of General Hammond:

"To the memory of the brave volunteers of Crown Point who gave their lives for their country and humanity in the suppression of the Great Rebellion of 1861–1866, this monument is erected by their grateful fellow citizen, C. F. Hammond."

Close by is another shaft ten feet high that General Hammond erected to the memory of his faithful war horse, Pink. The inscription reads:

"This horse carried his master 25 years, was never known to show fatigue while other horses of the cavalry and flying artillery were dying for want of food and from exhaustion. He was present in 88 skirmishes and 34 battles."

Beside these monuments are a field piece of ordnance used in the First World War and fragments of a cannon dating to the Revolution and recovered from Mount Independence, near Fort Ticonderoga. These relics and mementos link our present with our past in a continuous historic sequence.

Today's exercises are held against this background. Red, white, and blue bunting drapes the lower part of the big monument and a framed portrait of Lincoln has been placed there. A boy from the high school stands in front of it and earnestly recites the Gettysburg Address. The throng of people standing around on the grass turns its attention to the bandstand, where an orator is being introduced. At the close of his address we all turn away with the feeling that once again we have been "here dedicated to the great task remaining before us, that from these honored dead we take increasing devotion to that cause for which they gave their last full measure of devotion…" ◼

1917. Ann Graham rowed a guideboat on investigations in and around Inlet, N.Y.
Courtesy Leigh Portner

MOTHER WAS AN OPTIMIST: ESSEX COUNTY LIFE IN THE 1880S, PART ONE

By Edna West Teall, *North Country Life*, Spring 1954

Mother had many of her happiest moments at the Brick House windows. She loved most of the things that filled her days, for she was an innate optimist, even though her experiences were walled in by the restrictions of her environment—a farm woman with no close neighbors and but few contacts outside her small community. Her life span comprised the period from 1846 to 1919.

The first thing in the morning she looked out the front window for the view across the valley. Then she decided whether the day would be stormy or clear and glanced at the road to see if anyone was passing. These passings told their own story. It might be a neighbor going on an early trip to the village or some men off to work on a job miles away. She knew them all and their interests. If a stranger passed, it was a real news item. She would speculate as to who it might be and where he was going. Her before-breakfast glance was, in a way, her brief morning prayer.

Throughout the day she would look out to see what the men were doing on the farm, for her house duties must coincide with theirs. Should she have dinner ready when they came with this load of hay or would they want to draw one more? If Father was hoeing up on the hill or chopping wood on the mountain, would he watch the sun to tell him of the dinner hour, or should she ring the bell before it was prepared so he'd have time to come down before the food became cold?

In winter, she would hang her begonias and geraniums in the east window of the sitting room, the only one warm and bright enough to keep them growing in cold weather. As the day closed, summer or winter, she was at the west window reading or picking up her fine crocheted lace or some bit of sewing, and looking out now and then at the sunset in the niche of the mountains.

In between or at night I think she visioned the windows in her mind, for all that was outside them linked up so closely with the daily duties that took nearly all of her time: three meals a day, the house to keep in order, and the family sewing to do except suits, coats, and heavy underwear. She made Father's everyday shirts and his white ones for best, all her own and my dresses, and our muslin underwear, including the many ruffled petticoats in vogue at the time.

She made rugs and quilts and rag carpets. She skimmed the milk daily and seldom had help from the men with the churning and butter-making two or three times a week. In summer there were trips to the garden and fields for vegetables and berries, sweet corn to cook and dry for winter, and in the fall pumpkins to dry and apples, too. Tomatoes were canned, but canning other vegetables was not done very much in the eighties. In the fall, Father helped with the sausage- making and putting the meat into pickle or brine, but Mother tried out the lard.

All winter the wood ashes were saved. In spring Father set a bottomless barrel up on some boards, filled it with ashes, and covered the top.

For days a pail of water was poured into the barrel to drip into a pail set underneath. This liquid was black, strong lye for soap-making. There was one big iron kettle in the whole neighborhood which was borrowed in the spring, and into it went all the scraps of fat saved during the winter and the fall butchering. All of the entrails of the pigs had been cleaned for this purpose and bits of fat not tasty enough for lard making.

Into the kettle, which must have held a half-barrel, went the fat and the lye. A fire kindled underneath the kettle cooked the contents into a thick, slimy golden-brown mass of soft soap, guaranteed to take the dirt out of anything and the skin off your hands if you weren't prudent in using it. It was used for all kinds of cleaning and for washing white clothes, but it would take color from calico. Common soap from the store was considered something of a luxury.

Mother was always busy. She knitted Father's woolen socks and stockings for my brother and me. "I must get some cookies made," she'd remark. "And the bread's low; I must set some to rise tonight. Someone might come and I'd be so ashamed not to have a thing baked in the house. Frank's always asking someone to stop for dinner, even if they drive up the last minute. The day he brought in that city man that has the big farm down by the lake [Champlain] I had only three pieces of pie. I told the children not to ask for any and I tried to kick Frank under the table when he kept asking company if he'd like another piece. I hate to get caught like that."

Monday was wash day. If Mother were ill, Father would go over to Stowerville and get old Mrs. Longware. She talked in a continuous stream about neighborhood affairs as she worked. She brought two aprons, one to wash in and one to put on for supper when she tidied up. She was paid the same as the hired man, fifty cents a day. She had a rather expressionless, thin face, no upper teeth, and a little, round "tummy" that always seemed a little ahead of her as she walked, accented by the generous aprons, which were always of calico, dark for morning, a white print for supper. Mrs. Longware was drab from head to toe. Her wispy gray hair was parted in the middle and combed smoothly to a small knot in the back. Though I was too small to know, I dare say she dropped some colorful bits of gossip gathered from wash days around the community.

Wash day was considered fairly easy at the Brick House, for there was the big tub of spring water in the back room. Water didn't have to be pumped or drawn from a well outside. Unless he was too busy, Father usually filled the big clothes boiler and the two wooden wash tubs. Mother had a pounder which helped, too—a long thin tube, flared at the bottom, and a small wooden top with a tiny hole. Push it up and down in the tub and it sucked the clothes, swishing out the dirt, but there still was plenty to do with the washboard.

Summer or winter, the clothes went outdoors on the line. In bitter winter weather sometimes Father would hang them, Mother coaching by gestures from the window.

"He hangs them so crooked, I don't know what the neighbors will think," she'd say, as they stiffened almost instantly into an icy mass, wobbling and swaying in the wind, the underclothes having legs at all angles and the sheets up on one side and down at the other. By noon most of the clothes would be on the line and the kitchen would be mopped and shining before supper. ▰

MOTHER WAS AN OPTIMIST: ESSEX COUNTY LIFE IN THE 1880S, PART TWO

By Edna West Teall, *North Country Life*, Summer 1954

As for the meals, breakfast was pancakes and maple syrup from our own sugar bush; potatoes simmered in butter to a luscious, golden brown; coffee and sometimes salt pork in crispy slices, particularly when there was a hired man, and Father liked it, too. But rarely such things as baked beans and pie regardless of our New England ancestors. Once in a while we had oatmeal. That was a treat, for it came from the store and was a luxury. We always bought some if there was illness. The pork was excellent, sliced not too thinly, scalded in water, drained and dredged in flour and fried till it had a delicate, crisp jacket all over. The griddlecakes were tender and brown, made with sour milk or buttermilk, soda and a spoonful of cream. But alas, there's no recipe! Mother had a perfect eye-measure and knew to a dot how much soda was needed for milk so many days old, and couldn't have given the ingredients to save her. Anyway, they were different every time, according to what she had to use. In winter she made yeast-raised home-grown buckwheat flour pancakes. Some of the batter was kept each day to use as a riser for the next batch.

While meals were monotonous years ago, Mother had a way of making foods tasty. She cooked with a barrage of butter lumps. She'd heap up a dish full of creamy mashed potatoes, make holes in it with a spoon, pop in lumps of butter the size of a hickory nut and seal them in. By the time the dish went to the table the melted butter was oozing out in tiny golden rivulets, appealing to both the eyes and palates of a hungry family.

Dinner was potatoes, served baked, mashed or boiled and fried pork, as for breakfast, only milk gravy was made in the pork pan. After the pork was cooked, leaving behind a spoonful of crispy bits in the frying pan, nearly all the fat was poured off, about three cups of milk was added, and a bit of salt. It was thickened with two tablespoons of flour, then into the bowl a lump of butter was dripped on top, black pepper sprinkled over, and when it blanketed the boiled potatoes it was a dish for a king. In summer we had garden vegetables, lettuce, beets, carrots, string beans, corn, green onions, turnips, fresh shelled beans, asparagus in early spring and cabbages and cauliflower late in the summer or early fall.

There was usually one vegetable besides potatoes at noon meal. In winter there were the cellar-stored root vegetables—beets, onions, turnips, carrots and cabbages. There was also Hubbard squash, which kept only a few months and got pretty thin by late spring. So Mother used her dried corn, stewed dried red kidney beans, with plenty of cream and butter to make them tasty, and canned tomatoes. How we used to look forward to the first dandelion greens in the meadows in spring, and the cowslips in the brook a half mile away!

Mother never missed desserts at any time of year: sliced apples baked in a tin with a slightly sweetened cake batter on top, served with a bowl of thin cream; custard rice pudding and apple and berry pies following the seasons round.

One pie she made, handed down from her grandmother, or possibly an even earlier ancestor, is worthy of note, and readers are urged to try it by all means, providing they can get the chief ingredients, obtained only through some effort, for they are home-dried apples and boiled cider. I don't believe any commercially dried apple would have either the flavor or the color, when cooked, of this old-time home-cured product.

To begin with, they were sour, tart apples. They were peeled, quartered and dried on a rack in the kitchen, sometimes in the oven with the door open when it was moderately warm; otherwise the rack was set on chairs. They turned dark and shrunk to less than half their size when the curing was finished, looking like soft, brown chips and would keep for months in a cool, dry place. She often cooked them in a little molasses and used them for fruit cakes so she wouldn't have to buy raisins and citron.

When the pie was to be made, she soaked about two cups and cooked them to a soft mass, adding sugar to taste and a spoonful of boiled cider. A pinch of cinnamon or nutmeg was the seasoning. She made an under crust, high around the rim, spooned in the apple sauce with a liberal hand, folded in a beaten egg, put strips of dough across the top and baked it. It came on the table a warm, luscious queen of tarts in a flaky tiara, latticed with syrup-sprayed bands of deliciousness. For state occasions it was heaped with a snowdrift of fluffy meringue.

If you haven't the backbone to accomplish the dried apples, try it with rich, stewed damson plums and you'll get the idea. The dried apple store was a gold mine in the spring, when fresh apples were gone.

Supper was always a dish of potatoes, chopped, usually left over from dinner, simmered in butter or with milk poured over and slowly cooked till thick. No flour went into Mother's creamed potatoes. And if you want some with special flavor, use baked potatoes warmed over this way and don't stint the butter, a piece the size of an egg for a frying pan full.

With the potatoes were homemade bread or raised biscuits, hot apple-sauce, maple sugar or honey, baked apples or stewed fruit from the cellar preserve shelves, cookies, doughnuts or cake and tea. Berries and fruits came in season, beginning with strawberries in June, followed by wild raspberries, blackberries, blueberries and plums from the orchard.

The relishes were pickalilli, catsup, green tomato and cucumber and mustard pickles.

For variations at meals there were beans baked with crusty pork, eggs fried in the pork fat, it being carefully dipped over them till they looked like a pinkish jewel set in a frill of white marble. In cold weather there were pork spareribs with poultry dressing, pork tenderloins, sausages, bits of salt codfish in milk gravy, ham and once in a long time some beef or lamb. Beefsteak was hammered till lacy and quickly browned in butter, a real treat with baked potatoes. Another staple was salt salmon, not smoked. This was about the only kind of fish we ever had unless we caught them from the river. This can be purchased now in some shops. Let it soak overnight, skin side up with changes of water to freshen. Cook it gently, drain, smother with thick cream and a barrage of butter and you'll be glad you're alive with an appetite. Particularly good with mealy, boiled potatoes, let to dry out slightly, with a cloth over to keep in the heat and steam.

For two years I struggled unsuccessfully to teach a French-trained chef how to make Mother's chicken pie—and failed. First, there must be a flaky, soft, rich, baking-powder biscuit crust, rolled out a half-inch thick to line a deep baking dish. The chicken should be a chicken, not the grandmother or grandfather of a brood. He should make a quick trip from perch to kitchen with a short stopover at the chopping block to have his head removed, be scalded and plucked and drawn before cold and popped into the pot to cook till the meat is almost ready to fall from the bones and the broth reduced to a scant two cups.

A little salt for seasoning and not a single vegetable added to confuse the delicate flavor of the bird. Then pour in a generous cup of cream. Thicken slightly with flour and add a lump of butter. Take out the large bones, fill the crust with meat and gravy, roll the top crust a little thicker, make a fern leaf of holes in the center and lay it over the top with light fingers. Bake and serve with white onions, boiled to a pearly tone, with little rivulets of golden butter chasing down their sides. And that's a pie royale. ◼

Natural beauty was not the only prettiness found in the mountains. *Courtesy Leigh Portner*

❤ MOTHER WAS AN OPTIMIST: ESSEX COUNTY LIFE IN THE 1880S, PART THREE

By Edna West Teall, *North Country Life*, Fall 1954

But Mother's days weren't all housekeeping and cooking. She was the epitome of neighborliness and hospitality, carrying on these duties and pleasures as had her mother and grandmother before and generations of other families of Adirondack folks.

Back in my early childhood, when she used a funny little brown and gray stoneware churn with a wooden dasher, she would be talking about hurrying to get through " 'cause company might come." I can see her now with a big brown and white gingham apron spread over her lap and the front of her dress to protect her working clothes from the spatters of cream that would fly through the hole in the cover where the handle of the dasher went through.

Sometimes Father would come in to take a hand at it for a while, and Mother would remove the apron and tie it around his neck. We thought he looked funny. The cream dashed high when he went at it, and Mother was likely to shoo him out before it was finished, sputtering because of the "mess I'll have to clean up." He didn't like doing it and I've wondered if he didn't move the dasher with a little more energy than was necessary.

But whether it was Monday and wash day or mid-week baking, she was forever saying, "I must get through and cleaned up. Company might come."

And come they often did, all unheralded at the most unexpected moments. Mail was slow, often only once a week, and there were no telephones, but guests were always welcomed and usually she was ready. It was the custom to arrive so there'd be time to put extra potatoes in the pot, though there were a few who, it seemed to me, enjoyed the fluster of dramatizing their visits by driving up just as the family was finishing dinner. They were the ones who wanted to report on the efficiency of housewives who were able to rise to the occasion or hoped for an intimate peek into whether Mary and Frank set a good table when they were alone.

Mother was a good neighbor not only because she liked to be but also because neighboring was a necessity. There were few doctors and no professional nurses. It was a neighbor who came to watch over a sick one when members of the family were exhausted. When death came, it was a neighbor who prepared the body for burial.

Mother was often called on when neighbors were ill or in trouble. It might be at noon or two o'clock in the morning. Someone would have a broken arm or there would be a baby on the way. There were drives of miles over the rough country roads, frequently drifted with snow or gullied by spring rains. Then darkness would settle down like an enveloping mantle, pressing against the travelers as though it would hold them back. But they made their way by the light of a flickering lantern whipped by the wind.

I remember well, after all these years, one night on a country road when the howling wind blew out the lantern and the horses and wagon wheels were mired in the mud. It was the darkest night I have ever known. But it was an adventure, a gloomy one to be sure. The sickness and suffering awaiting at the end of the journey didn't brighten the situation. But the horses were patient, sagacious beasts, and the travelers usually arrived without serious mishap.

And were they welcome! The weary family could then perhaps creep off to bed. After a midnight lunch was set out and carefully covered with an extra tablecloth, the visiting watcher would be left alone with the patient and the voices of the night.

I know about those lonely vigils. Seldom were there friends and neighbors enough so that one had company. Several times I took my turn at watching and nursing. The first time was before I was in my teens. A nearby family had typhoid, one member after another. The little girl was the last. They were all worn out and half convalescent, for some of the neighbors were afraid of the disease. I went for one night. They had asked Mother, but she was ill, and the father and mother of the family were sadly in need of a night's rest.

By nine o'clock I was alone with the feverish little sufferer, the medicine, and my own thoughts. I had instructions to arouse the mother if there was any marked change. The patient slept fitfully. At midnight I ate the lunch left on the table in the next room. At one o'clock she was more restless. All the world seemed asleep but me. The wind moaned and dashed the rain against the windows.

Two o'clock—a whole hour had passed. It seemed as though there was only me between the little patient and the Great Beyond, and there was so little I could do and so much time to think. The very stillness was bearing me out on a rushing tide into an ocean of uncertainty. Three o'clock, four—she wasn't any worse. There was a faint glimmer of light in the east. Dawn slowly came; the ocean of night passed, and before the sun peeped over the hill, I was back—back safely across the bar. The voices of the day were around me, and I could look out to the harbor and fortress of the mountains so friendly and abiding.

It wasn't fully light when the girl's mother awoke. She felt so rested after the first night's sleep she had had for a week. I put on my coat and scurried along the drenched path, thinking as I ran how many times Mother and Father had spent such nights. Were they so long to them? Yes, of course, but I had never before realized how many minutes there were in those lonely vigils.

In the long winters Mother and her one sunny window of plants and their few flowers were always becoming involved in neighborhood contracts. It was with the blooming of her white calla lily with its stately, fragrant waxen blossom that the finest of her was revealed. She was endowed with a seldom-failing optimism. If there wasn't something pleasant to experience at the moment, she would recall something out of the past or expectantly prophesy something for the future. This trait seemed to find an outlet in her flowers. Their very brightness and the unfolding of their leaves and buds were a promise of pleasant fulfillment. Flowers grew for her summer and winter. Her begonias were just a bit more luxuriant than her contemporaries' when winter winds were blowing. Her few geraniums were a joy in their velvety foliage and occasional glowing blossoms. There was one geranium quite unique in the neighborhood. She called it a "Madama Pollack." It was locally a reigning queen, for few had success growing it. Consequently the mother plant was always being clipped for cuttings and rooted for friends and relatives.

But the calla lily was the queen of all the winter growing things. Day after day during the cold months, Mother tended it and watched for the slowly unfolding flower, and when it finally came into bloom, it was her greatest joy. She would hang over it with the unfailing ardor of a devoted acolyte.

It seemed like the weaving of fate that this cherished blossom should almost always be offered up on the altar of her steadfast neighborliness. But it was so. Anyone who has lived far back in the country in the old days when florists could not be reached will understand what it meant to see the casket of a loved one lowered into its cold resting place without a single flower or bit of green.

Many times in those days there was only one small wreath of geranium leaves. This meant that the window plants of the neighborhood had been culled of as many leaves as they could spare, possibly not more than a dozen from each home.

So many times in mid-winter, when the calla lily was in bloom, a neighbor would wade through the snow and knock at the door with a sad message.

"Did you hear? Yes, the MacDougal girl went last night. It's hard to find even geranium leaves, so many froze that last storm. Her mother's all froze. I guess she was so worried she forgot to cover them. We heard your calla was in blossom."

There never was a refusal, though she looked longingly at the blossom as she cut it down and wrapped it tenderly to send it on its sad journey, sacrificing the very finest of her window garden to soothe someone else's dark time when it could have given her pleasure for days.

Yes, Mother was a good neighbor. ■

❤ MOTHER WAS AN OPTIMIST: ESSEX COUNTY LIFE IN THE 1880S, PART FOUR

By Edna West Teall, *North Country Life*, Winter 1955

There were many times in the early eighties when Mother's optimism must have been strained almost to the breaking point. The farm was badly run-down when they bought it. The first year the farm produced only one load of hay. The next year there were several loads, which meant there would be need of less buying of this fodder for sheep, cows, and oxen. Buying hay meant debts added to the mortgage, already a heavy one for the small farm to carry. So hay came to mean success, reward of striving, anticipated comforts, little luxuries later on, and possibly a nest egg laid aside for oncoming age.

Whenever I smell a bunch of freshly-clipped clover, my memory leaps back through the years to "haying." Then Mother's optimism was soaring. The countryside was full of the fragrance of new-mown grass. Everywhere there was the c-clip, c-clip of whetstone against scythe, the whir of the mowing machine and the distant, not unmusical jangle of the horse rake, the bird songs and the hum of insects and bees.

Nature was smiling in haying time. There had been years when she had shown a dour face, for Nature can be a cold and cruel mistress to those who till the soil to earn their bread. This particular year Mother's face was wreathed in smiles, and past struggles fell away like a cloak cast off. Past failures were forgotten in present achievement.

Day by day, as the loads of hay went past the kitchen window, Mother peered out and watched them till they drew up at the barn doors. She had a pencil and a slip of paper hanging by the window and she would turn from her work at the sound of the wagon to mark a line on the paper for each load. The things those loads might mean—the interest on the mortgage paid, maybe the new clothes we would need for winter. She dreamed on; it was a good year and worries were stilled.

"There were two loads on Monday," she'd say as she told off the marks like a rosary. "Three Tuesday, and the meadow isn't done yet, and there's all the interval (sic) to do."

We children caught the undercurrent of her feeling and dashed after grasshoppers in glee or carried pails of fresh cold spring water to the sweating haymakers.

But Mother—Mother lived on wings. She mixed spicy cookies for supper and baked brown bread for dinner, served dishes of luscious creamed potatoes or buried fluffy biscuits into the oven, for "they'll be hungry when they come to meals." She stepped quickly, for at any minute might come the rattle of the wagon and the window would call her to watch another load go past to the barn.

Father and the hired men caught her spirit, too, and as the loads turned into the barnyard, they would call and wave to her, "Well, here's number three," and she would laugh, nod, and reach for her pencil.

"Sure you ain't putting 'em down twice?" they'd banter.

Had Mother lived today, she probably would have played a less passive part in the actual haymaking. Such a vital interest as hers in the pungent loads would have called a modern woman to the field, impel her to do something physical in the gathering of the crop. But she had been trained in a different school. She could bake and cook or grieve or pray or just wait on the others. A "lady" of that period didn't go into the hayfield.

When the hay was all in the barns, Mother settled down once more to the usual routine of her days. On the porch in the soft twilight she would grow dreamy with contentment as the sun's last rays brought long slanting shadows over the shorn meadows by the house.

But the picture that lingers is that of her face at the window—eager, joyful, happy with promise. Mother was an optimist. She gloried in the members of her immediate family. She believed in them to such an extent that they believed in themselves and in the possibilities of their own success. She looked forward to visitors and new friends as a happy adventure. There was a subtle something in her welcome, backed up by a full cookie jar, flaky biscuits, flapjacks and maple sugar, or a steaming chicken pie that pervaded the atmosphere of the Brick House. Nieces and nephews loved to pay her a visit. She had the joy of living wrapped up inside. We sensed it always, but knew it all too keenly when her face was no longer at the Brick House windows. ◼

⚡LIFE ON AN ADIRONDACK [FIRE TOWER]

By John Wilkins, *North Country Life*, Summer 1956.
Reprinted from the New York State *Conservationist*

If you—member of the mountain-climbing public—have ever pondered the problems besetting the Forest Fire Observer sitting on his Adirondack, you may have listed them in some such order of headache value: (1) fires, (2) the climbs with a pack full of supplies, (3) burglarizing operations of bears and raccoons.

But these are minor worries. From experience I can safely say that topping his list is YOU. Or to be more explicit, the effect he has on you; for make no mistake, the best and happiest observer is not the one who most successfully impresses the public.

The neophyte spending six months on a remote mountain must convince himself that he is admirable or else go nuts. And to convince himself he must also convince the public. This is not easy. Evolving techniques which can be modified to impress the various visiting types requires both talent and a considerable amount of patience. Consider, for instance, my experience with my first visitors.

It was late in May, and because the fire hazard confined me to my post, I hadn't seen anyone in three weeks. But suddenly I jumped for joy, for I heard voices. I ran outside the cabin. There (inspiring sight) stood a patrol of the Boy Scouts of America in full marching order.

"Hi, fellas!" I cried, giving the Scout salute. (A grave mistake, which shattered my carefully nourished characterization of a hardened woodsman).

"How do you do," replied the Patrol Leader with courteous reserve. The others eyed me with only mild interest and no one put any enthusiasm into his salute except the little fellow—a Tenderfoot, no doubt.

I led my guests up the tower stairs and proudly ushered them into my metal-and-glass cage. Stretching to the horizons was a panorama of forested ridges which here and there jumbled up into mountains approaching 5,000 feet. It was MY country.

"Let's see," I grunted, attempting to rally. "I reckon you lads drove up

Fire towers atop Adirondack peaks were the focus of many early climbers. Standing: Margaret Hibbard, Blue Mountain 1918. *Courtesy Leigh Portner*

by way of Old Forge and Inlet. If so, then you passed that lake over there. See it? Well, boys, that's Eighth Lake."

The Scout with three merit badges looked at the lake, checked the map, and straightened, going to another window and remarking casually: "I'm afraid you're mistaken. That's Brown's Tract Pond; the one beyond it is Eighth Lake."

So it was!

When we entered my cabin a few minutes later to take shelter from a storm, Merit Badges spoke up again: "That rifle could stand a little oil, couldn't it?"

I was starting to dislike this chap. "Shucks," I laughed, "Old Faithful don't know what oil is. Her barrel's so full of rust that if I cleaned her she wouldn't shoot straight." Expertly, I spat in the slop-pail; but unfortunately "Old Faithful" was Remington's latest model, and I had a feeling that Merit Badges knew it.

And so it went. While they reformed on the trail, a bit of flora caught their attention. The Tenderfoot said something about asking the Observer, but Merit Badges replied: "Oh, he wouldn't know." Bending down, he continued with a trace of doubt: "That's Chanaedaphne calyculata—rather rare around here."

"Oh, no it ain't!" I cried. "The nearest Chanaedaphne calyculata is near Shandy Pond." (This pond was dexterously incubated from *Tristram Shandy*, which I had been reading).

Merit Badges' reply was cold: "Where's Shandy Pond? I've never heard of it."

"Naturally you wouldn't; it ain't even on the map. It's formed by a beaver dam on a little creek about twenty miles from here. Mighty rough country in there." I smiled smugly. Me and Old Tristy!

But it can easily be seen that despite my quick action in the flora crisis and the degree to which I impressed the Tenderfoot, the affair was an almost complete fiasco for my ego. As a result I determined never again to slip from the role; I practiced every day, grew a beard, and eagerly awaited some victims with whom to redeem myself.

They arrived—a sweat-soaked and exhausted pair of newlyweds—on a sultry June day. Restraining the impulse to rush from my cabin and embrace them both, I waited until they collapsed on the porch, then clumped to the door and casually nodded. They sat bolt upright, blood streaming from black fly bites, and stared at my beard.

I passed them my fly dope. "Never use it myself," I remarked. "Been inoculated since they fed up on me three days while I was caught in a bear trap, when I was a little shaver."

As I stared at his wife, he asked if there was any nearby water, to which I replied: "Sure, there's a spring up that trail about sixty rods."

The girl sighed, "I'm exhausted. I can't move an inch." So I handed him a bucket and said that he could get some—but he hesitated, exchanging a meaningful look with her.

"Do you get down to the village much?" he asked.

"No more than I have to."

"Do you have many visitors? Do many women climb up?"

"Ain't had no women this year."

He returned the bucket and sat down. "I guess we'll wait awhile. It isn't good to drink too much."

"What's goin' on down below?" I asked. "Any wars or anythin'?"

The girl started to giggle, but was silenced by a frown from her mate, who replied, "No, not much is going on. Don't you have a radio?"

"A radio! I wouldn't have one of them danged things within a mile of here! The telephone is bad enough, but I need it to report fires."

Finally she recuperated enough to accompany him to the spring. Upon returning, they didn't even climb the tower. I was hurt but didn't show it.

"Well, goodbye," he said, and she gave a weak smile. Hand in hand they descended the trail.

This skirmish was of course successful in that I impressed the public—but I impressed it too much. This should be clear proof that a delicate balance is most definitely needed.

For the average visitor, the Alert-Young-Protector-of-Our-Forests gambit is often the best play. If on duty in the tower when the public arrives, you are off to a good start. You are in your element and the props are correct. Greet the visitor politely, but keep a stern eye on the far horizons. Of course it is disconcerting when someone asks you what you do up there all day and you have to reply with the one word, "Look." But remember that without actually lying you can add zest to your occupation by referring cryptically to the following duty.

Occasionally an illegal hunting or trapping shack is discovered in a remote section of the woods, and the Ranger may call on you to help him destroy it. The builders of these shacks are referred to among Adirondack natives as "outlaws." To impress your visitor, unless he is a native himself—which he won't be, because natives never climb mountains—you merely say with a slight tensing of the lips: "Oh, once in a while I clean out an outlaw."

This approach is especially effective with most types of young women. For the occasional older woman, who usually comes in a picnicking family group and who often has a pie or half a chicken left over, the gambit should be modified to that of the Nice-Young-Man. Answer her questions with "Yes, Ma'am," and "No, Ma'am." Take her elbow as she climbs the tower, make up names for the strange birds she hears calling, and tell her that you plan to plant a garden to keep yourself cheery. What does she recommend?

Probably the most annoying visitor is the one who skips up the tower, takes a glimpse at the mountains, and says, "Nice looking hills." This character has probably just returned from scaling the Tetons or fishing the Restigouche. An entirely different tactic is called for. The idea is to get them to at least peek into your cabin, where a typewriter (used solely for making out reports) is in casual but prominent display. You have seen all that life has to offer; you are tired of it all! You have hidden away to devote yourself to art. With the girl this has the thawing effect of a blast furnace.

In this matter of impressing visitors there are, of course, few hard and fast rules, and the totally unexpected can momentarily demoralize you.

One hot day my visitors were a very pretty girl and an escort whose sweater, which he certainly didn't need, supported a football letter the size of a billboard. The girl gratefully slumped to my porch while Superman remained upright, expanding his chest and reeling under the sun.

"You mean you stay up here all alone?" she inquired admiringly.

What luck! What a start! "You sweet little thing!" I purred to myself, and as Superman snorted in disgust I really began to apply myself. Just then the telephone rang.

I lifted the receiver: "Hello. Yes. Everything's fine. Yes. No, I'm all right. Of course! No. I said I don't need anything! Well, thanks for calling, goodbye! What's that? Of course not. Yes, I have two pairs. Yes, I'm warm at night. That's right, Mother, thanks for calling. Goodbye now!" ▰

🐦 THE PASSING OF THE PIGEONS
By Marjorie L. Porter, *North Country Life*, Fall 1950

We of this generation can scarcely picture the flocks of wild pigeons that were flying over this countryside 100 years ago.

"And he said that the wild pigeons was so thick that one time Joe Call—he was the 'Lewis Giant'—shot twenty of 'em with one shot from a small rifle and No. 1 shot."

Dana Lawrence of Keene Valley was recounting yarns that Uncle Bill McLenathan had told him some eighty-odd years ago. Dana himself recalled having seen a flock of 300 or 400—the last he ever saw—when he was a boy.

All Adirondack "old timers" agree that we of this generation can scarcely picture the flocks of wild or passenger pigeons that were flying over this country 100 years ago. Their estimated population ran into astronomical numbers of well over two billion.

The male of the now extinct passenger pigeon was fifteen to sixteen inches long with an eight to nine inch tail, making a total length of twenty-three to twenty-five inches. His weight was about twelve ounces. He was a beautiful bird—slate gray in color with iridescent violet, green, and gold feathers at the neck and shoulders. The female coloring was similar, though not so bright.

The passenger pigeon could outfly any bird of its size, a mile-a-minute clip being not uncommon. They were monogamous, the male and female working together to build a rather crude nest. In each nest two eggs were usually laid. The male carried food to his mate and occasionally relieved her during incubation, a period of fifteen days. Eight days after hatching, the young were full feathered and ready to leave the nest. A parent pair produced young from five to eight times a season. Their food was beechnuts, acorns, berries, rice, seeds, grain, etc.

The first written account of these birds is a Dutch report in 1625, stating that at New Amsterdam "the birds most common are wild pigeons; these are so numerous that they shut out the sunshine."

A long letter, dated April 24, 1823, from DeWitt Clinton to Dr. J. W. Francis is wholly on this subject.

The letter mentions that that the pigeons' migrations extended from Hudson Bay to the Gulf of Mexico and from the St. Lawrence Bay to the Rocky Mountains. Weld, an English traveler, wrote of a flock eight miles long, flying over Lake Ontario. Wilson, an ornithologist, reported a flock in Kentucky 240 miles long and a mile broad, containing 2,230,273,000 pigeons, which would consume, at a moderate allowance, 17,424,000 bushels of food a day.

DeWitt Clinton wrote, "They often resort to the seashore and the salines of the West for salt, and are frequently seen at the mineral springs of Saratoga enjoying the luxury of the waters."

He tells of a very hard winter in 1741, heavy six-foot snows and so cold that the Hudson River could be crossed on ice at New York City. Cattle starved, prices of food and fuel were exorbitant, sufferings were severe. In this crisis, five or six weeks earlier than usual, flocks of wild pigeons arrived, furnishing an abundance of food. At the time this was attributed to a special act of Providence.

The Indians moved to nesting places and stayed for a month or more to feast on the pigeons. What they did not eat were made into squab butter or smoked for future use. They made a negligible dent in the pigeons' numbers, however.

S. H. Hammond in his book, *Hills, Lakes, and Forest Streams*, or *A Tramp in the Chateaugay Woods* (published 1854), describes a flock of pigeons at Tupper Lake:

"We were startled, in the gray twilight of the morning, by a distant roaring; not like a waterfall, or far-off thunder, but partaking of both. We heard it several times at short intervals and were unable to account for the sound, until, as the light grew more distinct, we saw vast flocks of wild pigeons, winging their way in different directions across the lake, all appearing to have a common starting point in the forest, a mile or more down the lake.

" 'I understand it all now', said my guide; 'there's a pigeon roost down there, and, Squire, if you've never seen one, let me tell you it's worth going miles to see.'

"I had heard and read of these brooding places of the wild pigeon and was right glad to have an opportunity of judging of the truth of the statements in regard to them. We paddled down the lake to a point opposite to where it seemed to be and struck into the woods. We had no difficulty in finding it, for the thundering sound of those vast flocks, as they started from their perches, led us on. About half a mile from the lake we came to the outer edge of the roost. Hundreds of thousands of pigeons had flown away that morning, and yet there were hundreds of thousands, and perhaps many millions, old and young, there yet. It covered acres and acres—I have no idea how many, for I did not go around it.

"The trees were not of large growth, being mostly of spruce and stunted birch, hemlock, and elm, but everyone was loaded with nests. In every crotch, on every branch that would support one was a nestful of young of all sizes, from the little downy thing just escaped from the shell to the full grown one, just ready to fly away. The ground was covered with their offal and the carcasses of the young in every stage of decay. The great limbs of the trees outside of the brooding place were broken and hanging down, being unable to sustain the weight of the thousands that perched upon them. Evidently the wild animals had fattened upon the unfledged birds that had fallen from the nests, for we saw hundreds of half-devoured carcasses lying around. The hawks and carrion birds congregated about. We heard the cawing of the crows and the hoarse croaking of the raven in every direction and saw them at a distance, devouring the dead birds on the ground. We saw dozens of hawks and owls, sitting upon the trees around, gorged with food, that flew lazily away as we approached. Every few minutes would be heard the roar of a flock of the birds as they started from among the trees.

"After examining to our satisfaction this wonderful exhibition of the habits and instincts of this truly American bird, we took from among the largest of those in the nests what would serve for our breakfast and dinner, and turned to the lake. As we passed back, we saw just outside the roost two gray foxes stealing away into the thickets."

In his History of *Huntingdon, Chateaugay and Beauharnois*, Sellar mentions the flocks of pigeons which used to cross the St. Lawrence River:

"When the flocks of pigeons were seen coming from the Glengarry side, the men and boys hastened to the water's edge, each armed with a long pole. A peculiarity of the pigeon is that while crossing water it skims the surface and rises as it reaches land. Noticing this, the settlers struck them down with their poles just as they rose from the water's surface to wing a higher flight, and those who were dexterous sometimes killed four at a blow."

The real slaughter began when our transportation systems could carry large quantities to the markets. A report states that hunters and professional trappers took more than 10,000,000 pigeons a year in the decade 1866–76. Another record gives a figure of 12,000,000 taken in a single Michigan town in forty days.

One professional trapper, Albert Richardson (1821–1911), a man of sterling character, a total abstainer from tobacco and alcohol, and an active member of the Wesleyan Church, was spoken of as "Pigeon Richardson." He was a native of and always lived at West Chazy in Clinton County. He did a thriving pigeon business, having a number of men in his employ. His men put out rows of grain to attract the pigeons. When the birds found and visited these feed beds, a report came to Mr. Richardson, giving the time they arrived at each bed daily. With a couple helpers he would drive there with his net, which was then set by stretching it out with one side weighted down with stones at the rear edge of the feeding bed. The front of the net was held up by three poles. To these upright poles were attached long cords which extended to spots of concealment, where the three men waited.

When the birds arrived and covered the bed, a jerk on the ropes pulled out the poles, allowing the net to fall. The size of the mesh was such that the pigeons could get their heads and necks through but not their bodies. The men then bent each neck as far as possible with the hands and finished the job by putting their mouths over the neck and biting until the bone snapped. The kill was then loaded into a wagon and taken with other catches to Champlain, where they were shipped in carload lots to Boston markets. The nets averaged 800 at each setting. The favorite feeding beds extended from Point au Roche to Flat Rock.

Contributions to our pigeon lore have been made by such men as E. M. Merrill (Lem Merrill) of Merrillsville, Franklin County. Lem stated that there was a nesting ground on Lyon Mountain, where droppings were four or five feet deep. When fire swept the Adirondacks in 1903, Lyon Mountain was burned over and that entire deposit was completely charred.

Amos Blood of Fort Ticonderoga, aged 90, recalls that his father shot quantities of the passenger pigeons in Vermont.

Nathan R. Weaver, lately of Peru, wrote: "Numerous as they were, I do not remember that they were looked upon as a great calamity, though one instance went a long way to show that pigeons were not solicitous of the farmer's welfare. At home it was the custom to manure corn in the hill. The corn was dropped and the manure applied afterward. A field of nine acres had been planted and left over Sunday to be completed on Monday. But on Monday a surprise greeted us. Pigeons had scattered the manure and devoured the corn on the entire field."

Frank Atkins, formerly of Ellenburg Center, told visitors at his farmhouse-museum, that his mother, Lura Allen Atkins, a native of Grand

Isle, Vermont, said it was the common saying in that section that the pigeons would eat one crop and plant another.

Because of their great numbers, there did not seem to be any need for conservation of these birds. A few farsighted persons demanded laws to protect them, but most people believed it was impossible to exterminate them. In New York State a law was passed in 1862 which made it illegal to kill passenger pigeons at their nesting grounds.

But the netting, shooting, and clubbing continued so that by 1881 the estimated pigeon population had dropped from two billion to one million. By 1884 the birds were seen in flocks of only thirty to one hundred; in 1890 six were reported seen on Long Island; in 1900 ten were seen near Toronto, Ontario; in 1902 a solitary pigeon was observed at Canandaigua. This partial census indicated the startling downward trend in the pigeon population.

Finally, a solitary pigeon was in captivity in the Cincinnati zoo. No "Lonely Heart" appeal availed in locating a mate, and in September, 1914 the only existing member of a great bird race passed into that limbo peopled by countless numbers of the passenger pigeon.

⬦ THE ADIRONDACK GUIDE BOAT
By Roland B. Miller, *North Country Life*, Fall 1950
Adapted from the New York State Conservationist

There was a time, and not so long ago, when the Adirondack Guide Boat was to the North Country what the Brewster Buggy was to lower Manhattan. It was a good deal more than a pleasure craft. It brought the doctor to up-river settlements; it carried up-river people down-river to church; it brought voters to the polls and decided many a local election. It was also, as its name suggests, *the* boat for guides and fishermen.

If you want enduring testimony to the native ingenuity of upstate New Yorkers, consider the Adirondack Guide Boat. It is strictly a New York product. It is strictly a masterpiece of craftsmanship. There are still New Yorkers who can and do make them.

The guide boat, often referred to as the "light truck of the waterways," was originated over 100 years ago. Practically every section of the Adirondacks lays claim to its original design, but Donaldson, in his *History of the Adirondacks* (and few care to dispute that authority), holds that nothing of greater historical importance attaches to Long Lake than the fact that the guide boat evolved there. Its progenitors were Mitchell Sabattis, the famous guide, and one of the equally famous Palmers, who saw the need of devising something sturdier and swifter than the canoe. Their joint product must have been in use as early as 1842, for accounts of that time tell of little boats such as a man could carry on his back.

The guide boat of those days differed in one fundamental respect from the model of later years. It had a square stern, making for instability. This fault was soon recognized and corrected by Caleb Chase of Newcomb, an intimate friend and adept pupil of Sabattis. In addition to the pointed stern Chase tooled many a less conspicuous refinement into the guide boat, and after setting up his shop in 1850, he turned out a boat that for forty years was one of the mainstays of North Country traffic. Most authorities agree that there was only one improvement which Chase did not originate, and that was the decrease in weight successfully inaugurated by "Willie Allen's egg-shells."

"Willie Allen" was William Allen Martin, son of the William F. Martin who, as the first lessee of the Capt. Pliny Miller house, set up the earliest approximation of a hotel in Saranac Lake. The senior Allen required a large number of boats in connection with his hotel business because in the early days he hired all available guides and furnished each of them with a boat. Willie Allen went to work for his father in the boat shop on Lake Street and began to turn out his "egg-shells," and it wasn't long before every guide and camper in the Adirondacks wanted a Martin boat.

With Willie Allen the development of the guide boat reached its peak, but as late as the turn of the century there were a good many men in the Adirondacks who built guide boats and were well known for their craftsmanship. Among them were George Smith of Long Lake, Frank Blanchard of Raquette Lake, one of the Parsons of Old Forge, William McCaffery of Bloomingdale, William Kerst of Indian Lake, and Fred Rice and Theodore Hanmer of Saranac Lake. Hanmer's son Willard is right now turning out the genuine article in his shop at Saranac Lake. Except for some machinery to expedite his work, the process he uses adheres to the traditional procedure. It used to take Caleb Chase a month of "long days" to complete a guide boat. Now Willard Hanmer can turn out a boat in a good deal less than half that time.

The guide boat is still a very practical craft for Adirondack lakes and rivers. It isn't difficult to row one seven miles in an hour; the boat is easily handled, moves quietly, and leaves little wake in the water. It is light and sturdy. In view of their virtues and the pampering they have received at the hands of proud owners, it isn't surprising that there are still quite a few guide boats in the North Country, some of them still in use after almost a hundred years of service.

Nevertheless the Adirondack guide boat is fast becoming a collector's item. It is suffering at the hands of outboards and light metal craft the same fate it set for the birch bark canoe and crude flat-boats it replaced, and the day has already come when the few craftsmen who can still make a guide boat can no longer meet the demand.

Yet the guide boat is still, somehow the *proper* craft of the Adirondacks. It is the thing to be in when you round a bend and come upon a deer. ◾

◗ THE ADIRONDACK GUIDE BOAT

By Frances Boone Seaman, *North Country Life*, Fall 1950

A question by an outdoorsman on his first summer visit to Long Lake caused considerable amusement. He asked if a guide boat was used for paving the way, as a precaution, for a powerboat traveling on the lake.

His understanding of the term indicated a strange concept of the famous type of very light, round-bottomed rowboat, which is claimed by Long Lake residents to have been originated there many years ago. The term is applied to a seaworthy and portable boat used by the professional guides on the lakes of the Adirondacks. They, with their sportsmen patrons, depended on these light and maneuverable craft to cover long distances on fishing, hunting and camping excursions. Such trips could be extended from one lake to another by a mere shouldering of the boat with a yoke resting on the guide's shoulders.

In earlier years, in the absence of good roads by which to reach nearby settlements to get supplies, Long Lake residents also made trips in these boats to Axton and even to Tupper Lake, making the return trip the same day if necessary.

Regrettably there has been a diminishing supply of new Adirondack guide boats in the past few years. It was heartening therefore to find in recent years one source of output still active. At the then busy workshop of the late Charley Hanmer in Long Lake village, that old-time skilled workmanship was still being applied to the third one of these boats he had made during that winter of 1952–53.

This last specimen, sixteen feet in length and thirty-nine inches in width, had cedar sheathing sawed in strips three inches wide, which, besides being fastened to the ribs, were copper-tacked to each other. The edges of each one was beveled to make as smooth a surface as that of a finished canvas canoe.

When the Adirondack guide boat first appeared, it had a flat or square stern, but this was changed later to a pointed one like the bow. The ribs for the guide boat are procured by first sawing slabs from a large spruce tree root the curve and grain of which conform to the required shape of the boat ribs. From these slabs the individual ribs are sawed and finished. The curved stem and stern pieces are identical and are rabbeted for the sheathing to fit flush, completing the smooth, even-surface effect. The keel is laid flat, forming a solid footing for occupants of the boat. It is about eight inches wide midway, tapering at bow and stern.

Aside from about a square foot of decking at stem and stern, these boats seem to have always been made quite open. They are rowed with light oars at the gunwale sockets. For the sake of more leverage, the oars overlap slightly at the handles, which calls for a little practice and sometimes

Guide boat on Sixth Lake, Fulton Chain, in the early 1900s. *Courtesy John Chamberlain*

causes a little dismay for the uninitiated. Rowing is done from either the middle or bow seat, depending upon the number of occupants.

A guide boat, finished in varnished natural wood and equipped with polished metal fittings, is a work of art and an inviting vehicle for voyage and adventure, especially since it rows far more easily and with much more speed than an ordinary rowboat.

In water sports events on the mountain lakes, some remarkable records have been made in these guide boats. Howard Seaman of Long Lake was a recent winner in such a contest. His time for a mile, single, in the summer of 1952 was 5 minutes and 15 seconds.

Many a section of the Adirondacks claims to have been the birthplace of the guide boat, but Donaldson in his *History of the Adirondacks* says that the guide boat evolved at Long Lake. He gives credit for its origin to Mitchell Sabattis, the famous guide, and to one of the equally famous Palmers. Their joint product must have been in use as early as 1842.

John Chamberlain with his prize guide boat, 1917. *Courtesy John Chamberlain*

According to the late Wallace F. Emerson, a builder of Adirondack guide boats, the boat originated with Ransom Palmer and Reuben Carey.

Donaldson also credits Caleb Chase of Newcomb, an intimate friend of Sabattis, for having made outstanding improvements in the original design, and William Allen Martin of Saranac Lake for having reduced its width.

At the turn of the century, according to the New York State Conservationist, there were many who were well known for their craftsmanship in building guide boats. Among them were George Smith and Wallace F. Emerson of Long Lake, Frank Blanchard of Raquette Lake, one of the Parsons at Old Forge, William McCaffrey of Bloomingdale, William Kerst of Indian Lake, and Fred Rice and Theodore Hanmer of Saranac Lake. ✄

☎ "NUMBER PLEASE!"

By Marjorie L. Porter, *North Country Life*, Summer 1949

"LONG DISTANCE, please!"

Easy, isn't it? Conversation via telephone between Plattsburgh and distant points. Yet it was only seventy-four years ago that the first transmission was made by telephone and only sixty-seven years ago that the first telephone lines were put into use hereabouts!

Wire for a telegraph line between Black Brook and Saranac Lake was made in 1870 at Keeseville by the Keeseville Wire Company (the iron rods turned out were rolled by the Ausable Horse Nail Co. in the same village), but the first telephone in Clinton County was one used by the J. & J. Rogers Company at Ausable Forks for calls made more or less successfully to their iron works at Black Brook. In 1879 there were in Clinton County four short telephone lines, that from Ausable Forks being four miles long. The other three lines totaled one and three-fourths miles, including one at Rogers field (Lyon Mountain) which connected the mine office with nearby points.

The Northern New York Telephone Company was organized in 1881–82 with headquarters at Plattsburgh, its executive office being at Lowell,

Massachusetts. Warren Dow, later succeeded by C. A. Deifendorf, was general manager at Plattsburgh. With a capital of $30,000, the company began operations on May 1, 1882, the first telephone exchange having 25 subscribers.

In the late 1890s about 250 subscribers were listed in the Plattsburgh district, comprised of Plattsburgh, Ticonderoga, Port Henry, Keeseville, Rouses Point, Chateaugay, and Malone. Long distance communication was established with New York, Boston, and a number of other points about 1898.

Up at Saranac Lake, J. M. Bull, formerly of Ausable Forks, started telephone service along in the 1880s with a primary switchboard in his drug store and about ten subscribers. The central call was always, "Hello, Bull!" After Mr. Bull's death in 1893, two other Saranac Lake men took over the small exchange, and in 1897 the enterprise was sold to the Franklin Telephone Company, organized by Saranac Lake merchants to provide better and more extended service. The Hudson River Telephone Company bought out the older company in 1903, and in 1909 control passed to the New York Telephone Company, which put up a new exchange building at Saranac Lake. A competing company, the Mountain Home Telephone Company, offered rival service from 1906 to 1913, when it took over the field.

The Clinton Telephone Company, an independent organization set up at Plattsburgh in 1907 with I. H. Griswold as president and George H. Rymers as secretary, was one of a group which included the Mountain Home Telephone Company at Potsdam and Canton. In 1913 these independent companies merged and became affiliated with the Bell Telephone System under the name of the Mountain Home Telephone Company. The total number of employees at that time was 278, serving 11,668 stations. Also acquired by purchase were all properties of the New York Telephone Company in Clinton, Essex, Franklin, and St. Lawrence counties. During the next ten years additional properties at Ellenburg, Heuvelton, Ticonderoga, and Port Henry were acquired. Of the staff of 1913 at Plattsburgh, still serving at the present time are C. G. Folts, Thomas E. Mead, John S. Myers, and Anna Burke.

Mr. Folts, present plant superintendent, began his career in the field of telephone operation with an independent company downstate in 1898 and came to Plattsburgh in 1907. It was Mr. Folts who, with two officials of the Canadian Bell Telephone Company, directed laying of a cable across the St. Lawrence River at Ogdensburg during the 1920s, one of the longest cable in the United States. The cable was 8500 feet long, took three hours to lay, and replaced a fifteen-year-old cable. The new cable weighed thirty-nine tons, was reeled onto a scow in figure eights, and then guided off and submerged. It contained twenty-one circuits compared to the old cable's four circuits.

On January 1, 1923, the Mountain Home Telephone Company became the Northern New York Telephone Corporation, the territory of the organization having been extended to include a large part of the North Country. Properties of the former Thousand Islands Telephone Company with exchanges at Canton and Alexandria Bay and the Reynoldston Company near Malone were acquired together with that of the North-western Telephone Company at Carthage.

A new switchboard was "cut in" in Plattsburgh in June, 1925. It was a 3500-line board equipped with 1100 lines and consisted of sixteen operators' positions. At about this same time new switchboards were installed at Tupper Lake, Ogdensburg, and Elizabethtown.

On February 17, 1932, a merger was completed with the New York Telephone Company and headquarters were moved to Albany.

In the telephone building in Plattsburgh hangs a large oil painting executed by Haskell Coffin on commission from the company. The striking piece of work depicts Samuel de Champlain, discoverer of the lake which bears his name, standing on the shore of the lake, with an expanse of blue water and distant mountains in the background. A portrait of Jacques Cartier, early explorer of the St. Lawrence, hangs in the Ogdensburg exchange. This also was painted by Mr. Coffin.

Such is the history, chronologically and statistically told, of telephone operation in Northern New York. No history so told, however, can give the story of all that it means to maintain service in this region during stormy days and nights when working crews endure hazards and hardships almost beyond belief. It is a saga which matches tales of pioneer days, of heroic deeds performed by log drivers along Adirondack Rivers, of courage shown by adventurous surveyors and wilderness road builders a hundred years ago.

It records such episodes as the sleet storm and blizzard of December 29, 1942, when immense trees and telephone poles and wires lay tangled in a frozen mass across Northern New York and emergency crews worked under pressure in sub-zero temperatures that telephone communication might be resumed.

There are other episodes written only in the memories of men who faced driving rain on remote hillsides, who struggled through snow—white, stinging sand—that drifted along fence rows and rights of way, who strung and repaired wires from one rural community to another.

Older employees recall humorous incidents, too. Paul Seymour, who first traveled via bicycle as a line repairman, tells of the time he and several fellow employees were stranded at Valcour, six miles south of Plattsburgh, in a bad storm. They sought shelter at a farmhouse and were taken for convicts escaped from Clinton prison. It wasn't until the Clinton County sheriff, John Fisk, arrived that the matter was cleared up.

John B. Boylan, writing in the *Fortnightly Telephone Engineer*, recounts tales of the Gay Nineties. One yarn has to do with the occasion when P. J. Reilly, who rated himself a first-class trouble man, investigated a complaint at Tupper Lake. Upon arriving at the Harriman Camp, he found that a harness snap was hooked onto a bare drop wire, and fastened to the harness snap was a bare wire carried down to a metal collar on a hunting dog. The runway used by the dog had been well watered to insure ground contact.

Having located the ground, Reilly set out indignantly to find the person responsible for the trouble. "Poleon, the French-Canadian caretaker, was out back, chopping wood. When asked if he had hooked the dog on the telephone wire, he replied, 'Sure, I be damn busy feller. I don' know when M'sieur Harriman ring on telephone for 'Poleon mak' de trip for depot. Me, I don' lak sit on 'phone all tam to hear him ring, so de dog she help.

When does dog mak' two quick and wan long bark, dat's my ring for sure, so I go for house right 'way and say 'hello.' W'at is matter for dat?"

The saga is not ended, nor will it be while telephone communication continues. We, who benefit from that communication system, do well to remember the men to whom we so frequently owe uninterrupted service.

To what end?

That a father may call the doctor when Johnny is suddenly dangerously ill in the dead of night; that Dave may call Mom from San Francisco on her birthday; that Pa may call to order new parts for the separator or mowing machine; that Sue may make a date with "Slim," or Mom may ask Mrs. Flanders how she makes her topping for lemon pie!

And seventy-four years ago the telephone was a dream in most communities, and Grampa was afraid to touch the durn thing! ■

☠ ADIRONDACK MEDICINE

By Le Roy H. Wardner, M.D., *North Country Life*, Fall 1949
From *New York State Journal of Medicine*

Until a few months ago, Doctor Wardner was a practicing physician of Saranac Lake. His article, though written originally for members of the medical profession, deserves a wider reading, for it is, we are certain, of interest to the layman as well. Due to space limitations, it is here slightly abridged and the author's list of sources of information is omitted.

Outstanding pioneers of Adirondack medicine—from Rene Goupil in 1642 to the elder Trudeau in 1873—came to the mountain region through the influence of ill health. They met there the characteristic hardships of the frontier. The health-giving benefits of its climate gained wide recognition in Trudeau's time and spurred the medical advances in the treatment of chest diseases for which the region is noted.

The Adirondacks are the most prominent feature of a region long unsurveyed and unmapped formerly known as "The Wilderness" or "Great North Woods." Their name was first loosely applied to the entire region until the state set definite boundaries to it in establishing the Adirondack Park. In it are contained all or a portion of ten counties comprising a total area somewhat larger than the state of Connecticut. It was the state's last frontier.

Ill health has powerfully influenced the lives of outstanding physicians in the history of the Adirondack region. Early in the 17th century it prevented Rene Goupil from taking the vows of the French Jesuit Order. He was able to study the medical art, however, and his religious ardor brought him to New France as a Jesuit lay brother, perhaps a counterpart of the modern medical missionary.

In August, 1642, he set out in a party with Father Joques to travel up the St. Lawrence from Quebec on a mission to the Huron Indians of the Great Lakes. They were ambushed by hostile bands of Iroquois just above what is now Three Rivers, Quebec; both Joques and Goupil were captured along with a number of friendly Hurons. Their captors then set out with them to the Iroquois country through the watercourses of the Richelieu River and the Champlain Valley.

Torture was immediately their lot. They were beaten, their finger nails were torn off, and the savages chewed the raw quick with their teeth. Goupil retained composure through it all, ministering to the wounds of the other captives as best he could and even opening a vein for a sick Iroquois on the journey. Father Joques related that he bore himself with great humility and obedience, even to helping to paddle the canoe for his captors.

Their route carried them by water through Lake Champlain and into Lake George, skirting the boundaries of the present Adirondack Park. From Lake George their party followed an old trail near Saratoga to the Iroquois villages near the present site of Auriesville near Johnstown on the Mohawk River.

Then the ordeal of torture increased. For six days they were exposed to the cruelty of all the village. After six weeks, Goupil was dispatched by a blow on the head, thus gaining a martyr's death for the first physician to set foot within the Adirondacks. Father Joques was spared and later escaped to France with aid from the friendly Dutch at Fort Orange. His letters recording the martyrdom of Goupil are preserved in a volume of the Jesuit Relations.

History of the next century and a half leaves the Adirondack region relatively untouched. As the "dark and bloody ground," it was the private hunting preserve of the Iroquois, traversed only by occasional parties engaged in hunting or war. The Champlain Valley to the east saw the ebb and flow of Indian, French, and British fortunes through the Colonial wars and the Revolution, but the medical men of these armies came no nearer to the mountains than Goupil, and they lacked such historians as Father Joques.

After the Revolution, as the urge for westward colonization became stronger, two adventurous spirits from the little Vermont community of Panton crossed Lake Champlain on the ice and discovered by chance the natural beauties and agricultural promise of the valley of the Bouquet River. This was ten miles inland from the lake, extending in a southerly direction from the present site of Elizabethtown in Essex County.

Their enthusiasm inspired a small migration across the lake the following winter of 1792 to this "Pleasant Valley." They struggled inland over a narrow trail through deep snow without benefit of even a road for sleighs. They harvested a good yield of maple sugar, however, and prospered sufficiently through the year so that they were able to persuade their former physician in Panton to cast his lot with them.

He was Asa Post, then a young man of 27, who is reported to have come to Panton from Saybrook, Connecticut, for the "cure of consumption." Post served the young community with satisfaction until 1800, when the arrival of a colleague in the person of Dr. Alexander Morse enabled him to retire to a farm in the valley where he died at the age of 92. He was the first physician to settle in the mountains.

Alexander Morse, who followed him in Pleasant Valley, served the mountain community for half a century. His saddlebags and blood-letting lance are preserved as mute witnesses of the rigors of early medicine there. In 1809 he was a delegate to the State Medical Society, where he presented a paper on the "Effects of the High Altitude of Essex on Certain of the More Common Diseases." Hence, the mountain physicians lost little time presenting the advantages of climate and altitude in disease therapy.

A fringe of small communities grew up in the valleys of the northern and eastern Adirondacks in the fifty years after the coming of Dr. Post. Lumbering, iron mining, charcoal making, hunting, fishing, trapping, and farming occupied their rugged citizens. Gradually, medical pioneers moved in to make a hard life more bearable.

Outstanding was F. J. d'Avignon the Second, who escaped to Ausable Forks in 1837 under sentence of death for activities in inciting the Papineau Rebellion in lower Canada. F. J. the First had come from Avignon in France to practice in lower Canada. His son's adventurous spirit could not be held there, however. F. J. the Second found in the Adirondacks freedom and the opportunity to practice a brilliant and enterprising type of medicine and surgery in which he readily excelled. His Gallic mannerisms and wit lent him an almost legendary character, and his ability soon made him in demand far outside the confines of the Ausable Valley. He traveled on horseback, prepared to do his operating by lamplight on any kitchen table. County historians mention his outstanding work as regimental surgeon in the Civil War and then begin to speak of F. J. d'Avignon the Third, who became as able and equally in demand. His team of spanking blacks and the improving roads connecting mountain communities enabled him to range over an even wider area than had his father. The dynasty continues with F. J. the Fourth, who maintains today the colorful traditions of his family in his practice at Lake Placid.

But more isolated communities were late in securing their own physicians and were long dependent upon doctors miles away or lucky to have the incidental advice of medical men who came to hunt or fish in their vicinity. When the invalid Trudeau decided to spend the winter of 1876 and 1877 in the "miserable hamlet" of Saranac Lake, he became its first resident physician. In 1880, a contemporary historian recorded that the eleven families in the Tupper Lake region were dependent for medical care upon doctors thirty miles away. Under such conditions, the layman's knowledge of medicine often reached high standards of practical application.

W. F. Martin, pioneer resort hotel proprietor of Saranac Lake, was for many years on call to the sickbeds of the community. The winter of 1862 was unusually severe. His only daughter became seriously ill in March. A blizzard was raging and roads were practically impassable. The nearest doctor was forty-five miles away at Keeseville, but as the child became worse, Martin determined he must be obtained. He chose his most powerful horse and hitched him to a "pung," a handmade, woodshod, low box sleigh. He put in an axe and a shovel and started to dig and plow himself through heartless miles of drifted snow where drifts were ten to twelve feet high in narrow places. As he came to houses, he made his errand known, and all the men turned out to help him dig, often going a mile or more until fresh help was volunteered. In this way he reached his destination with his powerful horse exhausted and unfit for the return trip. Without resting himself, he secured a fresh horse and started back with the doctor. The return journey was comparatively easy and swift, but the great effort was in vain as the child died just fifteen minutes before the doctor reached her bedside. The Adirondack historian Donaldson termed the effort "an Erlking ride of the North Woods—one of those tragedies of distance that bring home to us the epic hardships of the pioneers."

After the death of his little daughter, Martin was deeply impressed by the fact that it was largely due to the remoteness of the nearest physician. Hoping to save himself or others from similar tragedy, he began reading medical books and seeking from medical men who stopped at his hotel fundamental instruction in the treatment of the most common diseases. The members of the profession were coming to the Adirondacks in increasing numbers for sport and recreation, and they recognized Martin's ability and the wisdom of his effort. Dr. J. Salvage Delavan of Albany was his chief mentor on his spring and fall visits, but all gave him suggestions freely and furnished him with authoritative books, pamphlets, and even medicines. His fame as an amateur doctor quickly spread in a community where there was no regular one, and he was called to sickbeds over a radius of ten miles about Saranac Lake until regular practitioners arrived in the early eighties.

Writers began early to attribute healing powers to the Adirondack climate. Dr. Morse's paper of 1809 has been mentioned previously. In 1857 Hammond's *Wild Northern Scenes*, a chronicle of a decade of mountain vacations, paid tribute to the tonic effect of the region. In 1869 a Boston clergyman, better known as "Adirondack Murray" for his *Adventures in the Wilderness* or *Camp Life in the Adirondacks*, was widely criticized for his account of the tuberculous invalid who was brought into the mountains on a stretcher and improved sufficiently to walk six months later. Many invalids jumped at the unwarranted conclusion that Murray had said the Adirondacks would infallibly restore health in any stage of tuberculosis. Consequently, without an investigation or reasonable preparation, they started for the wilderness and some of them died there. Winslow C. Watson, in his History of Essex County published in the same year, stated: "I have met with instances of individuals who had reached their forest homes in advanced stages of pulmonary affection, in whom the disease had been arrested, and the sufferer restored to comparative health."

The medical profession began to appreciate the advantages of climatic treatment in the next decade. In 1879 the well-known New York internist, Alfred L. Loomis, was able to address the annual meeting of the New York State Medical Society on "The Adirondack Region as a Therapeutical Agent in the Treatment of Pulmonary Phthisis." He recorded twenty tuberculous case histories of whom ten had recovered, six were improved, and four were failures. One of these was the case of Dr. Edward L. Trudeau, whose enthusiastic and logically written letters setting forth the values of the "salubrious" climate were fully reproduced. "Not only in New York but all over the country, the doctors evinced a sudden enthusiasm respecting the Adirondacks that was obviously kindled by Dr. Loomis' torch," wrote Marc Cook in his Wilderness Cure published in 1880. His was the first guidebook and curing manual for the tuberculous patient. By 1886 the concept of the mountain cure for chest diseases had so developed that Dr. Joseph W. Stickler of Orange, New Jersey, wrote a book called The Adirondacks as a Health Resort, containing numerous testimonials of doctors and patients. These form an authoritative record of early health seekers prior to 1880 and many to 1870.

Clearly the idea of climatic treatment of tuberculosis in the Adirondacks did not arise with Dr. Trudeau, but it was he who demonstrated its effectiveness and by controlled study placed it on a rational basis. When he developed the disease at the outset of a promising New York City practice in 1871, he was sent to the South for treatment. Later, as the disease progressed, he remembered good times on earlier hunting and fishing expeditions at Paul Smiths and asked to be taken there. He was quite literally brought in on a stretcher in the summer of 1873. He improved surprisingly that summer, but left the mountains in the winter only to return in much poorer condition in the spring. In the fall of 1874, he had improved so greatly that he determined to remain for the winter. The venture succeeded and he improved steadily all through the winter and the following summer. In the autumn of 1876, he moved to Saranac Lake for the winter, thus beginning a custom of 40 years. In the joy of returning health and vigor, his old love of hunting and fishing asserted itself. While he made no effort to practice medicine actively, his services were often in demand and he gave of them freely.

A handful of invalids had preceded Dr. Trudeau at Saranac Lake, led no doubt by the obvious advantages of the post office and telegraph station in the midst of the wilderness. His first five winters there brought him continued good health, and the publications of Dr. Loomis and Marc Cook widened its fame as a health resort.

The increasing number of patient arrivals began to tax the village capacities, and Dr. Trudeau pondered the problem of care for those unfortunates who came with high hopes but inadequate means. His renewed interest in medical literature brought him by chance upon the theories of the German physician Brehmer, who tentatively advocated the outdoor and institutional treatment of tuberculosis. Then in 1882 Koch's epoch-making discovery of the tubercle bacillus fired him with great enthusiasm. He began at once fundamental experiments with the bacillus and, working in a laboratory heated by wood and lighted by kerosene, he succeeded in growing tubercle bacilli in a homemade thermostat for only the second time in this country. In 1884 wealthy friends supplied the capital, and his guide friends bought land to make possible the humble beginnings of his inspiration, which has become the Trudeau Sanatorium of today.

The next decade saw almost unceasing labor accomplish great strides. A surprising number of scientific papers based on his laboratory studies came from his pen as he struggled to care for the ever-increasing load of private patients, to supervise the administrative and medical problems of the growing sanatorium, and to solicit funds to make up the yearly deficits. The sanatorium treatment of tuberculosis proved successful and gained wide acceptance. This experience was plainly the inspiration for companion sanatoria of the region—Gabriel's, Stony Wold, Ray Brook, and Sunmount.

To quote Donaldson: "Trudeau's was the first laboratory in this country devoted to original research in tuberculosis, and from it the doctor began to turn out work that was soon attracting attention all over the world. The experiments made and the papers written in Saranac Lake became the last word in tuberculosis. Gradually, the doctor gathered around him a growing group of younger men, imbued with his ideals and trained to his high standards of research and experimentation. Under his guidance and inspiration, they have done yeoman service in the great battle and achieved results that no man could have compassed singlehanded."

By 1900, both the Sanatorium and the Laboratory were well established, and the good doctor delegated almost all the active duties to his assistants, although he continued his efforts to raise funds for their support until the last. He had frequent relapses of his old disease in his later years, but again and again he rose from his sickbed to continue.

Dr. Trudeau died in 1915 in his 67th year. His friends and colleagues took immediate steps to preserve and expand the gains of his lifetime by forming the Trudeau Foundation. This serves as a governing and planning body for both the Saranac Laboratory and the Trudeau Sanatorium. To these were shortly added the Trudeau School for Graduate Teaching in

Tuberculosis, so that yearly several score of disciples of the "Beloved Physician" go forth to practice his teachings and humanity in all corners of the earth. His life had spanned an era in Adirondack medicine from backwoods practices to advances that won the continued admiration and attention of all in the field of tuberculosis. ✂

I REMEMBER THE NORTH COUNTRY BOOTLEGGING DAYS

By Charles Mooney, *North Country Life*, Spring 1959

In the 1920s Charles Mooney was a reporter on the Plattsburgh Daily Republican. He later served on the staff of the Albany Knickerbocker News. In December 1958 he put down a short memory of the many miles of wild, undeveloped North Country land in New York State along the Canadian border, remembering "It was fertile territory for the bootlegger during the prohibition era" that ended twenty-five years earlier.

I was a police reporter during most of that period, and my ears still ring with the gunfire.

Motorists who roll along the modern highways in the vicinity of the border find it difficult to realize that in the mid-20s—the real heyday of prohibition—the international boundary was an ill-defined line across which wound narrow dirt roads that were a special invitation to the rum-runner.

The names of the communities are the same—Champlain, Churubsco, Rouses Point, Plattsburgh, and the Pok-O-Moonshine Trail—but the times have changed.

The bootleggers who loaded up across the Canadian border and ran their cargoes over the dirt roads in the dead of night were a swashbuckling crew who realized they were facing not only the law but a deadly menace in the form of hijackers. The latter were the men who took none of the risks but waited not far below the border, guns handy, to rob the bootlegger of his cargo.

Dirt routes were typical connections between Adirondack towns and villages until the late 1920s. *Courtesy Leigh Portner*

Prohibition brought a windfall to farmers whose lands lay along the border. Many rented storage space in their barns to bootleggers.

There were times in the mid-20s when residents of the city of Plattsburgh thought they were at a rodeo. Route 9 runs through the city, and more than once a bootleg car would roar down Margaret Street, the main thoroughfare, with border patrolmen or state troopers in pursuit. Around the old traffic standard at the head of Bridge Street the chase would go, and out Peru Street to the road south, sometimes with shots being fired.

One who remembers is Paul D. McGinnis, Secretary of the New York State Department of Corrections. In the mid-20s he was a young state trooper at B Troop, Malone, and central figure in a hundred bootleg pursuits. He recalls many a hectic night along the Pok-O-Moonshine, a winding dirt road that ran from a point three miles below Keeseville into Elizabethtown and the favorite route of the bootlegger headed for Albany and New York City.

Rum-runners' boats plied Lake Champlain and the St. Lawrence River.

Also, many a cargo of whiskey and Canadian ale came across the border in boxcars, consigned as hay.

Beer and whiskey "drops," as the temporary storage places were known, dotted the landscape about Albany, Glens Falls, and Saratoga Springs. After having run the gamut that far, the bootlegger still risked arrest by the Prohibition Bureau, whose agents roamed far and wide from headquarters in Albany.

Albany was pelted with wet goods the way the Florida coastline has been pelted by hurricane rains. Bootleggers were running liquor in from the north. Another mob was running beer in from an illicit brewery at Newark, N.J. Vannie Higgins and his mob were smuggling whiskey in from the Berkshires. And the Jack (Legs) Diamond gang had muscled in on the lucrative moonshine traffic in the Catskills and were flooding the Albany market.

New York City was the mecca, of course, where the roaring 20s roared the loudest, even while "speaking easy" for the speakeasies that catered to the thirsty who had the magic password: "Joe sent me."

Probably the thirstiest night of the period was December 5, 1933. Utah voted that day to become the 36th state to ratify the end of prohibition. ◼

❧ THE OLD KITCHEN STOVE

By Glenn Neville, *York State Tradition*, Winter 1966

I have a wood stove in my summer home in Keene Valley. It is old. Its firebox needs repair. The drafts are getting rickety. But polish her up. Heat her up. She is a beauty and a joy. In my language, the cookstove is always feminine.

Here is a notation from my diary of Friday, October 23, 1964. My wife and I had decided to push our 'summer' home's capabilities and use it until November 1st. Thanks largely to our Stewart cookstove, we succeeded.

"It is an adventure to climb out of bed these mornings. Darkness is not all gone even by seven o'clock. I race with the chill to get the fire going. It seems that those reluctant, first-starting flames can never heat all that cold iron. But in a few minutes the pine, birch and oak splitlings perform their miracles. The iron that had seemed so aloof now turns like a newly-won woman and begins to work in your favor. The teakettle simmers over the hole, where you put it in place of the lid; it fits the hole perfectly and the bottom of the kettle is directly above the flames. The children come cringing down from their chill bedrooms. "Free-ee-zing!" They thrust their hands to the stove. They knee the oven door as they struggle into their school clothes. Soon the mounting heat drives them back to the table and their breakfast."

Once I roasted an 18-pound turkey in that woodstove. I sat beside it for seven hours, giving the pan a quarter turn about every half hour. Wonderful smells of meat and spiced stuffing filled the room. It was the best turkey our family ever had.

Finally, I got curious about the origins of my faithful stove. A few words of inquiry in the village revealed that the Stewart stoves had been made by Fuller, Warren & Co. of Troy, New York, and that these superb stoves are still serviced by that company.

But why "Stewart"? Who invented the Stewart, and when, and where?

Through the efforts of my local librarian and correspondence with Fuller, Warren & Co., I got from the Troy Public Library a unique little volume: *P. P. Stewart, a Worker and a Worker's Friend; a Life Sketch of the Great Stove Inventor*. It was printed in New York in 1873, five years after Stewart's death, and was evidently assembled by his widow.

I read the words, "Great Stove Inventor," and thought to myself, surely this is a widow's exaggeration—the wood cookstove must have been invented long, long before the mid-nineteenth century.

I was wrong. Until the era of Philo P. Stewart (1798–1868), there wasn't enough work done on the cookstove, as such, to make our foremothers glance up from their occupational crouch at the hearth. Up to and beyond Civil War times, most of America cooked its meals over the open hearth. Women tended their cranes, tripods, spits, grills, Dutch ovens, spiders, and soot-blackened pots and kettles. They baked in crude brick ovens installed adjacent to fireplaces or in the outdoor adobe ovens of the Southwest.

Of course, neither Stewart nor anyone else was the inventor of the cookstove. It took man an incredible number of centuries to come to anything like the familiar "old-fashioned" black kitchen range, which most of us think of as having been a fixture for several hundred years.

Probably the invention of the chimney in the 12th century was considered such a marvelous thing that it stifled further progress. This was the millennium. How could it possibly be improved on? The good wives had a relatively safe fire inside the house, the smoke drawn out through a brick, stone or wattle pipe instead of swirling unreliably out of a hole in the roof or wall.

The parlor stove, strictly for warming rooms, preceded the cookstove and reigned queenlike—or more appropriately, kinglike—for a long time before anyone gave thought to the stooping cook. The first room-warming stove I find record of was in Alsace in 1490. There may have been others earlier, and there certainly were many later. Quite a body of literature describes the elegant parlor stove in use in different parts of Europe. At this point, I'm sure some American will exclaim, "Oh, but you are forgetting Benjamin Franklin."

Never! The great doctor invented his Pennsylvania fireplace in 1742 and gave it to the world unpatented. The Pennsylvania fireplace, however, was not a cookstove. Dr. Franklin, noting the sufferings of himself and his friends in draft-plagued rooms, was thinking only of warming human beings. The base-burning principle of his fireplace was incorporated much later in box stoves for cooking. Franklin proved that stoves are far more efficient than fireplaces. They conserve 30 to 70 per cent of the heat value of the fuel, as against 10 to 20 per cent for fireplaces. He designed his stove to sit out in the room, delivering heat from all its surfaces.

He purposely did not give his name to his stove. But to Americans, whose benefactor he was, his "Pennsylvania Fireplace" will always be the "Franklin." It is still in use today and is being manufactured in increasing numbers. There never has been any need to change Franklin's basic design!

How do we get to Philo P. Stewart and his cookstove—my cookstove—warming my back at this moment? Allow me two more brief excursions, and we'll be with him.

Before the Christian calendar, the richer Romans warmed their villas by means of underground furnaces, called hypocausts. Stokeholes sunk at the side of the house held fires. Heat issued under the main floor and went up through wall flues. If the Romans had stuck to it, instead of getting diverted to pastimes that you see in today's movies, they might have made "central heating" and "modern kitchens" household phrases long before our times.

At the other side of the world, in China of the Second Han dynasty, 25 to 220 A.D., one unnamed Chinese manufactured a workable cast-iron cookstove, 28 inches long, 18 inches wide, 13 inches high, and inscribed: "Great felicity! May it be serviceable to the lords."

The stove was found in a tomb. I suspect its maker meant his lords and masters rather than the Lord above. But by one of those coincidences made for authors, when the cookstove emerged in 19th century America, its maker had a religious and benevolent turn of mind very similar to the unknown Han ironmonger.

Philo P. Stewart asked, "How can I, through these stoves, best serve God and humankind?" Like Franklin, getting a patent and making a fortune was not his ambition.

Stewart noted the disproportionate attention given to warming the human body as compared with feeding it. Said he, "They (the American people) have been liberal to prodigality in procuring embellishments for the parlor, but miserly in the extreme in reference to conveniences for the kitchen." How the ladies of that time must have exclaimed, "Amen!"

Philo P. Stewart was a noted, if eccentric, moralist, a missionary to the Indians, and co-founder of Oberlin College, the first coeducational institution in the United States. But he is best remembered for the stoves, which were manufactured in Troy, New York.

The idea—or ideal—of a cookstove had not gone unattended in this country even before the years of Stewart and his contemporaries. In Lynn, Massachusetts, in 1642, one of the first ironworks in America turned out a round-bottomed kettle with a lid, adaptable perhaps for teakettles, and believed to be the first stove of any kind manufactured in the colonies.

Many, and smoky, experiments followed, but none that seem to have left a literary trace. Stewart, living in "stringent poverty" in New York City, in 1836–37, set himself to make a stove for poor families that would "work on three sticks of wrist-size wood" for baking and cooking, and only one stick at a time, laid over the embers, for heating a flatiron.

He curved his firebox so that the three sticks would burn together and hung his oven in the middle to absorb heat on the bottom and both sides at once. He fitted a reservoir to provide hot water at no extra fuel cost. Waste heat warmed it. What emancipation for the housewife from food half-scorching over an open flame and hot water for washing up in a back-breaking kettle hung from a crane!

There were other stove inventors of Stewart's day: Dr. Eliphalet Nott, president of Union College; Jordan L. Mott, Mott Haven, Westchester County; Henry Miller, Worcester, Massachusetts; James Spear, Philadelphia; James Atwater, New York City; D. G. Littlefield, Albany. The ideas that had been germinating for so many centuries flowered almost simultaneously.

Stewart suffered tribulations, failures, and lawsuits against copyists. He was constantly experimenting, constantly improving. Finally he gravitated to a solid arrangement with Fuller, Warren & Co., which manufactured the cookstove still in use in so many kitchens today. "All that is of value in other stoves is taken from the Stewart," wrote Eliphalet Nott, who must have been singularly free of professional jealousy, for he held numbers of stove patents himself.

The inventions of Stewart and his contemporaries came at the time of the final expansion of America. Cookstoves were carried by wagon, barge, and steamboat to the West and other parts of the country. They followed the 49ers by ship around the Horn. Disassembled, they went by pack train into the mining camps of the Rockies. Let it not be forgotten that Leadville Johnny Brown and his Unsinkable Molly accidentally burned up their first fortune in an old wood stove.

Willa Cather, in *Death Comes for the Archbishop*, describes my beautiful boyhood home town, which was then (1858) a huddle of dirty shacks: "At Camp Denver there was nothing to be bought but tobacco and whisky. There were no women there, and no cookstoves."

By contrast, Miss Cather wrote from personal experience when she recalled, in My Antonia, "On those bitter, starlit nights, as we sat around the old stove that fed us and warmed us and kept us cheerful, we could hear the coyotes howling down by the corrals…"

Laura Ingalls Wilder, author of the "Little House" books (written for children but perhaps the most authentic of all accounts of Upstate New York and late-frontier Western life) refers often to the cookstove:

"Pa came in from the stable, stamping the snow from his feet. He broke the ice from his moustache and spread his hands in the warmth of the stove." And, "The room was warm from the glowing stove. Mush was frying on the long griddle. The teakettle was boiling and the table was set."

It was the railroads that gave the stoves their universality. When the golden spike was driven at Promontory, Utah, on May 10, 1869, tying America together by rail at last, the way was open for a vast commerce, human and inanimate, including the cookstoves that were more prized than gold by the pioneer women. As the people surged westward, the industry left its cradles in New York, Pennsylvania, and New England, and went with them. Manufacturers and brand names multiplied. Many are still famous.

My own first experience with the cookstove, long before I reversed the pioneer journey and found the Adirondacks, was in Fort Morgan, Colorado, on my uncle's ranch. My cousin and I were sent out all summer to collect cow chips by the wagonload. Dried to tinder in the blazing sun of those plains, they were known as "prairie coal." They sent up a quick, clean, blue-green flame, very hot but having little holding power. Nonetheless, they were an important part of the ranch economy. They could warm a room and cook a meal. They conserved the real coal, which was expensive. Only the rifle, the axe, and the plow contributed more to the final settling of the West than the old kitchen cookstove.

It is gratifying to know that the cookstove is now in a mild renaissance. At the end of World War I its future looked dim—stoves by the millions went to the rust heaps or were broken up for scrap. But the decline has been slowed. The end is not yet. Between five and six million old kitchen cookstoves are still in use. Manufacturers in 1958 (last available figure) shipped 29,974 new coal and wood ranges and 14,734 coal and wood cookstoves, according to the Bureau of the Census. A range is just a large cookstove.

The renaissance may be due in part to the mushroom growth of second homes—shacks, weekend camps, ski roosts, and summer homes— to which Americans flee from their over-civilized first homes. In homes that have furnaces and modern cookstoves, many keep an old stove for its comforting glow and its insurance against utility and power failures. Barely a month after I wrote in my diary that loving account of our Keene Valley woodstove, I read in the papers of thousands of families in Albany, Saratoga, and Warren counties stranded in freezing modern houses after an ice storm.

Of course, it'll never be like the Good Old Days. One of my Keene Valley village friends said to me, his eyes squinting into the past, "It was so beautiful here…winter mornings…the wood smoke standing up straight from every house, blue, over the white snow. You could smell it, along with the bacon."

He didn't know his own eloquence.

PART ONE

Culture, Lifestyles and Mountain Air

COLLECTION ONE
Points in Time

COLLECTION TWO
Adirondack Land

COLLECTION THREE
An Adirondack Past

➡ COLLECTION FOUR
Adirondack School Days

Harold and Dorothy Nyber, September 1930. Mae Nyber's 1978 self-published *Siblings, Scribblings and Borrowed Children* is her remembrances of teaching at Moose River Setlement in the 1930s.
Courtesy Mae Nyber

🖋 I DON'T KNOW "B" FROM BULLFROG
By William J. O'Hern

Thomas C. O'Donnell was a well-known North Country author in the 1940s and '50s. "His four regional histories," said friend Thomas F. O'Donnell, himself a writer (and of no relation) and professor at Utica College of Syracuse University, "not only left the stamp of his warm personality on the ancient lands he wrote about, but will be read and read again by others who will come to love the [North Country] and to find it, as he found it, forever various and forever new."

Well into Thomas C's later years—long after the publication of *Sapbush Run, Snubbing Posts, Birth of a River*, and *Tip of the Hill*, histories covering an expansive part of the lower Adirondacks—he put pen to paper for his own benefit.

As the author wrote the memories of his youth he went beyond being a mere chronicler. The unpublished narrative that resulted is a rewarding read for anyone curious about American life in unusual situations. He said his sources were simple—"memories which have not dimmed with the years," correspondence with principals involved with his family life, as well as correspondence and conversations with his sisters and brother.

When the red schoolhouse closed for summer vacation, a trip over mountain by-roads made in a two-wheeled gig with a horse that was slow and steady and not averse to frequent stops often ended at Lake George where a trained bear act entertained onlookers.
Courtesy John Chamberlain

O'Donnell's writing describes his rural life in delightful first-hand prose. The effort, he said, proved to be "a rewarding experience." Had it ever been edited and published, interested readers would have felt as richly rewarded.

"I Don't Know B from Bullfrog" is a collection of various school experiences. There were little community schoolhouses throughout the Adirondacks.

Thomas O'Donnell remembered his earliest school experiences. He recalled he was informed at breakfast that it was "high time that I got some schooling."

O'Donnell recalled, "It was a lot of nonsense…I could pick out "cat" and "dog." More than that, Mother was teaching me the entire alphabet and I could, with a terrific scrawl, make a go at writing my name. School indeed!"

Over a short time he "accepted them as something you had to attend." Seventy years after his first year in attendance, he recalled in detail the log school house he attended.

I recall along either side of the schoolhouse ran a bench, and in front of it, supported by upright pieces, was a wide board, on a tilt, to serve as a desk. Underneath was a narrower board on which we could keep our books, when not immediately in use, ink, pens, pencils, slates and slate pencils and slate rags. One bench was dedicated to the girls, and across the room, facing them, was a duplicate arrangement for the boys. The wide space between the two benches was a kind of neutral territory.

No regulations covered the manner of getting to the particular place on the long bench which was yours, be it at or near the end, or in the middle, a half dozen feet from the end. It seemed to be within the rules, if you were a boy, to go up to the spot and step over the bench. The more brazen of the girls used the same technique, and there were occasions when the tinier of them went to their respective places and crawled under.

Fred and Will Jones used whatever method would attract most attention at the time. Their favorite way was to come in, just before the bell rang, from the front end, squeezing in between the seat and the desk in front. This compelled everybody to rise, and the trick was to see how many sets of toes could be stepped on. Eight out of ten was par for the course.

A blackboard ran across the end of the room back of the teacher's table. Along the blackboard ran a projecting strip for holding the sticks of chalk, while at one end, on a nail driven into a log, hung a cloth for making erasures.

A child's school life appears so unadorned compared to modern times. The authors of Collection IV's stories must have found contentment during their elder years recording memories of their school days—familiar scenes that brought back memories of life as it was lived in the Adirondacks of a century and more ago. ▰

Hoffmeister School. Closing day, June 1900. Parents, children and friends in attendance. The building is now the Hoffmeister PostOffice. *Photo by Grotus Reising. Courtesy Edward Blankman (The Lloyd Blankman Collection)*

♥ MY FRIENDS

I had watched for days my friends
As one by one they walked
Down the long halls
Of that cherished school.

Hand in hand, arm in arm,
Laughing, rejoicing, at their own wit;
Finding it difficult to believe
That youth someday would pass

—Louella Waterman
North Country Life, Spring 1955 ◢

Adirondack Schools developed a friendly rival sporting competitions.
Courtesy Winfred "Slim" Murdock

★AN EARLY ADIRONDACK SCHOOL

By Edwin A. Juckett. *North Country Life*, Winter 1952

Adirondack historian, Alfred L. Donaldson, said in the
History of the Adirondacks, *that Keene Valley had the first*
public school in the Adirondacks. But "first," or "early,"
the record of the establishment and growth of this school
system is an interesting saga.

The initial stumbling blocks were not unlike present school problems, for the records of district meetings, starting in 1813, are full of references to "building a schoolhouse," "getting a good teacher," and how to get the where-with-all to run the school. The last problem, the where-withal to run the educational system of this really pioneer settlement, was probably eased by the New York State law of 1812 to pay state aid to local school districts. Although there is no mention of state aid in the records until 1820, it may be assumed that there was a connection between state participation and the opening of the first or at least an early school in the Adirondacks in 1813.

According to the records of the first meeting, held on July 6, 1813, the people of this beautiful valley got off on the right foot by electing a moderator and clerk of the meeting, and then electing two trustees, Joseph Bruce and Otis Estes. This first meeting was followed by five other meetings during the summer and early fall, with these results:

1. It was voted to "set a schoolhouse on the nole where Moses
Ware's house formally stood."

2. The trustees were instructed "To notify the inhabitants of this
district in building a schoolhouse when they shall think proper."

3. On Nov. 1, 1813, it was voted "To keep a school 3 mos.
This winter."

It seems that school must have been "kept" during that winter, and according to the records, there have been no lapses since that time.

It took several years, however, to get the first schoolhouse. In 1817 and 1818, school sessions were still being held in private rooms or homes. On Dec. 8, 1817, a district meeting voted: "To give Luther Walker one dollar and twenty five cents for ye use of his room to keepe school this winter."

On May 18, 1817, there was still no schoolhouse. The people voted: "We will have a school three months this summer if the trustees can git a convenant place for the school to be kept in." And in the following year of 1818, the building problem was still in the forefront. The record for June 9, 1818, carries this notation: "To build a schule house and fit it in Luther Walker's north line nigh to Stevin Estes log barn. To set up a block house to bild the huse twenty by twenty four." And on June 15 this: "To choose a committee to draw a draft of the school house that we are about to bilding. Joel Spooner and Nathan Ward. To git a stove to put in the schoolhouse. To have the house biginnuf for forty sitters."

These votes would make it appear that the school would soon be erected, but apparently a community jangle over the merits of frame and block construction consumed the next year. The next positive action came at a meeting on Sept. 7, 1819. At this time, the controversy over the type of construction must have been settled (in favor of frame construction), for there was an optimistic note in the resolution, "To hold the next meeting the First Tuesday in May at the schoolhouse or the most convenant place." And on May 2, 1820, the die was cast, when this vote was passed: "To raise a tax of one hundred and fifty dollars to build a schoolhouse to be paid in labor and materials for a school-house." And from then on, the action must have been fast indeed. For the next district record only one week later, on May 9, 1820, states that : "A meeting was held at the schoolhouse. An additional tax of $18. to be raised for building purposes. $23. was received from the Commissioner of Schools."

The district records indicate that it had taken seven years to get that first schoolhouse, the construction of which was completed in one week. It was "biginnuf for forty sitters," and according to the records cost $168, paid mainly in labor and materials. During those seven years, school sessions had been maintained in rented quarters.

The minutes of district meetings indicate that heating was a problem. Originally, each family was asked to furnish a quarter cord, then a third cord, then a half cord of "good hard wood, bech, burch, or maple for each scholar." But this plan was dropped in 1824 in favor of buying the wood outright.

The first schoolhouse was good for thirty years, and the second plant cost the Valley residents $238.00 in 1850. A third building was constructed at a cost of $1,400 in 1887, and a fourth in 1911 at a cost of about $13,000. The present building was erected in 1935 at a cost of $232,593.08 and serves the Keene Central School District, a consolidation of nine original districts.

The early records of the school district do not carry the names of teachers, but in November, 1827, it was voted that:

"Arzy Finney be hired to teach the school at the price he offered." Other entries indicate that the school sessions were generally held three months in the summer and four months in the winter. Apparently the district residents tried to get a woman teacher for the summer months and a man teacher for the winter term. That these teachers were not overpaid can be concluded from an entry of the April 26, 1825, meeting: "Voted to have a school three months and to pay a teacher $8.00 in money, and the rest in iron and grain at the going price, when the school is out." By 1838 the records indicate that the teacher was being paid $13.00 per month for the winter session and that forty-six pupils were in attendance. Records also indicate that teachers were paid more for the winter session than for the summer session. Could it be that those big boys demanded a stern master in those winter sessions?

Although it is not mentioned in the original minutes of meetings, it may be assumed that teachers "boarded around" for a week or more at the homes of each family that sent children to school.

The where-with-all to run the school in the early days was a combination of labor, grain, iron, money, materials, and service. The records do not carry a complete list of annual expenditures until the year 1872, when these items appear to be the costs of running the school for that year:

Wood	$11.75
Teacher's wages	56.00
Philo Estes pd.	4.00
Shingling house	49.00
Painting	20.00
Building woodshed	35.00
Total	$175.75

State aid, first mentioned in the local records in 1820, became more and more important. In 1839, for instance, the district received $29.58 from this source, and collected $18.64 in taxes. Using this total cash figure of $48.32, and the figure of "forty six sitters," reported for 1838, it becomes apparent that the per-pupil costs per year for that era were approximately $1.05 per "sitter."

As the nineteenth century wore on, it is apparent that materials and services became less important as a means of running the school, and cash became more important. The records portray the advance of civilization: In 1837 it was voted to buy a lock for the door; in 1859, to raise $5.61 to pay the costs of a lawsuit; in 1882, two coats of red paint made it "The Little Red Schoolhouse;" in 1896 it was voted to insure the building against fire; and in 1899 secret ballots were used for the first time. So it went. In 1902 water was piped to the schoolhouse, and in 1904 the trustee was told, by a 15-3 vote, that he couldn't hire a relative as a teacher.

In 1938, 125 years after those humble beginnings in 1813, the students of the Keene Valley High School depicted a century and a quarter of educational growth in their local district. This was done in pageant style, on the stage of a modern auditorium housed in a modern two-story brick and steel structure. This building, still a center for community activities, as its other predecessors had been, provides the services of a modern curriculum for elementary and secondary school pupils. It not only serves the children of the "flats," but also those of the eight other school districts of the Town of Keene that formed a central school district in 1930. ▰

John Chamberlin prodded his parents with a promise of being careful if they would allow him a little freedom alone in the water. Following school recess, summer vacation at the family's Sixth Lake camp in the Fulton Chain of Lakes was always a high point in his childhood. *Courtesy John Chamberlin*

◆◆THE COUNTRY SCHOOL AT THE CROSSROADS

By Carroll V. Lonergan. *North Country Life*, Fall 1946

One evening not long ago I stopped at a crossroad near an abandoned one-room school. Snow billowed over both shoulders of the ploughed road and drifted against the side of the forgotten structure. The sinking sun cast reflections on the interior, cold and dismal.

With no necessity for haste, I sat in my car with the windows closed and the heater running and indulged in a few moments of pure fantasy. In imagination I drew again to mind some probable happenings about the old school in years gone by. While enjoying this type of daydreaming, common to anyone, I suppose, who enjoys the study of the past, I was suddenly startled by a shadow on the snow. A deer had crossed the meadow at the rear of the school and had entered the mountainous woodland again to my left. "It must have been wild country," you will say, and you will be right, for this school is about ten miles from any town in one of the most desolate hollows of Buck Mountain.

I was about to resume my flight into the past when the little school bus, which carries the students from the backcountry to the village school, came over the knoll ahead of me. As it passed me, I saw laughing faces inside and one small nose pressed against the windowpane. A minute later the bus stopped at a house a short distance away and a small boy went running, with a shout, up the shoveled path to the kitchen door.

"What a transition!" I thought. "But do they get an education that is so much better? Do they appreciate their education as much? Are they getting soft from too much riding in warm school buses and too few chilblains from cold feet on winter nights?" And as the whole situation revolved itself in my mind, these are some personal conclusions that I drew.

The rural school depended for its success almost entirely on two things: the ability of the teacher and the aptitude of the child. Beyond that there was little to work with. We all know that many of our great men and women are products of the one-room school. We also know that many of our best educators began their careers in one-room rural schools. Fortunate indeed was the rural community which obtained the services of a real teacher, for the bond of fellowship and cooperation between such a teacher and her students surmounted all obstacles then, even as it does in some cases today. Lack of space and material or the limitation of subject matter were as nothing in the path of a willing child in his search for learning if he had the love and guidance of his friend and inspiration—a good teacher.

Yet good teachers are scarce. I believe that the fundamental improvement of the modern schools over the rural one-room schools is that in them a child will learn often in spite of poor teaching or his own unwillingness to apply himself. This, of course, is due to the teaching materials, visual aids, unlimited subject matter, and association with large groups of other students, through which he is exposed to a great variety of ideas and by which he is bound to absorb a certain amount of learning. I feel then that the modern school insures a greater amount of education in spite of occasional poor teaching, pupil lack of interest, or other handicaps.

We all look wistfully on the passing of the rural school. The feeling is as natural as any other human emotion. When something is gone which we have known or which our parents have known, we miss the old and we're slow to make friends with the new. We look on the things of the past with loyalty and affection. Great heroes of our past, old homes, old friends, the country school—they are all the same category.

You have often heard an elderly person recall with humor and pride his pranks and hardships in the rural school. What he is recalling actually is his youth, and for a few moments he is again a carefree young daredevil cut loose from the responsibilities and leashes of adult life. It is then that we hear tales of putting snow down the school chimney, snakes in the teacher's desk, or of playing "hooky" on a sunny afternoon in May to go trout fishing.

I have often heard my mother tell of the rural school, which my older brother and sister attended. Because they were the smallest children in the room, the teacher gave them seats near the big pot-bellied stove. One morning two reckless, unthinking pupils threw two 30-30 bullets in the stove.

The subsequent explosion broke open the stove, sent one projectile into the wall a few inches from my sister, and lodged the other in the ceiling.

Yes, schools have progressed a long way. Today in Crown Point we have a fine modern school—a far cry from the first school opened about 1800 by Mrs. Elisha Rhoades in the one-room log cabin, which also served as a home for her family and as a store. A far cry, too, from the early school in this vicinity to and from which the teacher escorted her students with a rifle to protect them from wild animals.

These were my thoughts as I sat musing by the country school at the crossroads. It was growing late as I drove away down the road toward home. When I looked back, the little school stood proudly silhouetted against the mountain and the sky like a child's drawing, a humble monument to our country's past. ◤

"Smile for the camera," the camera-toting shutterbug said, and agog with inspiration directed the children to cup their hands on their mothers' faces and to act like they were helping stretch their smiles to document on film how excited the mothers were to have chased their young'uns to the summit of Bald Mountain. "Holding their heads toward me will make a cat's meow of a memory of your summmer vacation climb in the Adirondacks."
Courtesy George Shaughnessy

222

🏠 THE ONE-ROOM COUNTRY SCHOOL

By Dorothy Pitt Rice, *York State Tradition*, Winter 1967

The store across the street, the nearby church, and my mother's school bounded my first memories. In this partly pre-World War I time, every country town in the state was divided into districts, each district having its own one-room school. One room and eight grades—that was the type over which the remarkable and conscientious teachers of that time presided.

And such a one was the school at Crown Point Center, where my mother taught for a number of years. I never think of it without recalling a golden, gentle fall day, a profusion of wild asters around the sturdy little building, and inside, always a lingering smell of school house dust, a combination from the bare wood floors and chalk dust.

The hours were long. Except on Fridays, school kept until 4:00 p.m. However, the recess periods were substantial. There were an hour at noon and two recess periods of 15 minutes each. This gave plenty of time for active youngsters to put on their wraps and play out of doors, but "Run, Sheep, Run" or "Hide and Seek" were always most exciting just when teacher rang her hand bell to call them back inside.

The custom of having several grades in one room was not so confusing as it now sounds. Each class moved to front seats for recitations, and the grades seated behind them could, if they desired, gain information from the senior groups.

There was no hot lunch program, although some teachers attempted serving hot cocoa to supplement the lunches the children brought from home. The lunches the farm children brought were usually a joy to behold: cold roast pork between homemade bread spread with homemade butter; pieces of pie, often made from wild raspberries; sugar cookies with a raisin in the center, or molasses cookies shiny with sugar. Who needed cocoa!

There were two eagerly awaited chores. These had to be carefully assigned so that no child would feel he, or she, had been slighted. These were cleaning the erasers and going for the drinking water.

The first was a simple enough process. The erasers were carried outside to a carefully selected spot, usually behind the schoolhouse, and pounded hard against the wall until no more dust came out. Since most of the chalk used then was the soft variety, the dust really billowed forth, to the delight of a small child.

Going for water was more time consuming and a delightful break in school routine. Usually two children went, carrying the big pail between them. At the Crown Point Center School we went to a little spring where one could dip up cold, sparkling water. Then, between the same lively twosomes it was carried back to school, and what remained upon arrival was that day's supply.

Each child was supposed to bring to school his own drinking glass, but many forgot it. It really tasted much better out of the communal tin dipper.

In addition to the Crown Point Center School, there were a dozen other one-room schools in the town. Most of these district schoolhouses still stand in 1967. Some of them have been made into charming homes. One has been converted into a firehouse, one is now a Grange hall, and the one at Crown Point Center now belongs to the American Legion.

But gone forever is that pleasantly remembered school house smell of bare boards, blackboard dust, and the crackling wood fire, with woolen mittens and rubber overshoes drying nearby.

A few of these little schoolhouses stand lonely and unused, monuments to a way of life that can never return. If you approach one of these on a day in early fall, when the air is mellow and a few colored leaves float down, you may in fancy hear the muted tones of a hand bell calling for the return of youngsters long gone their separate ways. ◼

Wilmurt District school house built by Henry Conklin himself on land he donated.

Photo by Lloyd Blankman (The Lloyd Blankman Collection)

⊨ PART TWO ⊭

North Country Characters

I must confess that I have a passion for Adirondack history and discovering fascinating men and women who have left a lasting mark on the Adirondack Park.

And as a history buff, I knew *Adirondack Kaleidoscope* would not be complete unless it included profiles of some of the North Country's interesting figures—some well-known, others not so well-known, but all the same noteworthy in their own right.

The list of absorbing characters runs from historian to sporting guide, preacher and conservation man, hotelkeeper, artist, a picturesque hermit and philosopher, forester to physician, numerous pioneers, and Granny Rhoades, who on her 100th birthday spun as much yarn as most young women could during a full day's work!

Perhaps more than anything, *North Country Characters* is a priceless scrapbook that takes today's readers and introduces them to a catalogue of interesting folks—drops them somewhere in the Adirondack Mountains—sometimes more than a century ago—and rewards them with north country magic. ⊯

Hermit-guide Alvah Dunning. "Alvah was well liked by some sportsmen. Admiring sports he served referred to him as 'Uncle Alvah.' But Dunning also had his share of distractors, and among the Fulton Chain guides he was, for some reason, an unpopular man-in-the-woods." *Adirondack Characters and Campfire Yarns. Photo: S.R. Stoddard. Courtesy Maitland C. DeSormo*

◘ ADIRONDACK SOULS

By William J. O'Hern

Every year the trout lie sleeping in still cold pools waiting for an Adirondack winter to change to the warmth of summer. With each cycle, new people find the old footpaths up mountains, around the edges of boggy ponds and alongside streams that twist toward distant lakes and rivers. This annual freshness has a history. Earl Kreuzer, also known as the Mayor of Hoffmeister, was part of that history. He traveled those Adirondack trails before me, rode logs on the Hudson River and owned a general store. His father, a former lumberman, owned and operated the Henry Kreuzer Hotel in Morehouseville.

I am a huge fan of Adirondack characters. I enjoy their tales, recollections, and personalities, and throughout my travels I've been fortunate to meet and interview a fair number of Adirondack characters—each one as unique and varied as sunset scenes.

"You've got to talk to The Mayor," I was told, to get the lowdown on the logging operations in the West Canada Creek basin. "Earl knows everything from way back. Besides, he has the best collection of old lumbering operation stuff around."

My best memory of meeting him is the clouds of black flies and the smell of his

PART TWO
North Country Characters

➡ COLLECTION FIVE
Noteworthy Adirondack Folks

Adirondack characters—cantankerous and otherwise. Phil Christy, a guide at Wellington Kenwell's Sportsman's Home along the south branch of the Moose River was an astonishing marksman. *Courtesy Winfred Murdock*

Protecting vegetables he grew and "E.T." Earl M. Kreuzer, June 1992. *Photo by the author*

house, best described as poorly-ventilated cigarette smoke and old stuff, mixed with burning woodsmoke. I made two trips to his small cabin along West Canada Creek. The interior was cluttered with relics of another time, hunting and fishing stuff, old logging tools and memorabilia. Old Earl told nonstop stories—one after another. I loved those stories but I never grew used to the swarms of black flies or the perpetual cloud of tobacco smoke. I snapped a favorite photo of Earl on my last visit. "Want to see a trick?" he asked, following my comment that his well-cared-for vegetable garden did not have a protective wire fence. For the life of me I didn't understand how he protected the crops from the forest critters.

"Sure," I replied. "What're ya gonna do?"

Earl's next moves sealed him in my folklore mind as a legendary hero of the Adirondacks. Earl picked up his .410 shotgun, grabbed a handful of unshelled peanuts, sat down on a log stump at the edge of the garden, and laid the rifle across his lap. "Watch this," he said as he placed a peanut on the top of his bald head.

It was only a matter of minutes before a chipmunk appeared. Chippy darted toward Earl's motionless body, raced up his side, grabbed the nut, poked it into his paunch and leaped off on a mad dash to who-knows-where.

Earl's 80-plus-year-old body bolted to life. The years had not slowed his reaction time. As the animal scurried off, Earl raised his rifle, aimed and fired. "There!" he declared in a big way, "That's how I keep my corn to myself."

I didn't think much of the slaughter, but Earl was just giving me a bit of insight into the ways of the old-time people of the Adirondacks. His behavior was simply part of his Adirondack character.

I rather doubt anyone consciously sets out to become a character. Character traits merely develop in accordance with one's personality. There's no recipe for being a colorful individual. The men and women I call characters were just unique in their own way.

Red Perkins was called "Perk" by most Old Forge folks, though some knew him only as "Red" because of the color of his hair. He was the first character I interviewed in the early 1980s. I was told those closest to him used his given name, Donald. I took that bit of advice as a gentle word of warning not to use his birth name. Perkins was a well-known story-teller, local guide at the Adirondack League Club, and an example of a priceless old-time Adirondack character.

Thankfully, a native of New Jersey, Ed Levine, arrived in the Adirondacks in January 1975 and at once became entranced with the mountains. Levine's background was in journalism, so it was natural for him to want to capture in print Perk's life accomplishments and "friskiness" in *The Adventures of Red Perkins*.

Regrettably, most characters don't get a book written about their lives, although their stories are historical treasures. Their lives reflect the mountains that gave them the skills to survive and the love to take pleasure in them. Most often their names and the tales of their adventures have been passed down by word of mouth.

Readers of Glyndon Cole's North Country Life and York State Tradition magazine helped to perpetuate the lives of North Country characters by sharing memories that were printed from time-to-time in Cole's column, "From the Editor's Mail."

W. J. Griffin Sr. of Oswegatchie, New York, is an example of a resourceful reader.

> *April 23, 1958*
> *Dear Editor:*
> *I was interested in your article on W.H.H. (Adirondack) Murray.*
> *[I was] born in 1863 on a farm where [I have spent my life and am] doubtlessly the only living person in St. Lawrence County who ever met Adirondack Murray.*
> *Much to my regret, the date of this meeting is lacking, but I distinctly remember it. I was a boy in my early teens. It may have been Murray's last trip in 1877.*

At that time Gouverneur was the nearest railroad station to the point where camping parties took to the woods on foot thirty miles from Gouverneur. My father's house was located close to the point where foot travel left the highway for the six-mile trek through the forest to the stillwater where they took the boats.

The Murray party arrived at my father's farmhouse in the evening, where they had come by team from Gouverneur. Murray was a large, handsome man. His party consisted of both men and women, about thirty in number. All stayed in the house or in the barn or wherever they could find shelter.

The following morning, after local guides had assembled, the party started out on foot for camp up the timberland and waters of the Oswegatchie. Three saddle horses were provided in case some might tire. How distinctly I remember the line of march starting out, mostly single file, Murray riding on horse up and down the line like a general reviewing his troops!

In the course of a few hours all had arrived at the destination except Murray and the charming young widow of the party. I was delegated to go back on the trail with a saddle horse to meet them, lest the lady had become weary on the march. I met them, and the lady mounted the horse.

The party soon took to the boats and headed for the campsites. In the bow of each boat flew the U.S. flag, making a scene long to be remembered.

The party was too large, resulting in discord. They came out a few at a time with feathers drooping and little to say of the pleasures of camp life.

Charles Holmer, a traveling man who lived near Gouverneur, was the promoter of the party. ◤

▮ WOODSLOAFER

"Have a chew." Acorn Charlie, North Lake, 1920, is one of the hundreds of North Country characters contributors related stories about in Cole's magazine.
Courtesy Doris and Tom Kilbourn

A woodsloafer needs no other reason,
For there is the lake, and here is the season;
And in the deep woods, and out on the stream
A woodsloafer is stopping to dream.

Here is the place where the river parts,
Here is the spot where the inlet starts;
There swim the trout of yesteryear,
There run the amber-spotted deer.

Here is his boat by the water's edge
And under a spruce, near a rocky ledge,
There is his tent by the drifting stream.
This is the pathway to his dream.

The noisy world is a mist blown by;
All that he hears is the plover's cry.
He smells pond lilies' night perfume;
His compass is the crescent moon.

Now that it's summer, the perfect season,
A woodsloafer needs no other reason.

—Elsie Wilkins
North Country Life, Summer 1956. ▰

♛ADIRONDACK MURRAY

By Glyndon Cole. *North Country Life*, Spring 1958

undreds of vacationers went home from the Adirondacks "mad," for they had been "gypped."

This was in 1869—the year of the first great influx of vacationers. That summer, people came from the cities in droves to relax in "comfortable" hotels, to camp out in the great health-giving wilderness, or to catch some of the fabulous trout abounding in the cool mountain streams.

One person was responsible for this—a Boston clergyman, the Reverend William Henry Harrison Murray, better known as Adirondack Murray. In April he had published his first of several books dealing with the Adirondacks. This was *Adventures in the Wilderness, or Camp Life in the Adirondacks*. By June of that year, the stampede of city people into the mountains was on. But by August there was another in the opposite direction—a stampede of disillusioned, bitter people cursing Adirondack Murray, who had "tricked" them into coming to a rough and rugged country where "comfortable" hotels were not adequate for the hundreds who wanted them. There was such a demand for bed and board that rates became exorbitant. Yes, "Murray's Fools," as they were called, went home with fire in their eyes.

Murray's book brought more people to the mountains in proportion to the current population than any advertising medium ever used to induce tourists to visit this part of the country. What kind of person was this Adirondack Murray, who could write a book that would have such an effect? And what was there about the book that caused people to feel that they had been duped?

Murray was born in 1840 on a farm near Guilford, Connecticut. His career is an example of the "self-made man." Born a humble New England farmer, by the time he was 30, he was enjoying world prominence and was considered one of the intellectual giants of the times.

As a young man, he attended Guilford Institute and worked on a neighboring farm in order to pay his tuition. In school he was popular

Camp Rustic, Lake Placid, a grand log structure built during the gilded era.
A Seneca Ray Stoddard photo. Courtesy Maitland DeSormo Collection

with his fellow students and was a leader among them. After Guilford Institute, he worked his way through Yale, graduating in 1862.

Attendance at a theological seminary followed. Then he became pastor of a Congregational Church in Washington, Connecticut. He caused considerable gossip among the inhabitants of this conservative New England town by organizing a rifle club and competing with members of his congregation in rifle matches. It was even more scandalous that he coasted and skated on moonlit nights with the boys and girls of the town. "It took stiff New England grit," wrote his biographer, "even to advocate, much less practice, in those days habits of thought and conduct which today are universally accepted as right and wise."

He held Congregational pulpits also in Greenwich and Meriden, Connecticut, acquiring a reputation as a brilliant speaker. From Meriden, at the age of 28, he was called to the Park Street Congregational Church in Boston, then one of the most prominent pulpits in the country. Within a few weeks he became nationally known for his masterly oratory. His sermons were circulated and quoted throughout the country and even in Europe.

A lover of horses, he was accused of owning race horses and betting heavily on them. The gossip caused him finally to resign the pastorate at Park Street after serving the church for seven years, whereupon he founded the Music Hall Independent Congregational Church. Here he reached the pinnacle of his fame as a platform speaker.

Suddenly in 1880 he left this church without farewell and disappeared. He was reported in turn to be engaged in the lumbering business in Texas, to be traveling in Europe, and eventually to be managing a restaurant in Montreal. After this he is said to have lectured again, or more frequently, to have read from his published works. "How John Norton Kept His Christmas" he read to 500 audiences, receiving as high as $500 a night.

In 1864, while he was still pastor of the Park Street Church, he made his first trip to the Adirondacks, and he continued to come every year until 1877. He cruised countless Adirondack waters and explored wild and remote corners. He became an expert rifleman, angler, canoeist, yachtsman, trailer, naturalist, and camper. He studied every phase of forest and frontier life and came to love and know the woods thoroughly.

His favorite campsite was Osprey Island in Raquette Lake near the mouth of Marion River. For a time the island was commonly referred to as Murray's Island. His favorite guide was "Honest John" Plumley of Long Lake, who became celebrated as the leading character in the stories Murray related in his *Adventures in the Wilderness*—the book which caused so much furor in 1869.

Newspapers and magazines attacked Murray, calling the book a "monstrous hoax." Noted preachers declared that he had "disgraced his high station by practicing upon the people, especially the weakly and sick, a cruel joke."

An impartial examination of the book now seems to indicate that Murray was hardly the liar people called him. Apparently readers inferred misinformation which Murray did not state or even imply. Ignoring his warning that life in the wilderness would be very simple, they came ill equipped for it. Apparently readers expected to find the Northern Wilderness dotted with hotels furnishing the comforts of home. Actually he named only five: the St. Regis House at Paul Smiths; Bartlett's on the carry between Round Lake and the Upper Saranac; Mother Johnson's at the lower end of the carry below Long Lake; Uncle Palmer's at Long Lake; and Martin's on the Lower Saranac at the terminus of the state route from Keeseville.

With reference to fishing, he cautioned the reader: "If one expects to find trout averaging three or four pounds, eager to break surface no matter where or when he casts his fly, he will come back from his trip a 'sadder and a wiser man.'"

As for the health-giving qualities of the wilderness, perhaps Murray erred in citing in detail and at considerable length the example of a consumptive invalid who came to the woods on the verge of death and after a few months in the mountains was able to go home a well person. Though Murray termed this definitely an exceptional case, people apparently concluded that a few months in the woods would be a certain cure for tuberculosis.

The first part of the book gives directions and instructions for a vacation in the Adirondacks—where to go, clothes and provisions to take, where to buy tackle, how to select a guide, and how much money to bring. The second part relates some of his experiences and some fictitious tales, including a ghost story. In this part of the book "his exaggerations were so obvious that a literal construction of them reflects on the reader rather than the author," comments Donaldson in his *History of the Adirondacks*.

In spite of all the adverse comment and name-calling, the fact remains that Murray did more to popularize the Adirondacks as a vacationland than any other single person. He certainly created a new interest in the region. In 1872 the state legislature ordered a complete topographical survey and appointed Verplanck Colvin as surveyor. A state park commission was created to inquire into the expediency of converting the Adirondacks into a state park. By 1875 there were more than 200 hotels in the area.

The years that followed—1875 to 1901—have been called the gilded years of the Adirondacks. The fame of the luxury of Adirondack hotels, the lavishness of private camps, the saltiness of Adirondack guides spread far and wide. By 1900—before the day of the automobile—a quarter-million visitors were coming to the region in a single summer.

"Murray's Rush," as the influx of 1869 was called, seems never to have stopped. "Murray's Fools" of today, counted in the millions, go home happy and satisfied, for accommodations of every type are plentiful, and the recreational opportunities are so varied that the Adirondack region has become known as the family vacation paradise.

Murray really started something in 1869.

Many types of Adirondack characters found comfort of various types in the forested mountains. There were other clergymen, and there were hermits, hoteliers, and mountain guides. They injected a rare flavor to the already rarefied atmosphere—one that is not seen nearly so often these days. ◾

★FRANKLIN B. HOUGH, FATHER OF AMERICAN FORESTRY

By Ralph S. Hosmer, *North Country Life*, Winter 1955

Forestry in New York State and in the nation had its real beginnings in the decade from 1875 to 1885. Then were laid the initial foundations on which has been built the superstructure that we know today.

To lay foundations that will endure requires men of vision who also have the zeal and the ability to make their dreams come true. The state of New York has produced many leaders in forestry. Of those of the early days, none is more outstanding than Dr. Franklin B. Hough, a native of this state and long a resident of Lowville in Lewis County.

Franklin B. Hough's contributions to the beginnings of forestry in the United States were twofold. He was one of those who labored effectively for the New York State Forest Preserve and the state forest policy, which supports it. He was the first man to be appointed by the federal government specifically to study the forests of our country and to make recommendations for their proper care. In both tasks he rendered notable service. It is the purpose of this article to enumerate some of the salient features of what he accomplished.

"Uncle" VanDyke's place near Sand Lake is typical of an old-time Adirondack home.
Courtesy Edward Blankman (The Lloyd Blankman Collection)

While forestry has a background of centuries in Europe, the need for the systematic management of forests in America came only slowly to be realized. It was a virgin continent, unequalled by any other land in its natural resources, which welcomed the early colonists. As these sturdy and adventurous people and their immediate descendants pushed out farther and farther into the wilderness, they found an apparently un-limited supply of forests, of wild life, and of minerals. It is not surprising that among them developed the "Legend of Inexhaustibility," which, coupled with the attitude characteristic of any frontier, led to consequences of improvidence and waste, from which it is only in recent years that we are beginning to escape.

There were some, however, who realized that spendthrift ravaging of the bounties of nature could not go on forever. Even in colonial days occasional voices were raised in warning, although their pleas were usually discounted or quickly forgotten. Later such protests became more frequent, as when, a little over a century ago, Governor DeWitt Clinton and James Fenimore Cooper voiced their feelings as to the dangers of forest destruction in New York State.

In the two decades following the Civil War, some attention at last gradually began to be paid to the arguments of those who spoke for the forest. In this group belongs Doctor Hough. An organized drive by the American Association for the Advancement of Science finally led in 1876 to the beginning of national forestry by the appointment of Doctor Hough as special agent under the Federal Commissioner of Agriculture. From this humble start has developed the United States Forest Service of today.

Dr. Franklin B. Hough was born in Martinsburg, Lewis County, on July 20, 1822. He was the second son of a physician, Dr. Horatio Gates Hough, the first of his profession to settle in Lewis County, and Martha (Pitcher) Hough. Dr. F. B. Hough was in the sixth generation of descent from an English emigrant who settled in Connecticut.

As a boy, young Hough became deeply interested in botany and in geology, particularly mineralogy, and through wide-ranging excursions of his own planning came to know Lewis County intimately as well as the surrounding region. Preparing at Lowville Academy and the Black River Institute at Watertown, he entered Union College, where he was graduated with the degree of A.B. in 1843. During his course he was elected to Phi Beta Kappa. After teaching for a time in New York and Ohio, he took the regular course at the Cleveland Medical College, receiving the degree of M.D. in 1848. Much later, about 1880, the Regents of the State of New York conferred on him the honorary degree of Ph.D.

Before taking up his residence in Lowville, Doctor Hough practiced his profession in Somerville, St. Lawrence County, from 1848 to 1852. He also served as surgeon of the 97th Regiment, New York Volunteers, in 1862 and 1863. While he always retained his interest in medicine, it became with him from that time essentially an avocation, since his other interests led him more and more into the fields of local history, statistics, and finally forestry.

As Doctor Hough studied the botany and geology of Northern New York, incidentally becoming well acquainted with the Adirondacks, he became impressed with the importance of recording the local history. This led him to prepare and publish from 1853 to 1860 histories of St. Lawrence, Franklin, Jefferson, and Lewis counties, which for accuracy and comprehensiveness rank as noteworthy contributions in that field. A compilation of meteorological data and the New York Civil List, both published by the State in 1855, led to the selection of Doctor Hough as director of the New York State Census for 1855, a post which he held again in 1865. A Gazetteer of New York State and several important monographs on the State Constitution and related subjects also belong in this period. As one of his biographers says, Doctor Hough was "preeminently a New Yorker." He was an indefatigable worker, with the ability to bring order and sequence out of a mass of details. He never spared himself in his search for all the information that was to be found, whatever the subject he undertook to investigate. He made statistics alive and vital.

Perhaps Doctor Hough's most notable service to forestry in New York State was in connection with his membership on two state commissions that had to do with the creation of the New York State Forest Preserve, one in 1872, the other in 1885. In the seventies the Adirondack region was just becoming known to the general public, for it was still a wilderness. But large areas of the state-owned lands had been sold to railroad and other corporations at the ridiculously low figure of five cents an acre. Trespass on state land was the order of the day, indiscriminate logging the only known practice. How to handle the problem so present led to acrimonious controversy.

In 1872 a commission of seven members was set up, with Horatio Seymour as chairman. Verplanck Colvin, who from his surveys of the region perhaps knew the Adirondacks best of anyone, and Doctor Hough were members. To the latter was assigned the task of preparing the exhaustive report submitted by the commission in 1873. Most unfortunately, this report was pigeonholed by the Legislature, but it was not forgotten and ten years later helped to bring about the definite action that was taken in 1885.

In view of subsequent developments after Doctor Hough's death, especially the inclusion in the State Constitution of the famous Article VII, Section 7 (now since 1838, Article XIV, Section 1), it is well to remember that Doctor Hough stood for a plan that recognized the place of the lumberman in forest management and that provided for what in more recent years has been called "perpetuation of the forest through wise use." In this article he was opposed by Mr. Colvin, who held that a great state park was the right solution.

When this problem came to a head again in 1884, Doctor Hough was brought in to work with a special committee appointed by the Comptroller at the request of the Legislature, of which Professor Charles Sprague Sargent of Harvard University was chairman. This committee framed the bill authorizing the Forest Preserve and setting up the administrative machinery to handle it under the New York State Forest Commission, the first predecessor of the present State Conservation Department. This bill became law on May 15, 1885. It is "the foundational law of conservation in the State," for the basic state forest policy then adopted has been in operation ever since. New York is the only state that can show so long and continuous a record.

It was while working on the draft of the law of 1885 that Doctor Hough was stricken by his final illness, but many of his ideas were embodied in the act as passed. In all his efforts for forestry in New York, Doctor Hough exhibited the qualities of full knowledge based on intensive study, fairness to all concerned, and vision for the future. These traits won the respect and admiration of all who knew him.

The second significant contribution made by Doctor Hough to forestry was the service, centering in Washington, which he gave when he laid the foundations of the Division of Forestry under the federal government. Lack of space prevents more than touching upon that aspect of Doctor Hough's work, but at least the high spots must be mentioned. In 1873 at Portland, Maine, Doctor Hough read a paper on "The Duty of Governments in the preservation of Forest" before the American Association for the Advancement of Science, which so impressed that body of scientific men that a special committee was set up to prepare and present to Congress a memorial embodying a plan for the careful study by the federal government of the forests of the country, looking forward to the better care and management of the forests on the public domain plus related matters demanding government attention. Although presented to Congress with the endorsement of President Grant, this memorial at first failed to receive attention. But, the effort was continued and in 1876 an item was at last secured, as a rider to an appropriation bill, which created the position of special agent in forestry under the Commissioner of the Department of Agriculture. To this post Doctor Hough was appointed. He served until 1883.

With an appropriation of $2000 for the first year and only $2500 for the next three years, Doctor Hough set to work to compile in statistical form various sorts of information concerning the forests of the United States. Between 1878 and 1883 he brought out three reports and contributed to a fourth, which for a number of years constituted the best, indeed almost the only, available data on the subjects covered. That the worth of this material was recognized more than locally is indicated by the fact that for the first two reports Doctor Hough was awarded a diploma by an International Congress held at Venice in 1882.

Under Doctor Hough the work in forestry developed steadily so that in 1881 it became a division, which in 1886 was officially recognized as such by Congress. From this meager start has developed the Forest Service of 3000 technically trained workers to administer more than 175,000,000 acres of national forests, to conduct the activities at twelve forest experiment stations and the forest products laboratory, and to cooperate with the several states in a variety of projects.

As the man responsible for the initial start of this enterprise, there is good reason why Doctor Hough should be called "The Father of American Forestry," even if he did not have the advantage of professional training in forestry to equip him more completely for the duties to which he was called. At a time when forestry was little understood, when continued opposition had to be met and inertia overcome, Doctor Hough handled forestry matters tactfully in dealing with those in authority in Congress and elsewhere in the government. He made friends for forestry and so paved the way for his successors.

In 1882 and 1883 Doctor Hough conducted for one year the *American Journal of Forestry*, the first forestry magazine in the United States. It was discontinued because of lack of support, but it is worth remembering. In 1882 he published his *Elements of Forestry,* a textbook. This stands as one of the first modern books on forestry in the English language.

Doctor Hough passed away at his home in Lowville on June 11, 1885, leaving in his varied contributions to human knowledge a memorial that is enduring. As has been said of him by one of his successors in the office of chief forester of the U.S. Department of Agriculture, "Doctor Hough was perhaps the chief pioneer in forestry in the United States."

♛ "PANTS" LAWRENCE IN NEW YORK CITY

We waited at Delmonico's
And finally he came
After a light exchange of blows
When the doorman asked his name.
Pants' strength comes not from words but deeds.
Intrinsically fine,
Secure within himself, he reads
The menu line by line—
It's mostly French, we feel him freeze.
"Green corn" makes sense to him.
We hear his voice, "Just bring me, please—"
Pants' French is rather slim.
We wonder, will these strange words daunt?
Not him! To the manner born,
"Yes, bring me please, here's what I want—
A dozen ears of corn!"

—Helen Hays, *North Country Life*, Fall 1953.

"Pants" Lawrence, West Canada Lake. *Courtesy Edward Blankman (The Lloyd Blankman Collection)*

♛ "PANTS" LAWRENCE OF THE ADIRONDACKS

By Donnal V. Smith, *North Country Life*, Fall 1953 version was abridged
from *New York Folklore Quarterly*. The Quarterly's entire story appears here.

This is a "letter to the editor" about the "North Country" that I don't
know very well, but for which I have a deep affection. The people up
there, at least the ones I know, are all genuine folks and have a charm and
character all their own that designate them as a part of the most distin-
guishing feature of our state, the Adirondacks.

The man about whom I really want to write I never knew, but in one
way or another I have heard so much about him that I have to tell you a
few of the stories. You may be able to get others to recall his stories,
which must have been almost endless. If they are like the ones I know,
they are amusing and illustrative of both the country and his time. Let
me begin this way: "Pants" Lawrence died about a year and a half ago. In

a way his passing marks the end of an era—the end of an era when the Adirondacks, almost uncrossed by east and west roads, had only a few trails north and south—up along Lake George and Champlain, up the Fulton Chain, and through the Black River Valley; a few trails followed by a few men, supported by dreams of one kind or another. Once it was an engineer who thought a string of lakes might be connected so that there would be ready travel between the St. Lawrence and the Mohawk. French explorers, English explorers, Indian traders, Indian raiding parties, British armies, and Green Mountain Boys made the pathway up the lakes well known. And then in the 1830s when the people in the Black River Valley believed that it would be the great dairy section of the State, just ordinary families made a trail up to the North Country. Only a few hardy souls who crossed back and forth, east and west, knew the interior of the Adirondack country. One of these was "Pants" Lawrence.

Before I tell you the few stories I know about "Pants," I have to tell you how I heard about him. We have, at our camp up on Raquette Lake, a Camp Director by the name of Arthur L. Howe. For a number of years Art was physical education director and a chief citizen of the village of Hamburg. For almost thirty years he not only was the physical education director in the public schools, but put up the lights at Christmas time, was chief *factotum* of American Legion events, and in a thousand and one ways was a leading citizen of the village. Before the dial telephones were installed, his phone number was 1. And when he left Hamburg to join the staff of the State University Teachers College at Cortland, a fine new athletic field, with stadium, baseball diamonds, football gridirons, and playing fields of all sorts was dedicated as the Arthur L. Howe Athletic Field. Art has a genuine love of the North Country too, and he finally knew Hamilton, Essex, and St. Lawrence counties so well that he became a licensed guide. Art is the one who told me about "Pants" Lawrence. In many ways the stories he told won't have the flavor when I repeat them, because as you watched and listened while Art remembered "Pants" and the many hours they spent together, there was a flavor of the Adirondacks that will never be put in print. I am very sure, though, that if you would preserve the folklore of New York State, a good old American stock best represented by characters of the strength of "Pants" Lawrence must be recaptured. Paul Bunyan stories, "French Louie", the Émigrés, the French explorers: they are all part of the lore, but fundamental to the country we know today are the life and experience of that relatively small number of "American stock" that went into the Adirondacks in the early days to establish their families, in many instances through the years right down to the present.

The elder Lawrence was such a fellow, and "Pants" was born up there in the 1860s while the War Between the States was going on. He got his name, as might be imagined, from the fact that the elder Lawrence made all too little to provide his family with clothing bought at the store. So young "Pants," in trousers made over from his father's, got his name. Of course, in the beginning "Pants" wasn't a guide, because the only people in the Adirondacks at that time didn't need guides. Before Prohibition, "Pants" entered business and operated a tavern up Speculator way. He might have followed that profession indefinitely, but Prohibition cut short his career, and when the State began licensing guides, giving each a number, "Pants" became licensed guide Number One.

By that time "Pants" was a man grown tall and spare, six-foot-three or better, with long arms and powerful hands, and a voice like the Bull of Bashan. He was suited to be the guide for sportsmen who came up from the city to fish the streams and lakes, and hunt deer and bear in the mountains. Tall and not given to wasting words, "Pants" would on occasion, particularly after a drink or two, become quite loquacious. He himself boasted that when he began drinking he limited himself in amount to the quantity necessary to float a ship, but felt as he grew older that he would have to give up because they were making the ships bigger and bigger.

Many a famous name in the sports world had "Pants" for a guide— Jimmy Slattery, Dempsey, and Tunney are only a few of the better known. When "Pants" in his old age became ill, it was they who contributed to send him to a nursing home down in Gloversville.

Of course, as might be expected, "Pants" was not only the No. 1 Adirondack guide, but to this day at the Osborne Inn up in Speculator there is a framed license hanging behind the bar which is testimony to "Pants" ability as a story teller. In bold print it declares that "Pants" also had the No. 1 "Adirondack Liar's License."

It is funny how once you become conscious of a character in the North Country his name pops up in unexpected places. Not long ago I met Donald E. Sharp, an executive of the Libbey-Owen-Ford Glass Company, out in Toledo. And in casual conversation, when stories were being told, he told one readily identified as a part of the "Pants" Lawrence legend. And so, he too contributed something to the collection of the few I know. To be sure, these stories were told with all seriousness—told by "Pants" to his clients, and told by his clients to me as gospel truth. And while I don't want to lay myself open to charges of gullibility, I nevertheless have the feeling that there is something true in all of them. And speaking of gullibility, "Pants" could never be charged with that. In fact, he was something of a scientist in his own right. He believed in experimentation. An anecdote will illustrate the point.

When smokeless powder was just coming into use, the sportsmen were bringing it into the mountains instead of black. "Pants" looked upon it with the greatest of skepticism, and he tried it out with great care, and after his experiment, went back to black powder because it packed the real charge. The experiment all happened one day when "Pants" was hunting up the Kun-Ja-Muk. "Pants" was such an excellent marksman that he could take muskrat with a rifle and didn't have to bother with a lot of traps. Given anything like a decent sight, "Pants" could hit a muskrat in the eye as far as he could see it, and so he was very careful when up the Kun-Ja-Muk to be ready to take a pelt here and there.

For his hunting that day "Pants" was using an old muzzle-loader which he commonly charged with a heavy black powder. But just to prove to himself whether or not smokeless was better, on this occasion he filled his horn with the new smokeless powder. As he walked up the creek, he spotted a muskrat, drew a careful bead, and fired. He walked over to where he thought the 'rat would be, but he found that it had slipped into the water. And so he lost a skin that was worth 35 or 40 cents. Shaking his head, he paused to reload his rifle, and no sooner had he rammed the ball home than he saw another 'rat about the same distance away. This time he aimed carefully, and as quickly as he had fired, he ran to the spot, but the 'rat, unharmed, had slipped away. By this time "Pants" was getting a little hot under the collar. So for the next charge he took almost twice as much powder, and exercised special care in ramming it home. He took off his mackinaw, pushed back his cap, and carefully surveyed the bank for another 'rat. This time, before he sighted, like a runner on his blocks he made ready to dash away. After he had drawn his bead and fired, he was away like a flash, scarcely knowing whether the gun had cracked or not. He ran up the bank to the exact spot where he thought the muskrat would be, and as he was stooping over to pull it out of the water, where he felt sure it would be, along came the ball out of his own musket and hit him in the seat of the pants. Surely this is proof enough for any scientist. "Pants" gathered up his gun, his mackinaw, and cap, and made his way back to the canoe in the stream, cursing smokeless powder, and thankful he didn't have to sit down to paddle home.

A further indication of the scientific quality of "Pants'" mind was his experience up on Swort Mountain. He had ranged far away from the camp looking for black bear. While he hadn't seen any bear, as he was coming down he took a shot or two at some small game, and had a try at a couple of deer with the result that as the sun was going down he found himself without much powder and no lead at all since he had loaded light when he started out that morning. Carrying his rifle in his hand, he came walking down the mountain, thinking about whatever it is a guide alone on a hunting expedition thinks about as he comes home in the evening almost empty-handed, when a little movement beside the trail attracted his attention. His eyes flashed to the right, and there just above the grass he saw a panther's tail whipping back and forth, to and fro. Well, "Pants" knew from the movement of that tail that here was a panther ready to spring, so he watched, and sure enough, right out of the brush came the body of that black cat; but since he was on the alert, "Pants" ducked, and the panther sailed right over his head. Flicking his eyes to the left side of the trail, he saw at once that the panther had whirled and was ready to spring again. And just in time "Pants" dropped to his knees as the cat, already in the air, again sailed over his head. This time "Pants" knew the cat would turn quicker, and as he looked out of the corner of his eye, he could see it, tail lashing in fury, ready for another leap. So, crouched on all fours, hands fumbling for his knife, he was ready for the next spring, and as he dropped flat on his face, "Pants" could almost feel the touch of the cat's body as it passed over. Rolling to his back, if one can wait in an instant, "Pants" waited for what might well be the last jump. But the instant lengthened and nothing happened. So, slowly "Pants" raised his head, and then on his knees looked to the left over the ground that sloped gently up the mountain. There, through the weeds he could see a movement that indicated clearly that the cat was going up the mountainside. For almost a minute he watched, for he couldn't make out why it was that a cat hungry enough to jump a man not once, but three times, would finally give up and go off up the mountain. Impelled by curiosity, "Pants" followed, and stalked that panther for more than a mile. Finally, up where the timber began to thin out and there was a relatively flat, grassy area, "Pants" parted the "popple" switches and looked through. There, on the outcropping of rock, "Pants" watched in amazement, watched while that panther practiced shorter jumps.

Lee Fontaine for a long time ran The Whitehouse up Speculator way. In summer it was a popular resort, and people from down-state would come up to rest. They would eat their dinner at noon in the large, cool dining room, and after their meal they would saunter out on the porch and see "Pants" sitting on the stoop, his back against the rail post, looking off over the mountains. The outlanders, appreciative of their leisure, would comment on how lovely and cool the weather was in July in the Whitehouse Inn. "Why is it," they would ask "Pants," "that it is so cool in the Whitehouse dining room?" And after several had asked, "Pants" would tell. "Well, it's this way," he would say. "Up the West Branch of the

Sacandaga there whips up some powerful winds in the winter, and as these winds wind up the mountain to Mud Lake Notch, they are for sure cyclones. Now, since there ain't much going on around Speculator in the winter time, we decided last year to go up there with two barrels of old molasses and paste it on both sides of the Notch just ahead of a blow. When the high winds got up the river, they hit the Notch, slowed down some, and then got stuck there. Then two of the boys and me went up there, and with the long cross-cut, in one day, we sawed off enough of that cyclone to fill the ice house, and now in the summer time all they have to do is chip off a chunk and hang it in the doorway of the dining room to keep it right cool."

If you go up to Speculator today, you come to the Osborne Inn. Once the bar had fine pine paneling, but "Pants" always declared it was hickory. "But how," people asked, "did they come by such fine hickory paneling?" And "Pants" told the tale:

"It come about a few years back that I was logging up Whitaker Lake way. I was kinda' late getting out of the woods one day. And you know how it is when you're late and anxious to get home; you hurry up a little. So the team was jogging down the trail road, and the empty wagon was jouncing around, with me holding on every way I could. It was one of those nice days, the first real warm day that comes in spring, and the snow was all gone, except in the northeast hollows. It was so warm that I druv all the way home that evening in nothing but my red underwear. Just as I pulled around the last bend before you get to the flats, I slowed up the team and leetle before they hit the flat rocks that go clear across the trail. And it was a good thing I did, too, 'cause there, sprang in the middle of that big warm rock, I see coiled the biggest rattler I ever seed, with his rattle a-ringin', all ready to strike. I yanked back on the lines and the horses reared up, the sparks a-flyin' from the shoes on the rock. I saw the rattler strike, and quick as I could get the team stopped, I jumped down and run around to hold their heads and see which horse would have to be shot. But you know what I seed when I got there? That snake had missed both horses, and had struck that wagon-tongue right back of the yoke. It had hit so hard that its fangs were in clear to the back of the jaw. Its tail was a-lashin' every which way, but I finally grabbed on to it, and pulled as hard as I would, I couldn't jerk it loose. I finally had to take out my hand axe and chop off its head. Well, I saved the rattles, gentled the horses, finally got going, and pulled into the mill yard just about dark. I unhooked the team and tied up in the stable, and hung up the harness ready to go the next morning.

"Well, you know, the next morning it wasn't light yet when I got out to hook up the team. I led them out into the yard where I had left the wagon, and backed them over the tongue, and tried to get the yoke to fit. But I fumbled around there in the dark, and I couldn't get the tongue to go into the ring; so ruther than fool around any more, I just led the team over to the next wagon, which was an extra anyway, and drove up into the woods. A couple of times that day I looked at the yoke, thought maybe the ring was bent or broke, but I didn't see that it was. So that night while I was going home, I got to thinkin' why it was I couldn't get the ring of that neck-yoke to fit over that wagon-tongue. So when I got down to the mill yard and unhooked the team, I went back and looked at that wagon tongue that was three inches at the tip and it was now about a foot across. I couldn't figure that out, but I was tired and I just went on in to bed. The next morning after I had made my first trip, I got to thinking again, so I stopped at the yard and took a look at that tongue in the full light of day. And you know what? That hickory tongue was now a log better than a foot across. So I just hooked on to it and took it over to the mill and got it sawed into half-inch panel strips and them's the pieces we used to panel this here barroom wall. And you know every spring, just when the snow is gone except for the northeast hollows, just a little bit of snake oil comes oozing out of the hickory panel, and the hired girl gives it a swipe or two with lamb's wool, and it has a polish as good as a looking glass."

Of course, there are other stories about "Pants" Lawrence and his friends: Willie Cook up Glen Falls way, folks over in St. Lawrence County who used snakes to cool their milk, and others who gave up the woods and went into the "black dirt country" above Batavia. There are memories too of people who hunted with "Pants" Lawrence, and listened to his, shall we say, "picturesque speech," as he made a drive chasing deer down for city folks to shoot at. I am sure many more of these tall tales and anecdotes are alive today. This letter may serve as a means of soliciting some of them from folks who will say, "Sure, I knew "Pants" Lawrence. Did you ever hear the one—?" ▰

❧ MITCHELL SABATTIS

By L.E. Chittenden, Reprinted from *Personal Reminiscences, 1840–1890*
York State Tradition, Spring 1964

Mitchell Sabattis, 19th century Adirondack guide of the Long Lake area, was a full-blooded Indian of the Abenaki tribe, noted particularly for his skill in woodcraft. He was a small man, gentle, unassuming, and reticent, but with "the strength and endurance of tempered steel." Addicted to alcohol, he overcame this weakness and became "for the last thirty years of his life…a kind husband, and a most reputable citizen." How this change in his life came about is here related by L.E. Chittenden, who refers to him as one of the finest characters he ever knew.

I spent my last night at Mitchell's home in Newcomb, [New York], where a conveyance from Elizabethtown was to meet me. Mitchell and his wife appeared depressed by some impending calamity. I made them tell me their trouble. There was a mortgage upon their home and little farm. It was due, the property was to be sold about four weeks later, and they saw no way of avoiding this, to them, ruinous result. If his home was sold, Mitchell's habits would be worse than ever.

Mitchell's wife assured me that he was proud of the fact that he had never broken his word; she said he was a kind husband, and if she could induce him to promise not to drink, she would even be reconciled to the loss of her home.

Eagle Bay, N.Y., 1925. In order to survive, Adirondackers once did an immense amount of physical labor. *Courtesy Marilyn Breakey*

The next morning when the horses were at the door and I was about to leave, I called Mitchell and his wife into their little "square room," seated myself between them, and asked:

"Mitchell, what would you give to one who would buy your mortgage and give you time in which to pay it?"

"I would give my life," he exclaimed, "the day after I had paid the debt. I would give it now if I could leave this little place to my Bessie and her children."

"It will not cost you so much as that," I said. "I am going to Elizabethtown. I shall buy or pay your mortgage. Your home will not be sold. On the morning of the second day of August of next year, I want you and "Lon" with your boats to meet me at Bartlett's, between the Upper and Lower Saranac Lakes. If you there tell me that you have not drunk a glass of strong liquor since I saw you last, your mortgage shall not trouble you so long as you keep your promise not to drink. If you break your promise, I do not know what I shall do, but I shall lose all confidence in Mitchell Sabattis. Your wife and children will not be driven from their home until you get drunk again."

He promised instantly, solemnly. He rose from his chair. I thought he looked every inch the chief which by birth he claimed to be as he said: "You may think you cannot trust me, but you can! Sabattis when he was sober never told a lie. He will never lie to his friend."

For a few minutes there was in that humble room a very touching scene. The Indian silent, solemn, but for the speaking arm thrown lovingly around the neck of his wife, apparently emotionless—the wife trying to say through her tears, "I told you you could trust Mitchell! He will keep his promise—he will never get drunk again. I know him so well! I am certain that he will not drink, and we shall be so happy. Oh! I am the happiest woman alive!"

"Well! Well!" I said, "let us hope for the best; we must wait and see. Mitchell, remember the 2nd day of next August—Bartlett's—and in the meantime no whiskey!" And so we parted.

I bought, took an assignment of the mortgage, and carried it to my home. Other duties occupied me, and Sabattis had long been out of my mind. One evening late in the following February, just at nightfall, I was watching the falling snow from my library window in Burlington [Vermont], when a singular conveyance stopped almost in front of my door. It was a long, unpainted sled, the runners hewn from natural crooks, with stakes some five feet high enclosing an oblong box of rough boards, to which were harnessed two unmatched horses. The driver traveled by the side of the horses, carrying a long gad of unpainted wood having no lash. He wore a cap and coat of bear-skin, which concealed his features.

Taking him to be some stranger who had lost his way, I went to his assistance. As I made some observation, a voice deep down inside the bear-skin said: "Why! It's Mr. Chittenden. I was looking for you and your house."

"Mitchell Sabattis!" I exclaimed. "In the name of all that is astonishing, what are you doing here?"

For a moment he made no answer. As I came nearer, his arms worked strangely, as if he would like to throw them around me. His voice was tremulous as he said: "I am so glad. I was afeard I should not find you—this town is so big and there are so many houses and men and roads. I was looking for a place where they would feed and take in the horses."

"But what has brought you here, a hundred and fifty miles from your home in Newcomb?"

"Yes! Yes! We have been very lucky this fall and winter. My wife said I had better come. I have had good fortune. Sold all my furs and my saddles of venison for money. Just now the season is over and I had nothing to do. So we talked it over, my wife Bessie and me. You remember Bessie. Somehow I can't get the right words. I would like to tell you tomorrow. Do you know of some place where they would take in the horses?"

"But what is this sled loaded with?"

"Nothing—much. Only a little game for you. I will tell you all about it tomorrow."

I went with him to a stable where his horses were taken in and his load put under lock and key. I took him to my house, although he protested that he had his own supplies and could just as well stay in the stable. His personal neatness, his civility, and the oddity of his expressions delighted every member of my household. A warm supper and a like welcome soon opened his heart, and I gathered from him the following details:

Good fortune had attended him from the time when he was relieved from anxiety about the mortgage. He had employment as a guide until the season for trapping and shooting for market began. He had never killed so many deer nor got such good prices in money for venison. He had paid all his little debts and saved one hundred dollars, which his wife said he ought to bring to me. They thought I would like a little game. So he had built a sled, borrowed two horses, made up a little load, and he had travelled that long and hard road from the head of Long Lake to Crown Point and thence to Burlington, not less than one hundred and fifty miles.

A refusal of his gift was not to be thought of. The next morning I took my butcher to his little load of game. There were the saddles or hindquarters of twenty-five fat deer in their skins, two carcasses of black bears dressed and returned to their skins, the skin of a magnificent catamount, with the skull and claws attached, which he had heard me say I would like to have, a half-dozen skins of the beautiful fur of the pin martin or the American sable, more than one hundred pounds of brook trout, ten dozen of ruffed grouse all dressed and braided into bunches of a half dozen, and some smaller game, with some specimen skins of the mink and fox. There was more game than my family could have consumed in a year.

I selected a liberal supply of the game and took the skins intended for myself and family. For the balance my butcher paid him liberally, and this money with his savings would have more than paid his mortgage. But I would not so soon lose my hold on him. He had told me that if he could build an addition to his house, his wife could keep four boarders while he was guiding in the summer. I induced him to save money enough for this addition, and to purchase the furniture then and there. He paid the interest and costs and a part of the principal of his mortgage, and went home loaded with presents for Bessie and the children—a very happy man.

On the 2nd of August, this time with two gentlemen and their wives, all safe companions in roughing it, as we approached the landing at Bartlett's, Mitchell and Alonzo were waiting for us. There was no need to ask Mitchell if he had kept his promise. His eye was as clear and keen as that of a goshawk. The muscles visible in their action under his transparent dark skin, his voice, ringing with cheerfulness, all told of a healthy body and a sound mind. His wife, he said, had her house filled with boarders, his oldest son had been employed as a guide for the entire season, and prosperity shone upon the Sabattis household.

Where shall we go? I consulted him about the location of our camp. He said that "Lon" and he knew what kind of place we wanted. We didn't want visitors or black flies—we wanted a beautiful location, with mountains, lakes, brooks and springs and an abundance of game. He and "Lon" knew such a place—they had left home, built a camp for us there, and if we would make a long day of it, they would row us there at once.

This chapter is already too long. I have not time to tell of the beauty of our camp, the abundance of the game, the sympathy of all our party, the fawn we caught, tamed and enjoyed, and left in its native woods, and the fidelity of our guides, which made those weeks a green oasis in all our lives. Nor can I describe the subsequent lives of those guides.

My destiny led me far away from the Adirondacks. The last I had heard from Mitchell was when he sent me a draft from New York for considerably more than the balance due upon his mortgage. The locality had become too easy of access—visitors were too numerous. It had so few attractions that I did not visit it for many years. But in 1885 the old feeling came over me, and with such of my family as had not gone out from me into homes of their own, I went to a new and fashionable hotel some thirty miles from Long Lake. From an old resident who knew it thoroughly, I had the subsequent history of Mitchell Sabattis.

He had never broken his promise to me. He united with the Methodist Church and became one of its leaders, and in a few years was the leading citizen in the Long Lake settlement. In worldly matters he prospered. His wife kept a favorite resort for summer visitors. Their children were educated, the daughters married well—two of the sons served their country with courage and gallantry through the war, returned home with honorable discharges, and now guided in summer and built the celebrated Adirondack [guide] boats in winter. Mitchell, now a hale and healthy veteran of eighty-four years, still lived at Long Lake in the very house of which I was once the mortgagee.

The next morning I heard a light step on the uncarpeted hall and a knock at my door. I opened it and Sabattis entered. He was as glad to see me as I was to grasp his true and honest hand. But I was profoundly surprised. Had the world with him stood still? He did not look a day older than when I last saw him, more than twenty-five years ago. The same keen, clear eye, transparent skin with the play of the muscles under it, the same elastic step, ringing voice and kindly heart. His eye was not dim nor his natural force abated. We spent a memorable day together—at nightfall we parted forever.

This is a true story, and of course has its moral, which is that a kind word or an inexpensive favor may sometimes save a fellow creature and change him into a useful man. To him who bestows either, I could not wish a more delightful memory than that of my relations with Mitchell Sabattis. ▰

TOM PEACOCK, ADIRONDACK GUIDE
By W. H. Burger, *North Country Life*, Winter 1953

His grandson's eyes sparkled as he told me about him. The boy was 17 and already an outstanding person in Saranac Lake, where he was living with his grandfather and two younger sisters. I was fascinated by the boy and what he told me about the man he worshipped. Said I to myself, "Here is a person I must meet."

In five days I was back in Saranac Lake for a long talk with and 88-year-old man, who was keeping house for his three grandchildren, and while he could no longer roam the woods, was doing the finest guiding of his career. The man was Thomas L. Peacock.

His earliest memories, I found, clustered about one of the most exciting figures in American history—John Brown. His family and the Browns were near neighbors, and he vividly recalls, although he was only six, the night John Brown left home for his Harper's Ferry expedition. He and his father had been planting potatoes on a piece of Brown land which they worked on shares. They were returning past the Brown home about sundown. Small groups of men were talking in the door yard; others were within. Childlike, the boy sensed the suppressed excitement. His father and he lingered, and about dusk John Brown rode up on the horse. There was more talk. Then he remembers that he and his father went on, and John Brown bade them good-bye.

When Brown returned, it was in his coffin. It was a snowy day in December, and a big crowd had followed the body from Lake Champlain and other places. Again the child was profoundly impressed.

He also recalled how surviving members of the Harper's Ferry party furtively returned, slipping from house to house and barn to barn. A couple of them came to his home for food.

Mr. Peacock was still corresponding with the then 84-year-old granddaughter of John Brown, who was living in Hollywood, California.

Tom Peacock started on his hunting and guiding career when most boys are now entering high school. When he was thirteen, he shot his first deer with a flintlock musket owned by Henry Thompson, John Brown's son-in-law. At seventeen he was guiding through Indian Pass and up the Saranac Lakes. When he was eighteen, he blazed the first trail from the top of Ampersand to Middle Saranac, or Round Lake as it is known locally.

He was one of Grover Cleveland's party when the president-to-be made his headquarters at Prospect House (Saranac Inn) in 1878 and 1879, and he was with the New York State Surveyor Verplanck Colvin on his first trip.

He recalls W.H.H. (Adirondack) Murray as being very strong. Once while Murray and his friends were lolling around, someone egged Murray and Peacock into a wager about "hefting" a huge pack basket filled with stones from a sitting position on the ground. Murray tried, but only half-heartedly, Peacock said. Peacock did it by rolling against a log and grasping a protruding stub.

His father had a contract to supply food to lumber camps at Big and Little Wolfe Ponds, near the present Tupper Lake station. This was the late 60s or early 70s, when Tom was a young man.

They would load hay onto lumber sleds in the evening. Next morning, rising hours before daybreak in the dead of winter, they would put 25 to 30 bushels of potatoes and two or three quarters of beef on the hay. The start was usually made about half past two or three, but Tom remembers driving through Saranac Lake as early as 3:00 AM. They planned to get out onto the Lower Lake by daylight. The sleds would usually arrive in camp about 9:00 PM to be greeted by the lumberjacks with great enthusiasm. They not only carried food for man and beast but brought mail. Mr. Peacock remarked that in those days mail was carried through the woods by Tom, Dick and Harry.

Since North Elba was his home town, he knew every inch of it and the village of Lake Placid. Mr. Peacock could recall only four buildings on the road past Mirror Lake when the Lake Placid Club bought the property on the opposite side. There was no store in town.

Tom remembered when the Stevens House blew down. It was May along in 1880 or 1883. The hotel had burned down and was being rebuilt. It happened during the night. The cause was the first thunderstorm of the spring. The place simply collapsed to kindling wood. The kitchen wing, in which forty men were sleeping, stood up through the storm. After the storm, the North Elba people went into the woods and cut timber, and although the spruce was green, the hotel was built and in operation in July.

Tom vividly remembered the red schoolhouse in North Elba, which did duty through the 1850s and into the 1880s' first town meetings, elections, funerals, church services and for classes for teaching the three R's to mountain kids.

Tom Peacock must have been a man of prodigious strength. He was no boaster, but his quiet account of some of his feats gave convincing evidence of his prowess. He was sitting in the Guide Room at Martin's on Lower

Tent scene on the Saranacs. Guides were an essential part of a "sports" experience.
Kollechar photo. Courtesy Maitland DeSormo Collection

Saranac Lake one evening when old man Martin came in and asked if anyone wanted to take a telegraph message up to Big Tupper. Nobody answered,
and as Tom said, he didn't answer either. But finally, when silence was getting strained, Tom said "I'll take it," although he didn't like going through
the Seven Pole Rapids at night. The dam had raised the water in the Raquette River fifteen feet in places, and thousands of acres were flooded.

The trip was arduous but uneventful. The lights were on at Bartlett's
as he made the carry. He carried over Sweeney's, cut across the Oxbow,
and rowed into Big Tupper just as it was coming daylight. Forty-three
and a half miles in one night—not bad for one man and a guide boat.

Unlike most Adirondack guides, Peacock traveled widely and guided
in other regions than our North Woods. He hunted moose in Canada for
fifty years and made several trips "out west." During one of these he visited the Theodore Roosevelt ranch in North Dakota. One winter he kept
a railroad construction gang in Colorado supplied with elk and deer

Hotel at Conklingville, N.Y. This town was flooded with the construction of the Conkling-ville dam. A century has brought a nearly ceaseless demographic shift to the Adirondacks. *Courtesy Marilyn Breakey*

meat. He worked at the Hotel Breslin in Lake Hopatcong in New Jersey for ten summers and lived in New York for many years.

The last time I saw Tom Peacock he was dying, though neither of us realized it. He was in bed, and as he lay there he said his whole life seemed to come back to him. Out of this flood of reminiscences, I recall his impressions of "T.R." in North Dakota and the story of Ike, the tame moose.

Tom and another fellow had just swum their horses across the little Missouri and got plastered with mud. They went on toward the ranch house and saw Roosevelt coming up a hill, leading his horse. The sun was shining on his glasses and his buck teeth stuck out. He was carrying a string of sage hens he had just shot. Roosevelt mixed with the men, cooking for them, sleeping with them, and telling stories, and Tom added, "What stories!"

And here in Tom's own words is his valedictory—the Ike tale.

"Back in 1903 and 1904 I had a camp in the Narrows on Long Pond. We had just arrived at my house in Saranac Lake when a boy came in. He was badly scared. He had just come from camp and said he had seen the 'awfullest' animal there.

"We went right up on the train. When we arrived at camp, we found a moose walking around. I went up to him. He reached out his nose and I patted it. He stayed around all summer.

"He seemed to be very tame. I called him 'Ike' after our game protector. He would always come when I called him even if he was way up in the woods. But he didn't like women. His eyes would turn green if he saw one and he'd start for her.

"One time some boys saw him on a ridge on Slang Pond. He started for them. They ran to their boat and he swam after them. They carried the boat across carry into Long, but he came right after them even to camp and followed them up onto the porch of a cabin into which they ran. Then he looked in at them through the windows and glass door.

"Finally I was down at my house in Saranac Lake. Old Mr. and Mrs. Turner were in camp. The boys came down and told me the moose had noosed up the swing, which was hung on 1½ inch rope. His horns got caught and hung up in the rope as he struggled to get loose. Gilbert Turner tried to cut the rope. He lunged at Turner, his horns broke, and he went wild. So old man Turner shot him. That was the end of Ike." ◼

JACQUES SUZANNE — MAN OF THE NORTH

By Terry James Gordon, *York State Tradition*, Spring 1973

The heritage of the North Country has been enhanced in recent years by a flow of publication on the lives of some if its outstanding men and women. Noah John Rondeau is now a household word, while "French" Louie and Seneca Ray Stoddard bring smiles to the faces of all who encounter them. David S. Kellogg, the North Country's "Doctor at All Hours," certainly loved and added to the region's heritage. Yet there are others equally as outstanding who as yet have been neglected by writers.

One such person is Jacques Suzanne (1880–1967), a man of many talents. Suzanne was born in Deauville, France, on April 17, 1880. His father, Armand Albert Suzanne, was a shoemaker, and his mother, Eugenie

Georgina Morel Suzanne was a housewife. His father's craftsmanship must have rubbed off on him, for in later years, Jacques was making his own shoes, moccasins, furs, and coats. In 1898 Suzanne left France with two bulls and four Spanish horses for Buenos Aires. He fought bulls in the arena in Argentina but left for the Pampas, because the Argentinos were not very polite with the foreigners, whom they called "Gringos." In the Pampas he painted and sketched the Gauchos and broke horses for the English army. From there Suzanne went to Australia, Java, and a number of other countries. At a very early age he was an enlightened world traveler.

Suzanne also studied art under masters at Paris, and it was this that eventually brought him, in a roundabout way, to America.

"As an art student in Paris," he wrote, "I read many books about explorers. I was so taken with them I put my studies aside and set out to discover the North Pole, striking toward it across Siberia. Although I started in 1905, I never reached it, for when I heard it had been discovered by Admiral Peary, I gave up. But now I was in love with the North and I thought, 'I will be the first to drive a dog sled across the top of the world, through Siberia, across the frozen stretches of the Pacific, across Alaska and Canada to Labrador.'"

Suzanne traveled for 20 months on this exploring trip, covering 5,000 miles by sled—the longest trek by sled ever recorded—but he never finished it, for he was caught by movie producers in Canada, and they eventually brought him to Lake Placid in 1921.

Suzanne settled on the Bear Cub Road in Lake Placid and named his ranch, which he built himself, the "Eskimo Camp," later more commonly called the "Movie Ranch." This was a fitting setting, for Suzanne still had that great yearning for the North, and this feeling was depicted in his Nordic style of living. His ranch was a piece of the real North Country, and civilization, such as we know it, seemed at least a thousand miles away.

On Suzanne's "Movie Ranch," many dozens of screenplays were filmed in which either Jacques or his Siberian malamute huskies starred. A few of these were *The Trapper's Wife*, with Kitty Gordon, *The Spell of the Yukon*, with Edmond Bresse, *The Broken Silence*, with Zena Keefe, *The Man from*

Beyond, with Houdini, and *Arctic Explorers*, with Captain Evelyn Baldwin.

The "Movie Ranch" was an interesting place. Suzanne not only lived there; he charged admission to see it. Thousands of people visited this strange little tourist attraction out on the Bear Cub Road. They included such well known people as Lowell Thomas, David Selznick, Adolf Friml, Leopold Stokowski, and Peter Tchaikovsky.

What would one see at the Ranch? First of all, it was surrounded by large estates, but the area retained the simplicity of the great North Woods. In fact, one almost needed a map (which the Lake Placid Chamber of Commerce supplied) to find it. If one could find it, as thousands did, the first thing one usually saw was Suzanne himself, for he greeted every visitor as soon as he saw him. He gave the visitor the strange feeling that he was meeting a person of Herculean strength and one endowed with Achillean courage. He bore many scars and claw marks attesting to the fact that he was not afraid of wild wolves, bears, or any other animal. Many of these scars were reminders of the battles he staged for an anxious movie producer.

After meeting Suzanne and listening to some "wild" stories of how he intended to live to be 100 and how he, not Admiral Peary, discovered the North Pole, one usually encountered his beautiful huskies. Papoose weighed 225 pounds; Vodka, a Russian wolfhound, cost $2,000; and Sampson, another Russian wolfhound, stood over six feet tall on his hind legs. Suzanne had sled dogs and wolfhounds from all over the world. He had giant Alaskan malamutes, descendants of Peary's North Pole expedition, Greenland dogs, Nova Zembla sled dogs, and descendents of Suzanne's own Trans-Siberian racing dogs. Next, one would see wolves, either caged or on long leashes, depending on whether they were trained or not. Suzanne captured, trained, and bred all his own wolves and aided the Conservation Department many times when wolf packs were a serious threat to Northern New York. Other animals at the Ranch included Golden Palomino stallions and Lipizzaner, wild cats, bears, hawks, ducks, etc. Next there was the museum of Indian and Eskimo costumes, relics of Arctic explorers, and copies of Suzanne's movie songs, such as "Tundra Song," "My Country," and "The Last Raid."

Finally one saw Suzanne's own paintings of outdoor life. Suzanne depicted his life travels, his animals, and his vast knowledge of Nordic living (by survival of the fittest) with such talent that life-sized dogs on canvas almost seem to breathe.

He painted about 92 murals, of which approximately 20 are known to exist [in 1973]. One of the most beautiful, which is owned by William F. Davis, Port Henry, is a 12' by 4' painting of Admiral Peary and his dog team. It shows Peary about to start out with his team of huskies in the bluish light of the midnight sun, depicted realistically on Suzanne's canvas in a soft blue color with a splash of gold in the background setting off a panorama of white swirling snow. The mural took three years to complete, all of it done outdoors.

Suzanne's paintings have hung in salons in Paris, London, New York City, and Petrograd, and some still hang there. They are in the New York State Museum of Art, the Adirondack Museum, [the former] Frontier Town, and some private residences in Lake Placid and Port Henry.

Jacques Suzanne died in 1967 at the age of 87. His famous Ranch on the Bear Cub Road has been leveled, and all that remains is a memory of bygone days. This account is but a minute description of a life filled with story after story from hunting tigers in Bengal, hunting wolves in Siberia for the Czar of Russia, taking New York Governor Whitman for a sled ride in 20-degrees-below-zero weather, to being a main attraction at the Tahawus Sportsmen's Show in 1952.

His life was as fascinating as any the North Country has ever known. It seems fitting that he is buried next to his friend and fellow outdoorsman, Noah John Rondeau.

Peggy Byrne summarized Rondeau's life by saying he lived in harmony with nature rather than trying to conquer it. I would summarize Suzanne's life by saying he lived because of nature, and his whole life was centered on experiencing it. ▰

Editor's Note: Much of the information contained in this article came from Suzanne's own writings, particularly his letters and journals, which were loaned, or in some cases, given to the writer by countless numbers of people from California to Vermont. Other sources of information were the Essex County Republican, August 23, 1963; New York Times, May 17 and 21, 1914; New York Herald Tribune, February 23, 1947; and Parade, April 1, 1945.

THE HERMIT OF COLD RIVER

By Clayt Seagears, *North Country Life,* Spring 1947
Reprinted from New York State *Conservationist*

There isn't a more bona fide hermit in the whole United States— including Sharktooth Shoal—than Noah John Rondeau, who has occupied a hole in a woodpile way the hell and gone back in the Adirondack wilderness for 33 years.

Noah John is not only the real McCoy in the hermit department; he looks like hermits are supposed to look. He lives the same way.

He has himself a Sunday suit fabricated out of a couple of deer hides and assembled with bear-tooth toggles. He hunts. He fishes. He traps. He uses the longbow. He keeps a diary in secret code and sets his calendar by the stars. He owns less household equipment that a Tenderfoot Scout would take on an overnight hike, and how he gets through a long, zero Adirondack winter in that layout of his is strictly a lesson in hibernation which any woodchuck would do well to look into.

Noah John is, in truth, sprang out of this universe.

Perhaps we shouldn't wait to the breathless finish of this yarn to give out with a rich moral. We have a state with darned near 14 million people in it [in 1946], the teemingest population in the nation. Yet here's a guy wanting to be a hermit who was able to be one with a minimum of outside interference, and in a peak-studded wilderness six hours by forest foot trail from the nearest hamlet. The moral thus seems to be that (1) Noah John is one in 14 million and (2) that despite a population density of 250 folks per square mile, we still have large quantities of country for people to lose themselves in when pressed (for various reasons) for a walk in spaces very wide and very wild.

Leave us draw up a hunk of balsam stump while Noah John cooks what very well may turn out to be his whole day's "vittles"—a few flap-jacks bogged down with his own brand of syrup.

This cooking function is performed (in summer) over a more or less perpetual open fire. He flaps the jacks in bear grease, rolls them up like a cigar, bites off about up to the band and then takes a healthy swig of syrup out of a bottle still ketchupy around the seams. Nuts, says Noah, to the napkin trade.

And let us gaze (withal, with awe) upon the unique living quarters of Noah John. What appear to be wooden tepees are, indeed wooden tepees—but of a variety more practical than anything ever described in the Manual of Carpentry and Tinkery for Growing Boys. Noah John lives in his own woodpile. Come spring, he has burned his kitchenette, his storage vault, his front parlor and his powder room behind him. Furthermore he has made it easy to do.

The system is this: When winter has run itself out down the mountain rivers, Noah John starts building his tepee village. He cuts long poles of efficient burning diameter. Every three feet he notches them nearly through. Then he stacks 'em up like a wigwam, leaving an interior recess large enough to stretch out in. Thus, when winter has piled the drifts high and our hermit's activity has been reduced to a minimum, the chore of keeping a fire is a cinch. Noah John merely reaches out the door, removes a pole, gives it a belt with the axe head, and the notched pieces fall apart. He admits it took him a few years to figure out the proper deal for this easy-living angle; but what do a few years amount to in a pattern of life such as his?

Noah John is 63 years old. He now finds it bad news to do his main sleeping under a drafty canopy of slanted poles. So he has a hovel made from a few boards off a long defunct lumber camp. Over the so-called door to this realm of retirement the old boy has nailed a sign: "TOWN HALL." Inside there's just room enough for a sort of bed and a crude stove. Every year the place gets smaller, due to encroachment of soot layers from the walls. On the bed is just what you'd expect to find on the bed of a better class hermit—a bear skin. The interior has touches here and there of

Noah John Rondeau and Mary C. Dittmar. 1943. *Courtesy Adolph Dittmar*

"Mm hum," Noah chewed on his whiskers. "Tell them I have become a cantankerous hermit and am living in a burrow with a raccoon."

"You reckon that'll satisfy the newspaper people?"

"Well," Rondeau replied, "there taint no way to *mollify* them."

gaudy décor—the stalagmite drippings of myriad red, yellow and white candles. There are no windows and none are necessary, because the occupant is, perforce, always close to the door. It's as simple as that.

He has another cubbyhole for the convenience of visiting firemen—the hikers who occasionally call on him. This jointed shelter does have a window, and more extensive decoration—the chalky shoulder blades of a dozen beavers, the antlers of bygone bucks and the skulls of two degreased bears. These rattle nicely in the breeze and add to the general cheer.

Noah John, despite his 33 long years of complete isolation, and despite the primitive aspects of his existence, is by no means uncouth or illiterate. By any yardstick of human behavior he is a distinctly bright gent. It would be difficult, in fact, to find a single button missing, except on his pants. He loves to talk—picturesque hermit talk if he thinks his hiker-visitor would be made any happier by it. He reads anything he can lay hands on, but leans to books on astronomy, philosophy and kindred subjects of the solitudes. This is quite understandable.

He likes people (if they don't crowd him), but it is suspected that he views them with some suspicion. Inherently honest himself, Noah John hints darkly that it was a sequence of sharp practices by others, when he was the youthful proprietor of a barber chair, which drove him from what he felt was a chiseling world to the honesty of open spaces.

Noah John's outdoors is built to order for a hermit. His spot is on a bluff high over the end of Cold River Flow, twelve miles as the crow flies south of Lower Saranac Lake, ten miles northeast of Long Lake Village and twenty

Starks Home. The Adirondacks was once a region where the great majority of people were natives existing off the land. *Courtesy Marilyn Breakey*

miles west of Keene Valley. Trails maintained by the Conservation Department lead all the way—about nineteen miles of hiking in any direction, except that eleven miles can be made by canoeing to the north end of Long Lake, thence into the Raquette and then a mile or so up the Cold. Most hikers go in via Long Lake Village and Shattuck Clearing, although some prefer the hoof route via Corey's (just south of Upper Saranac) and Mountain Pond. Four miles to Noah John's east are Preston Ponds, nestling at the end of Indian Pass. He couldn't have picked a more isolated place to live with a Ouija board.

Nor could he have picked a spot of greater beauty. Towering across Noah's valley is Panther Mountain, and Santanoni and Henderson. Behind him rear Seymour, Seward and the Sawtooths. He lives on a strip of [former] lumber company holdings in the middle of a huge chuck of state land comprising about 130 square miles.

It's wild land, a stronghold of marten and fisher. Noah used to run a 40-mile trap line when he was more spry. Now he has all he can do to "come out" once a year for a pack basket of staples. Forest Rangers—like Orville Betters or Wayne Tyler—or deer hunters and hikers bring him his mail now and then, plus small supplies of food. Or Fred McLane, the Conservation Department's head plane pilot, may drop him bread and papers. Maybe the brook trout are biting in Noah John's Lost Pond or in Cold River Flow. Maybe a snowshoe rabbit rams its head against Noah John's sittin' log and conks out conveniently in time for a lonely, February meal. Maybe.

The Conservation Department has a great friend in Noah John. Spry or not—if anything went wrong in the woods he'd be out of there on all two cycles to tell the boys about it. He's a great friend of Man in General, too, for he's the magnet which lures many a hiker deep into some of the grandest country in the world, and that kind of stuff is good for what ails you.

Yep, everything considered, there's quite a guy behind all that alfalfa. ▰

❦❦ ADIRONDACK HERMIT: FERDINAND JENSON

By Elmer Owen Hoffman, *North Country Life*, Winter 1956

Finding the following clipping tucked away in my desk brought to memory a deer hunting trip that Doc, Griff, and I had taken several years ago. The notice read as follows:

> **Tupper Lake Free Press**, March 27, 1947
> *Aged hermit dies as fire sweeps cabin. Body of Ferdinand Jensen, age 87 years, found in the ashes of his camp in the woods, in Killdare country, 14 miles north of Tupper Lake, N.Y. Last seen by Lawrence Stafford, Superintendent of Killdare Club. Aged recluse was in the habit of hiking out to the road about a third of a mile to get mail and supplies brought to him by employees of the club. When his mail was left untouched for several days, George Littlejohn, an employee of the club, hiked in and found that the one room cabin had been burned to the ground, the unrecognizable body of the old man lying in the cold ashes near the remains of his bed.*

The details of his death never will be known, but it is easy for me to reconstruct the picture.

While staying at his camp, more than once I had awakened to see the old guide sit up in his upper bunk, fill and light his pipe, then throw the half-burned match in the general direction of the nearest stove. There were two stoves placed end to end, one a cook stove, the other a big sheet iron heating stove. Scattered around on the floor near these stoves were old newspapers, kindling wood, and trash. Is it any wonder that the cabin finally caught fire and burned while the old man slept!

If he smelled smoke he doubtless paid no attention to it, as smoke in the room was a common occurrence. On cold nights he usually covered his head with the blankets, so he probably did not discover the flames until his bed caught fire and then it was too late.

My first trip to this camp is an experience that I always will remember. The three of us were willing to put up with primitive living conditions and inconveniences in order to have the use of a warm, dry shack in this very secluded, wooded mountain region. Not everyone realizes that New York State is one of the best places to hunt deer in the United States. According to the records of the New York State Conservation Department, there were 26,677 deer shot in this state in 1947.

It was a beautiful autumn morning when we started on our hunting trip. The 200-mile drive from Albany was not a hardship as the weeds were aglow with color and the many lakes we passed sparkled in the sunshine. About eight miles northwest of Tupper Lake, we came to the gate which marks the entrance to the property of the Killdare Club. There we parked our car and transferred our hunting equipment and supplies to the Killdare Club station wagon.

"Sports" arriving in Newcomb, 1930s. Outing parties looked forward to hearing stories about old-time guides and other Adirondack characters. *Courtesy George Shaughnessy*

One of the rules of this club was that their private road, which they maintained, could not be used by the public: but they were glad to take us in to Jensen's camp in one of their own cars. The road winds in and out through state land and through the forest belonging to the Oval Wood Dish Company. Occasionally in the distance, we caught glimpses of Mt. Matumbla, a conspicuous landmark. After a few miles we came to the Jordan River, a deep, slow moving stream, teeming with brook trout. The nearby scenery was beautiful, with imposing rock cliffs to the west, too steep to scale excepting in a few places.

At last we were deposited with our duffel and supplies beside the road at the trail leading through the woods to Jensen's camp. It was a quite a job toting our supplies and rifles up the steep trail to the camp as this was a rude change from our customary desk work.

At last we came to the end of the trail and there was old Ferdie in his doorway, beaming us a welcome. His eyes were keen and blue and his hair and mustache a grizzly grey. He was then over eighty years of age although he did not seem that old to me. Of short, stocky build, he had been a strong man in his prime, but of late years he had been unable to tramp through the woods guiding hunting parties as he had done for so many years. All that he could do now was to share his cabin with deer hunters and keep the fires burning.

In his 18 x 20 ft. room were two tiers of double bunks. Ferdie always climbed to an upper bunk while we occupied the lower ones. An old home-made table, covered with annual layers of white oil cloth was always set with dishes and a motley array of jars of peanut butter, jam, mustard, ketchup, vinegar, and Ferdie's old glass tobacco jar. In the center of the table was a kerosene oil lamp, the only source of light in the room. Innumerable pots, pans, and skillets hung from the rafters. He took great pride in his cooking utensils, many of them aluminum. Woe unto you if you used the potato kettle for prunes!

He gave us plenty of advice, not only about hunting but in regard to cooking also. Coffee must be boiled thoroughly or it was just no good, in his opinion. As one approached through the woods when Ferdie was making coffee, the pungent aroma could be detected a quarter of a mile away. It smelled good, I admit, and better than it tasted. As for tea, our practice of using tea bags was held up to ridicule and scorn. It's too weak," he complained. "Put in another tea bag, Ferdie," I advised. Still dissatisfied, he grumbled, "It tastes raw, it ought to be boiled."

Because we were hunting in such a wild and remote section of the mountains and had to do our own cooking, we were careful to take an ample supply of food to last for our ten days' stay. We made sure that we had more than enough, as old Ferdie always was delighted to accept any surplus as a gift. Some of the items on our list were old fashioned buckwheat pancake flour, genuine maple syrup, bacon, eggs, coffee, tea, and sandwich material. In our hunting coat pockets, we always carried our lunch of sandwiches, hard candy, and at least one chocolate bar for emergency. As it was war time and meat was rationed, we took no fresh meat but counted on killing at least a spike horn buck the first day.

The morning after our arrival at camp, Griff and I started hunting at daybreak to get our much- needed venison to supply us with meat while in camp. There are many ways to hunt deer, but we were devotees of the method known as still hunting. Usually each man hunted alone, but sometimes two of us went together. A compass was indispensable, and we constantly watched our landmarks, occasionally clipping a blaze on the far side of the tree. These white marks are visible at quite a distance through the woods, even at night with the aid of flash lights which one always carries. By using care and observation, we were able to cover large areas in the trackless forests. We walked together until we were about a mile from camp, then separated, taking parallel paths about a hundred yards apart, moving through the forest toward the northwest, Griff on my right. Slowly and cautiously, one step at a time we proceeded, being careful not to step on any dry branches. Most of the time we were not in sight of each other, but when I came to an open space, where I might see Griff off to the right, I stopped and waited until he appeared and waved me on. After several hours of this slow progress, a shot echoed through the woods, a signal that Griff had obtained a fleeting glimpse of a deer and was warning me to be on the lookout. My old Savage rifle in readiness, I stood motionless. Suddenly a deer came bounding through the woods.

Being a poor shot when a deer is running, I hoped the deer would come close enough to give me a fair chance.

Luck was with me! The startled deer stopped about fifty yards away when he saw me. Very little skill was required to drop him at that distance. He proved to be a spike horn buck in excellent condition.

Well! We had deer liver and bacon for breakfast the next morning and choice venison every day for the rest of our stay in camp. Needless to say, there was very little left but the bones when we departed.

As I did not hunt as far or as steadily as my companions, I spent quite a bit of time in and around the camp and became very well acquainted with the old guide. He told me a great deal about his life.

He said that he was born in Copenhagen, Denmark, in 1859. When he was about twenty-nine years old, his sweetheart died and he left Denmark and came to America. He tried to forget his sorrow by living alone in the northern Adirondack Mountains. He was an expert axeman and found work with Raquette River Paper Company when they lumbered this region many years ago.

After the pulp wood had all been cut, he built a log cabin and remained as sort of watchman or fire warden. When this property was sold to the Oval Wood Dish Company of Tupper Lake in 1916, it was brought out in court that the old man had been living on the land for at least ten years.

Many years later the Killdare Club wanted to buy the two square miles where Jensen had squatted, but the late W.C. Hull, Sr., then the President of the Oval Wood Dish Company, would not sell. Mr. Hull said that, since Jensen had been permitted to live there unmolested for so many years, he should not be disturbed in his old age: so Jensen had practically the undisputed use of two square miles of excellent deer country.

The Killdare Club land joined his property on two sides and State land on the remainder. The employees of the Club were very good to the old man, picking up his mail as they went by and making purchases for him in the village of Tupper Lake. Beside the road he had an old trunk in which they put his mail and packages. On rare occasions they would take the old man to the village for some business or special celebration, but in general he lived alone, away back in the woods, seldom seeing a human being, with only the deer, foxes porcupines, and other wildlife for companions.

However, thanks to his radio, he was surprisingly well-informed. Being so far from power lines, he obtained excellent reception from his battery set. I can still see him sitting on his old trunk listening to his radio. He had worn a clean, shiny spot where he had sat on the lid year after year. He did not care for musical programs but listened to all the news and had decided opinions on almost every subject. He was extremely partisan with several pet phobias. The less said about them the better.

The little cabin in which he lived he had built unaided, using rather small seven-foot softwood logs, set up in a vertical position and toe nailed together at top and bottom. By using this original method, he was able to use shorter logs which he could handle alone.

One day, returning from hunting, I was puzzled to see a black and white striped cabin off the in the woods. It proved to be Ferdie's shack. A snowfall the previous night had covered the roof and the heat from inside the cabin had melted the snow over the wide spaces between the roof boards. To save lumber he had left a two-inch space between each board and covered the gaps with rolled roofing. Hence the odd zebra-like striped effect.

I had been told by my companions that the camp was supplied with running water. The joke was on me when I discovered that the running water came from a clear mountain spring 100 yards distant and had to be dipped up and carried in a pail to the camp.

Ferdie bought most of his tools, equipment, and clothes through mail order catalogues. These catalogues were very much in evidence, not only in his cabin, but old numbers were plentiful in a small building some distance from the camp, just over a knoll and facing towards the woods.

This little building had a back, a roof, and two sides which were only four feet high. It had no door. I asked the old hunter, "Why no door or sides?" He replied, "Well, when I am here by myself, I always carry my rifle and more than once I have shot a deer from this hide out."

As his garbage disposal plant was down toward the woods, not far away, the deer probably were attracted to this place by the salt.

With all his eccentricities, he was a kind-hearted old man. He loved the birds and hung up meat and suet outside a window to attract them and also threw out bread for them, calling, "Biddie, Biddie, Biddie." Many birds came at his call to enjoy their breakfast.

Once he bought two young chicks, hoping eventually to get a supply of eggs. They grew to be huge, white roosters.

When I suggested that he sell us a rooster and we would all have a feast, he indignantly replied, "Kill one of my pets, never!"

The next year when we returned the roosters were gone. Old Ferdie could not afford to keep them in food so he gave them to a man who kept a hennery.

Occasionally he visited a family in town, and after these old folks died he practically adopted their married daughter and her little girl. Although old Ferdie had very little money he saw to it that this little girl was remembered on her birthdays and at Christmas.

After a few years the child's father died and the mother neglected her little girl. One time when Ferdie dropped in to see how things were going, the mother took advantage of the opportunity to step out for the evening. About three o'clock in the morning she returned half drunk and started to abuse her child. The rumpus awakened the old man, who immediately took charge of the situation. "What did you do, Ferdie?" I inquired. "Well! I took her over my knee and spanked her bare bottom, till she hollered," was his startling reply. At least old Ferdie did his best to reform the wayward mother.

On this, our last hunting trip to the old guide's camp, we each shot a deer, and on the brisk, cold morning near the end of the season we said a cordial goodbye to Ferdie, hoping to return the next year.

Little did we realize as he stood in his doorway waving a goodbye to us that it was the last time we would see our old hermit friend.

Poor, lonesome old man, with no kith or kin on this side of the Atlantic, dying as he always had lived, all alone back in the woods. He was buried in the clearing near the site of his burned cabin.

On his grave an unknown friend planted some of the narcissus that he had loved and tended so many years. There the spirit of the old guide rests, gazing across the woodlands toward Mount Matumbla, under whose shadow he had lived so many lonely years. ◤

OLD MOUNTAIN PHELPS

By Rev. Frederica Mitchell, *North Country Life*, Summer 1950

This tribute to one of the most colorful old-time Adirondack guides was delivered on the occasion of the Haystack Centennial, August 20, 1949.

You who are gathered here this afternoon are well acquainted with Orson Phelps, if not by personal contact when he walked these mountains, then by reading Donaldson's *History of the Adirondacks* or *Warner's Character Study*, or by hearing mention of this famous Adirondack figure. Therefore, in paying tribute to him at this time, I will speak briefly of a few things known about him not found in books.

He attended the church services in the Valley at intervals and was a good listener. Once when a minister candidly asked him what he thought of the clergy in general, he received this startling reply: "They don't preach the living God."

His answers were always unconventional, and hence in the Bible class he was a source of some anxiety to the teacher, but the answers showed that he did his own thinking and was not beholden to the opinions of others. For awhile he himself taught a Sunday School class, and that must have been an experience for the pupils. When Otis Estes was spoken of as a religious man, Old Mountain Phelps commented, "Otis Estes probably is the piousest man in town, but I enjoy religion more."

One can easily imagine such a soul as his worshiping God with joy in the sublime beauty seen from a mountain height, or along a trail he had cut, or deep in the woods, where he could never lose himself even though it might be "on a reg'lar random scoot of a rigamarole." He had a very keen aesthetic sense and a refinement of feeling within, which was belied by his exterior. To many he seemed a part of nature which he so passionately loved. He took pleasure in the forests and streams and high peaks and dropped into reveries about them quickly. Standing on the top of his "Mercy" mountain, and exalted of spirit over its majestic wonders, he called it "heaven up-h'istedness." He boasted of having climbed Marcy over 100 times—what a record!

Although he preferred the woodland creatures to a town meeting, we are told, he was not an ardent hunter. Perhaps he loved the animals too much. Certainly he knew their habits and characteristics. He could name the birds also and the wild flowers. The latter he enjoyed hunting as truly as the partridges on the hill near his home. Every year likewise he sought the wild bees for their honey. This was an expedition upon which he allowed his grandchildren to go with him. The results were a tasty spread for the bread.

In the spring he and his wife, Lorinda, played a little game with each other. They slipped away separately, seeking the first sky blue violets. It was a personal triumph for the one who was first to bring back a bunch of them for the table.

Another of his warm loves was children. He delighted in having them around and often greeted them with a hug and a kiss. Frequently they would come over to spend the day. Mrs. Phelps welcomed them to the noon meal and tried to serve what she believed they especially liked— such as parsnip stew. Mr. Phelps would talk with the children as to adults, sharing his views and ideas, sometimes reading aloud to them. But lax though he was in certain matters, he was strict with the children when he thought they were about to get into mischief. That he would not tolerate, and the children apparently approved his attitude because they always returned.

Old Mountain Phelps, 1888. *A Seneca Ray Stoddard photo. Courtesy Maitland DeSormo Collection*

Old Mountain Phelps was skilled in making fishing poles and pack baskets. For the latter he would buy, for a nominal sum, the privilege of cutting in the woods a few black ash trees of the right size. These he split into logs, and then on an anvil hammer them until they parted into splints. The baskets he made stood hard use, never going to pieces and only wearing out in time.

In his younger days he smoked a pipe. Then he developed "stomach trouble" and was advised by the doctor to stop smoking. He went home, laid his pipe in the cellar way, and never touched it again. Occasionally in the beginning when the desire came strongly upon him, he would go to the place, reach for his pipe, pull back his hand, and take up something else to occupy his mind. The stomach trouble was cured finally, but he did not return to smoking.

Before this happened, though, he had a hot experience with his pipe. He never indulged in profanity, I am told. However, one day he slipped slightly. Thinking his pipe had gone out, he dropped it into his pants pocket. A couple of sparks burned through to his skin. Surprised, he suddenly clapped his hand to his hip and cried, "Damn."

Yes, Old Mountain Phelps was an unforgettable character with his virtues and his faults like the rest of us, but as the years go by, our memories of him are of the wonderful qualities he possessed, and we let the others go by. He was a child of God, attuned to the heavenly harmonies heard in the silence of rocky heights or deep forests. His spirit knew Almighty God and reverenced Him, and for that we give special thanks, rejoicing that since 1905 Old Mountain Phelps has been exploring spiritual trails and climbing spiritual mountains in the Kingdom of the Lord. ▰

SOME CONSERVATION MEN (OF OLD)

By W. H. Burger, *North Country Life*, Summer 1950

John Gunther in his *Inside U.S.A.* states that New York is probably the best governed state in the country. Warren Moscow, for many years legislative correspondent of the New York Times in Albany, says practically the same thing in Politics in New York State. The Conservation Department is one of the most efficient of the state departments. It is also outstandingly creative. The following about some of the men who are or have been in the Conservation Department may help explain why.

WALTER RICE: Right under the peak of Ampersand you will find a bronze tablet with this inscription:

> *In loving memory of Walter Channing Rice 1852–1924*
> *"Hermit of Ampersand"*
> *Who kept vigil from this peak 1915–1923*
> *Erected by his sons – 1930*

When I last saw it, it was nearly ruined by the scratches and scrawls of people who have a yen to write or carve their names everywhere they have been. One of these days some curio hound will probably jimmy it loose to gloat over with his pals at home.

Walter Rice preceded the fire tower on Ampersand. In fact he built his own observatory, a neat little stone hut which has long since disappeared.

While Walter Rice was on Ampersand only eight years, he had the same sense of belonging to his mountain that Old Mountain Phelps had to Marcy. It possessed him to such degree that he must have written poems about it as he did about other things that took hold of him. Unfortunately, none of these survive and little information about the Hermit of Ampersand is available. But from what little we know and from the impression he made on some of us who met him on his peak, we sensed that here was a rare combination of woodsman, philosopher, poet, and gentleman, a kind of Robert Frost on a mountain top. Too bad Henry

Van Dyke didn't meet him. They would have had a rare time together, for both were in love with a lovable mountain.

A clipping from a Saranac Lake paper, dated April 26, 1918, reveals the essence of Walter Channing Rice. He is starting up his mountain for the summer season, and this is what he tells an inquiring reporter:

> *"I'm anxious to go back. People will tell me that they don't see how I could live up there all alone. But they don't understand. When they say I'm alone on old Ampersand, they are far from the truth. They don't understand that I have the best friends in the world up there—the wild flowers, the birds, the animals, and the many manifestations of Nature that go to make up the comradeship of the soul. The still life—that is the source of contentment on old Ampersand. Let them come up to that little world of mine and let me show them the joys that fill my existence there, and then, if they can see it all as I see it, they will no longer condole with the 'Ampersand Hermit'."*

THE PETTYS: Some of the marked differences between the older and younger breeds of mountain men are evidenced in a father and three sons. They are the Pettys of Coreys, New York. Coreys is about a mile off the shorter route from Saranac to Tupper, and if you went through it, you wouldn't know you'd been there. Father Petty is 86 and works as a guide and caretaker at a camp on Upper Saranac Lake. Mother Petty lives in the homestead where she was postmistress for 26 years.

They had three sons—all good, clean boys, as their mother says. They must have been, for here is their record.

William, a graduate of Saranac Lake High School and Cornell University, is now district forester for Essex, Clinton, and Franklin counties.

Archibald, also an alumnus of Saranac Lake High School and Cornell, is now aquatic biologist for the State Conservation Department.

Clarence, the third to graduate from Saranac Lake High School and an alumnus of Syracuse University, is district ranger for St. Lawrence County.

Shattuck Clearing, Cold River, Summer 1950. *Courtesy Ed Kornmeyer*

How's that for a real backwoods family? Must have had some Mom and Pop. I haven't met Pop, but the fact that he is 86 and still working shows he's plenty rugged. In his heart he must be as proud of his kids as I know their mother is, but I've heard he has little use for all this modern, scientific stuff, like blister rust control and such foolishness. Fortunately the little spores weren't flitting so blithely from gooseberry and currant bushes to succulent white pine when he was young. And how he must snort at the aquatic biologist business! Maybe he feels differently about the modern fire fighting organization, which is as efficient as the most up-to-date city set-up.

One day last summer I was in Bill Petty's office in Saranac Lake. And let's get this straight, except for fish and game matters, he is the chief administrative officer for the State Conservation Department in the most important Adirondack area. He was talking about the old hillbilly type of Conservation employee, with apparently no consciousness that he was a perfect example of the other extreme. Sitting at a big desk, facing a map of the Adirondacks, smooth, alert, efficient, he had the bearing of a trained executive in a big business corporation. In this combination of technician, administrator, speaker to garden and Rotary clubs, Adirondack Boy Scout Council member, and Forest Fire Chief, I sensed one reason why the New York State Conservation Department is probably the most potent agency of its kind in the United States.

No wonder the woods can be kept open during a drought. No wonder the pine blister is being licked. No wonder camp sites are being maintained to serve many thousands of motorists. No wonder hundreds of miles of trails are kept open and scores of lean-tos maintained, game protected, streams and lakes restocked, millions of trees grown for replanting, and a big battle fought constantly with urgent interests to keep at least part of the woods wild. All on a pretty slim budget.

No, the old boys couldn't do what men like Bill Petty and his brothers have to do. If they were running the show, the white pine would have followed the chestnut, and much, if not all, of the Adirondacks would be burned over.

LUCIUS RUSSELL: Shattuck's Clearing is about four miles up Cold River from Calkins Creek and a little farther from Plumley's near the foot of Long Lake. One day we noticed a new cabin had been built for the resident forest ranger. It was a very good-looking and substantial log job. Then a while later there was a new ranger who more than matched the cabin. He invited us inside, told us to help ourselves to jam and peanut butter and in general to make ourselves at home.

Good looking, smooth-shaven, and soft spoken, he somehow seemed a bit out of place, but that was a very fleeting impression. Behind the bland and gracious façade was as real a stuff as the old Adirondacks ever saw. For instance, when a big boy came bounding down the trail from Seward Lean-to at dusk one night to get help for a man who had nearly drowned, he ran back with the boy and stood by most of the night (I know about this, for I was the man). One hot July morning this ranger collapsed under a fifty pound pack on the trail going up to Plumley's, but he kept on to the cabin by dint of sheer grit.

After I got acquainted with Lucius Russell, I could understand why his cabin was such a popular hang-out. Every time I went by, there seemed to be someone there, and the stories over the coffee cups were pretty tall. After he had his stroke, I found Deputy State Conservation Commissioner Vic Skiff and his boy and Clayt Seagears, Educational Director of the Conservation Department, making themselves very much at home here one morning on my way up to visit Noah Rondeau. One of Lucius' city pals, a brain specialist in New York, thought so much of him that he flew to Long Lake to look him over and later had him down to New York for an operation. That's the kind of guy he is.

Lucius Russell was born at Long Lake. Anyone meeting him now is amazed to learn that he finished school with the sixth grade, for he could readily pass as a college graduate. Most of his life has been spent guiding, caretaking, and logging. It was not until eight years ago that he became a state employee. His first job was that of observer at Owl's Head Mountain (the Long Lake one) and in 1944 he became forest ranger at Shattuck's

Lou Russell with his donkey, Shattuck Clearing. *Courtesy C.V. Latimer, Jr., M.D.*

Clearing. Except for his eight months' illness, he's been on the job since, looking out for fires in his valley. In addition to maintaining a mountain fire station headquarters, with portable gasoline pump and other equipment, and sleeping quarters for fire-fighting crews, he keeps the eleven-mile trail between Plumley's and the Dam open and the lean-tos in good condition.

His attractive, well-kept home is located across the bridge in Long Lake on the road to Tupper. When the woods are well wet down, Lucius gets out to the house over week-ends and sometimes in between. He commutes by kicker the seven miles from Plumley's to the village.

Since his stroke he has had the help of a jackass to carry supplies, which like all worthy jackasses adds to the fun of living. A dog, and pet deer who pry into his private life early evenings, keep him from getting too lonesome. There's a tiny but fertile garden near the cabin. Lucius Russell's life is pretty full of a number of things.

CLINTON WEST: Clint West of Colden impressed me probably more than any mountain man I've encountered. My first contacts with him were at his cabin as I passed by. Later he loaned me blankets and utensils and entertained me in absentia in the snow-buried cabin one never-to-be-forgotten February night (we made an entrance by digging down to a window which we located by guess work). Once I met him with a group of kids he had taken up Marcy. One of them was his lovely daughter. And then I met a college graduate son down at the lean-to in the Gorge between Marcy and Haystack. Every contact with him or his family deepened my impression of character and ability.

Vic Skiff, to whom I am indebted for much of the material about these Conservation men, asked M. D. Mulholland of his staff to get together some data about Clint, and what he wrote I'm quoting without changing a syllable:

"Clinton A. West, former forest ranger, was born at Olmstedville in December 1886. He was first appointed forest ranger on

August 31, 1921, and assigned to Lake Colden, where he was stationed until November 1937, when he was transferred to Olmstedville on the death of Forest Ranger Charles Barnes. He retired from State service on April 10, 1947.

"Clint's first winter on the job was spent at Lake Colden, where his principal duty was the daily reading of snow and water gauges. This gave him plenty of time to run a trap line through some of the heaviest and wildest woods in the Adirondacks, and his catch of pine marten, or sable, as the old-timers call it, and of fisher was phenomenal for those days. It even exceeded the best hauls of 'Old Mel' Hathaway, the famous trapper of the Johns Brook country.

"During Clint's sixteen years at Lake Colden he became known to and helped and advised more hikers and mountain climbers than any other man in the Adirondacks. There are literally thousands of persons who, because they went into the big woods with more ambition than experience, carry a very particular warm spot in their hearts for Clint West. His cheerful willingness to help anyone at any hour of the day or night and his gentle hints to leave the kitchen stove or some other incongruous piece of impedimenta behind, endeared him to all comers.

"Clint, in his prime, was probably the best all-around woodsman that the Adirondacks has ever seen. He was resourceful, skillful, and tenacious. Few men were his peers in fly fishing for trout, and I have known him, when caught without tackle and hungry, to catch trout with bunchberries, a safety pin, and an odd piece of fish line from his pocket. I have seen him make impossible shots at deer, and only one man, Ranger Grover Lynch, was more skillful at still hunting.

"Clint West's versatility is well illustrated by his skill with both the axe and the skillet. Many a lean-to and the Lake Colden

and Shattuck Clearing ranger cabins stand as monuments to his skill with the former, while to eat one of Clint's breakfasts of flapjacks and trout was an experience never to be forgotten.

"Out-of-doors skills and accomplishments like those of Clint West are likely to give the impression of a rough, tough, he-man sort of person. He was anything but that except on rare occasions when aroused by the mean act of another. Clint is without doubt one of the gentlest and most considerate men who ever lived a hard life of practically unremitting labor. His reluctance to hurt any living creature unnecessarily is one of his outstanding characteristics.

"Like most men who have spent much time in the woods alone, Clint is not much of a talker. But in spite of that, one remembers most vividly, of the days spent in the woods with him, the feeling of companionship that those times always brought. It is always good just to be outdoors with him and good to remember all the rest of one's life." ▰

"We would often play outside until our lips turned blue." From left, Francis, Malcom and Douglas Blue; John and Annie Watkins. Old Forge, ca. 1925. *Courtesy Marilyn Breakey*

♥ GEORGE WEBSTER—AN ADIRONDACK MINISTER

By W. H. Burger, *North Country Life*, Summer 1954

The older Adirondack ministers and missionaries were a rugged breed. They had to be. For no lumber camp or deep woods village would put up with any slick theology from the city.

Way above average was George Orlia Webster, who was for the twenty years before he died at 77, minister of the Federated Church of Essex on Lake Champlain. Up to very nearly the end, he regularly conducted three services every Sunday and during the summer one or two more.

Nor did he stop there. He wrote songs, hymns, anthems, folklore, poems, and Adirondack history, raised prize gladioli, and when he got a chance, cast the brooks in search of the ever more elusive Adirondack trout.

The story of how he began his poetic career is fascinating. He thought he was born with a love of poetry. He said there was some great poetry in the early school readers. As family gatherings were then the chief occasions of entertainment, he was asked to read the selections he liked. One day when he was 15 or 16, he saw there was company in the parlor as he slipped by on his way home from school. Sure enough, his mother met him at the back door and told him Aunt Lucy was there. She was not a relative, but one of those community characters which flourished in small places before the movie and auto busted our intimate social groups into smithereens. Mrs. Webster said, "George, you must behave like a gentleman because Aunt Lucy wants to read your bumps." Like similar characters, Aunt Lucy made some pretensions to acquaintance with the more or less occult science of phrenology. So George went in and knelt before Aunt Lucy while the trembling fingers explored his cranial protuberances. Sure enough, Aunt Lucy found what she was looking for—the poetic bump—and in no uncertain tones pronounced her opinion.

While Orly, as he was then called, must have writhed under the ordeal, the whole incident made a profound impression upon him. He presently found himself turning sentences to make them rhyme. But it was not until after the death of his mother, when a real aunt sent him some dried flowers from her grave, that he wrote his first poem, a lovely little thing. It was the spring of '88 and he was 21.

He wrote thousands of pieces. At least 2,000 of his hymns have been published. Some of them have been sung around the world, the most famous being "I Need Jesus." One day a leading missionary from Burma came to tell him that this song was the most useful one in that great mission field. He said the boys sang it as they went to work in the fields. The people who heard asked, "Who is this Jesus?" This gave the missionaries their best chance to tell "the old, old story."

Just picture it. Here was a man without any musical training and with scanty general schooling, writing verses and even composing his own music for many of his songs. He was a natural. His songs spanned a half century, as the first was published in 1892 by Dr. Ufford, who himself wrote the famous "Throw Out the Life Line." He made no pretense to writing great hymn poetry, just simple gospel songs, which plain people love to sing. The quality of his spirit is revealed in a little poem he read me from one of his "Children's Days" book.

Conserving the Sunshine

If we could can the sunshine,
As we do the fruits and berries:
If we could serve it up like tea,
Like peaches, plums or cherries;
How fine, upon a dreary day,
To feel the sun's warm glow—
Just open up a sunshine can,
And let the sunbeams go.

If we could can the sunshine,
Like asparagus or peas,
Or store it on the ice box shelf,
Like potted meats or cheese—

But you cannot can the sunshine,
'Twasn't made to use that way,
And the only way to keep it
Is by giving it away.

If we could buy the sunshine,
As we do our breakfast food,
In a sanitary package,
Guaranteed as fresh and good,
Cooked and ready for the using,
Needing only cream and sweet,
Costing but a little money,
And as nourishing as meat.

Ah, but who would want a sunbeam
Purchased at the corner store,
Or the wagon of the huckster
As it passes by the door?
If the way to keep the sunshine
Is by giving it away,
Then the only way to have it
Is to make it fresh each day.

Keep your sunshine plant so busy
You will need an extra shift,
If you cannot use the output
Let your friends enjoy a gift;
You will find that your investment
Is like lending to the Lord,
And in dividends of sunshine
You will reap a rich reward.

George Webster was a native Adirondacker. He was born in Fort Ann, and has spent most of his life in the North Woods. His father was a Baptist preacher and presently followed his flock to Indian Lake, where many Baptists and others were migrating back in '75. George grew up in the North River region. As a young fellow he worked in lumber camps, ran logs down the Hudson, and worked a strip mine.

After his mother's death, which occurred soon after Aunt Lucy's visit, Mr. Webster went to a charge in Vermont and George ran wild. But not for long. Presently a famous lecturer and humorist, "Bob" Burdette, preached a couple of summers in the North River church. He got a grip on George, and this resulted in George's conversation. In January of 1886, the church sent for George's father to baptize him in 13th Brook, near North River. The ice was four feet thick. But George said it was nothing at all.

George now turned definitely to the Baptist ministry, in which he served fifty years. Significantly enough, although he said he could never be anything but a Baptist, at heart, thirty of the fifty years were spent in nondenominational work. His Federated Church at Essex contains Methodist, Baptist and Presbyterian groups, and he was also Methodist minister at Whallonsburg.

Because of ill health of the present Mrs. Webster, he was forced to spend twelve years on a farm near Glens Falls. But the old farm just couldn't keep George out of the pulpit. Before he realized what he was doing, he was conducting, with Mrs. Webster's help, four services a Sunday. The farm chores were sandwiched in between. This work had two important con-sequences. It resulted in the organization of the larger parish of the Glens Falls Presbyterian Church and in George's being called to the Warrensburg Baptist Church, where he cured a very sick situation.

George's children wanted him to write a book, the title of which would be "Story of an Adirondack Boyhood." It would intimately reveal the inside of home and community life in the Adirondacks during the 70s and 80s. Another project of Webster's was "My Story of the Adirondacks." He said Donaldson's *History of the Adirondacks* is fine, but it was written by a city man who could never get down deep into Adirondack folk.

George never got around to writing these books and left undone a lot of other projects. Men of his type could live forever. Maybe they do.

Several times I was tempted to ask him about retirement. But I didn't dare. For with that big strong body, firm rolling gait, boyish eyes, square jaw, keen mind and going spirit, it would be an affront. Such men don't retire. They keep at it to the end.

George died in an ambulance on the way to a hospital, with his boots on, as he surely would have wished. No lingering deathbed fuss for him. ▰

OLD MAN OF THE MOUNTAIN

Emil G. Kraeling, *North Country Life*, Spring 1955

The Adirondack guide has been a famous figure ever since Adirondack Murray first aroused popular interest in his kind over a century ago. But he now is about as extinct as the Grand Army. Those old enough to have known the type of guide that still existed up to the time of the first World War can only think of them and of the life they represented with a certain nostalgia.

A survivor of this hardy race of men is 93-year-old Walt O'Connor of Olmstedville in Essex County. Short of stature and well-knit of frame, with a merry twinkle in his blue eyes, he could not deny the Hibernian descent if he would. And indeed his home was in a district nearby called "Irish town," because Irish immigrants were decoyed there long ago buying land, sight unseen. Dumped into the middle of a wilderness, they had to wrest a living from it as best they could. Walt's father was such a one. They lived by Minerva Stream under the shadow of a mountain. To me the little man has always seemed to be "the old man of the mountain." He had the habit of speaking as softly as though there were a deer in the next bush—an obvious indication of his long preoccupation with the art of guiding.

The mountain that was Walt's domain has no name on the topographic maps and is less than 3000 feet high. It lies in the area of "Thorn's Survey." Some of its waters flow northward to join the Boreas River, but most of them flow southward, merging with the stream that, before Walt's time, bore its great pine logs to Olmsted's mill at Olmstedville. There was a little Irish settlement farther up that stream valley, and there under the shadow of the mountain wall frowning down upon it from the north Walt spent his life.

A few years ago his house burned down. For a while he lived in a small bungalow on the property with his wife. After her death he left the scene of his toil and his happiest memories to live with bachelor son James in a little house shaded by maples—a real "house by the side of the road"—in Olmstedville. When he stands on the side porch, he can look over to a mountain—alas, it is not his mountain—but another that hides his from view.

Walt refers to his mountain as "Green Mountain." If the name lacks distinction, it served Walt as well for purposes of identification as if it had been called "Ararat" or one of those fancy "Injun" names Charles Fenno Hoffman plastered on Adirondack topography a century ago. And if you had lived under that mountain's southern side and had seen it grow green in the glad light of spring while its opposite side with northern exposure still stood bare, you might think Green Mountain a most beautiful and appropriate name.

When my 88-year-old father and I visited the old guide not so long ago, his son James, returning from his day's work, began to get supper ready in the kitchen, and my mind went back to the day when I first saw Walt a half century ago. I was but a boy. Father and I had been fishing, and Father decided to drop in on Walt. He was a bachelor then, living with his aged father, Michael. He was cooking their supper in the house under the mountain. "I've a good son," said old Mike as he gratefully took a nip from the hunting flask offered him.

And now the cycle of life had gone around. Walt had taken his father's place—but at an electric range instead of the ancient black wood burner.

Walt had a camp on the mountain in those days, and it was there he took his parties. A road ran up to it from his clearing. It stood on the site of an old mining camp. The forge had been close to his house in the valley.

The ore beds were part of Walt's early life. The mine was opened in the Civil War time, when there was a great demand for iron ore. A Glens Falls man put all his money into the enterprise. The woods all the way up the mountainside went into charcoal for smelting the ore. The owner had a chance to sell a half interest for a half a million but refused it. Then difficulties arose. Diamond drills were brought and holes were dug deep into the mountain. Walt worked with the engineer supervising this and aided in the search for a possible connection between this vein and the "iron mountain" at Tahawus. The results were disappointing; the enterprise collapsed.

Walt kept one interesting relic of those days: the field book recording the results of the drilling which the mine owners had left behind. When, a few years ago, engineers for mining companies investigated the mine anew, they would have liked to have had that book. But it was burned in the destruction of his house.

After the mine had closed down, Walt, who had climbed the mountain so many times as a mine worker, became the guardian spirit of the mountain and roved far from his log cabin on the mining camp's site in search of deer and bear. It was not particularly productive hunting country; it took stamina to get game there, but Walt knew it like his vest pocket.

Back in the days when Walt was born, the settlers in the wilderness did little hunting. The Irish immigrants had no guns and were too poor to buy firearms. The older native population rarely had anything better than a flintlock musket. To obtain venison men would wait until the snow had crusted, and then, pursuing the deer with cur-dogs, would kill them with sticks as they floundered helpless in the snow.

In the years when the great Adirondack Survey was being made, Walt was among those who worked in that undertaking and so came to see much of the whole wilderness. Any reader who may have read Verplanck Colvin's reports will have gained an impression of the boundless energy of the man and the enormous labors he carried on in the service of the Empire State. When Walt reminisces about Colvin, one sees the big boss in the light in which those who worked under him saw. Axeman O'Connor thought him a rather vain man. When he came into camp for an inspection of how the work was going, he would be wearing patent leather boots and a plug hat! And was he hard to please! The maids at the hostelries where he stopped all complained about him.

Once Colvin came into the camp of the survey party to which Walt belonged at Preston Ponds between the Upper Works and Cold River. Surveyor Dan Lynch (for whom I as a boy once stretched the surveyor's chain on my father's newly acquired land) had sent a man named Lindsay over to Colvin to cook supper for him in a bark shanty across the water. Lindsay was grouchy all the next day. Toward evening Lynch told him to go over there again.

"Work for that S.O.B.?" said Lindsay. "I won't go. Why, he made me carry a cup of tea back three times!"

"Tut, tut," said Dan Lynch. "We'll let O'Connor go."

So Walt crossed over to cook for Mr. Colvin. The superintendent of the Adirondack Survey licked his platter clean and asked for a second helping. When he was through, he wiped his whiskers with satisfaction and said, "It tasted good tonight. It must be the atmosphere."

Walt still chuckles over that remark. It evidently did not occur to Mr. Colvin that the cooking had anything to do with it.

Apparently Colvin needed more such "atmosphere," for Walt graduated into cooking. Once when he was getting a meal for the whole crew including the big boss, the latter wanted some special service. Now when Verplanck Colvin wanted something, he wanted it right off. But Chef O'Connor had his hands full at the moment.

"I'll get around to you as soon as I can, Mr. Colvin," said Walt. "But if you be in a great hurry, get it yourself."

Mr. Colvin took it in good humor. That he thought no less of Walt for it could be inferred from the fact that when the others were discharged, the surveyor was directed by letter to keep "one axeman and O'Connor." Presumably Mr. Colvin foresaw the possibility of his drop in for a few meals.

When, after several weeks, Walt, too, was discharged, he waited in vain for his pay. Finally he wrote Mr. Colvin to ask for it. He received a reply that his "time" had not been sent in. This aroused Walt's ire. He wrote Colvin again, reminding him that he had been kept on by his own instructions and closed saying, "I expect my check by return mail." He got it.

Back in those hounding days deer were scarce and Walt often traveled many miles in his mountain area to start one after posting his sportsmen at some pond or runway. When hounding stopped, they became plentiful for a time. Walt now had to learn the art of still-hunting or "driving deer by hand."

The deer that stands out most in his mind was one that weighed nearly 400 pounds and had a big spread of horns, though only a few points—one of those old bucks rarely outwitted by the hunter. A Doctor Nicholas from Worcester, N.Y., was the sportsman who got him.

But Walt thinks less of all the successful hunts than of unsuccessful ones. There was the big buck he followed in the snow, whose track ended at a brook. Strange as it seemed, he must have gone up or down in the brook bed. Walt followed it down and found no sign. He went up a stretch and noticed how the snow-cap had been brushed off a stone sticking up out of the water. Some distance about he found the track where the buck got out of the brook. He followed him and finally came in sight of him. When he raised his gun to shoot, he stepped back with one foot to get a better position and, as luck would have it, stepped into a hole and lost his balance. The buck saw the motion and was gone before Walt could recover his equilibrium.

He likes to tell, too, of the trip he took in the dead of winter to the bear den he had found in November. He was still-hunting when he came to the spot where the beast had pawed out a hole for himself. Curiously it had left a stone about the size of a tea kettle lying in the hole. He wondered if the bear wanted it for a pillow, and he determined to go back and wake him up. But when he went back later in the winter, he found that the den had not been occupied. A bear had been killed on the mountain by one of his sportsmen that season, and Walt suspected it was the same bear.

Walt had a sense of rectitude. He gave good measure in his work, and when others treated him right, he became their friend. In the days when the deer season opened on September 1, my father once engaged Walt for a week's hunting and went up with him to the camp on the mountain. He had been there only a day when a telegram was transmitted from North Creek by mail summoning him to New York. The next morning we came down from the mountain and started for the city. My father paid Walt in full for the time he had hired him. Walt never got that.

The following summer he invited my father and me for a day's fishing. He hinted that he knew of a place where there were "some pretty good trout." We made a day of it, getting to the spring hole when the sun was high. While the men smoked, I was permitted to crawl to where I could peer down into the deep hole. It took my breath away to see those two and three pounders lying there gently moving their fins. We ate lunch and went away to fish lesser places. We came back before nightfall, however, and when we went away the second time, there were a half dozen of those great trout in our basket. Their tails hung out of it as we trudged up the dusty road from Walt's house in the gloaming. So Walt repaid justice with kindness and friendship.

One of Walt's most memorable experiences was a weary trek home from the Boreas country in a howling blizzard. He had been with a surveying party that was trying to clear up a dispute over a strip of land near Mount Marcy. The surveying compass went out of commission. There was nothing to do but to send it to Albany for repair. They started out and reached Nelson Labier's at Boreas River, where they spent the night. When they went on the next morning, it began to snow. From the "Durgin clearings" to the Old Dan Lynch clearing on Minerva Stream and on to Irish town by old tote roads was a long march on snowshoes on a good day. But on that day it seemed endless. It was the kind of snow that did not hold under the snowshoes, and thirty inches of it fell on that occasion. The men changed off breaking trail for a while, but one after another of Walt's companions gave out. The man who was carrying the compass finally could shoulder it no longer and asked Walt to take it. Some began to despair of being able to make home and thought of spending a miserable night in the woods. But to find a camping spot in that blizzard or try to start a fire to keep warm in such a night was no alluring prospect.

"You kin do as you like," said Walt in his quiet, determined way. "But I'm goin' home."

And the wiry little man, carrying his pack basket and the surveyor's compass, broke trail alone until, long after dark, he issued forth from the grim woods, while the north wind roared over the mountain. When he came to a neighbor's house, he stopped to tell of the stragglers coming behind and of their need for something to revive them. Then he crossed the bridge on a side road and went on to his own home. He no longer cared whether the others got out that night or not. He was too dog-tired. And grimly he thought that some had lain down on the job when they let him break trail those long hours. Anyone who knows what woods travel is in a blizzard will agree that it must have been a tough day. But the hardy little woodsman proved equal to the occasion.

Having reminisced of times past, we take leave of the Old Man of the Mountain. His big bony hand which swung the double bitted axe for so many years presses ours in firm farewell. He is ever glad to see old friends. Somehow he does not belong in the village. His place is under the shadow of the range on which his eyes opened at birth and that will be looking down like a silent sentinel on his resting place in St. Mary's church-yard, hard by the stream near his old home. It's eerie height seems to say, "Old Man, you climbed my back with pick and shovel, rod and creel, rifle and pack basket more than any other. When your spirit seeks me, I'll be there waiting." ◾

⭐ GI, 1863

By Julia Gardephe Simmons, *York State Tradition*, Winter 1964

What was he like—the GI of 1863? Why did he enlist? Under what conditions did he live? How did he spend his scant supply of money? What did he eat? What did he think about the war and the country? What did he write home?

Countless biographies of the leaders of our War Between the States have been published. Records of the common soldier have been less common, though these anniversary years have seen the publication of some letters of men in the ranks and some novels tell of their experiences.

One such collection of letters from a Clinton County soldier to his cousin and friend came into my possession some years ago. These letters have furnished me with many hours of interest. I should like to share them with you.

The soldier who wrote was Forrest Fisher. The recipient of the letters was my great-grandfather, Cornelius Fisher, who lived at Culver Hill in East Beekmantown. Both men had families. Forrest refers to a son; Cornelius had at that time four sons. In the first letter Forrest explains that though he is reluctant to leave his wife and son, particularly at a time when the farm work is not caught up, he has considered the matter carefully and feels that he must go. "We are so close to the Canadian lines that cowards and Tories drop over in droves, and thin our ranks. We were not going to be able to fill our quota of men without resorting to a draft. That I could not stand." He mentions that his health is not rugged but concern for his own well-being will not deter him.

Some time later he is even less enthusiastic about his army career. "It is very warm here, and unhealthy. Our camping grounds are mud holes. About one-third of the regiment is sick, including the captain and the lieutenant—but we're just as well off without them."

By the end of 1863 he had spent some time in the hospital himself at Point of Rocks, Virginia. Once he was convalescent he was kept on and he became chief ward master. He says that from six hundred to a thousand patients occupied this base. There were eleven wards and four more were being built. Each ward was being equipped with a brick furnace from which a long brick flue ran through a ditch in the floor of the ward. "It works like a charm," he remarks.

Food seemed to be plentiful at first, but plain, which would not have concerned farm boys. But as the months went on, conditions worsened. He mentions a small loaf of bread as rations for the day, supplemented by a cup of soup at noon and a small piece of meat at night. Then he writes, "It is no wonder to me that there are so many sick, eating such miserable fare. Most of us have to eat what is furnished in order to send our pay home. As it is I have used half my pay these two months to buy food, and I believe I should not have been alive if I had not done so." Boxes of food were occasionally sent from home, and in one letter he thanks his cousin for one such package, "my first really good meal in months." The home folks sent other things, too; cough medicine with which he promptly dosed an ailing friend, socks, and a dollar or so when one could be spared, for at one writing he states that he has been seven months without pay.

Of course this GI, like others, had his opinion about the war, his commanders, the government, and the freed slaves. Burnside was a favorite with the men, but highest of all in the hearts of the rank and file was "Little Mac." When the election year of 1864 approaches its climax, he urges his cousin to put in a word for MacClellan among his friends at home. "If his hand is on the helm of state we will soon see an end to this conflict."

The family had been abolitionist in thought for many years, but they had had no first-hand knowledge of slaves. Now the soldier finds himself face to face with freed Negroes for whom inadequate provision, or none at all, has been made. Freedom was all benefit, no responsibility. He is indignant and confused about what he sees.

The war as he now sees it is "cruel and fratricidal, a disgrace to a once happy nation." He deplores the seeming helplessness of the administration.

Most of all he writes of home and the people and things familiar to him there. He'd like to be home when the maple sugar season comes around. Pancakes with the soft maple sugar would taste good.

A neighbor boy who ran away from home to enlist at fifteen was captured in his first engagement. "He's now enjoying the luxuries of a Reb prison," the soldier writes. "If he lives to get home I'll bet he'll think twice about running away again."

Like all GI's he wanted people to write him. He urges his cousin to remind other relatives. Cornelius has a popular young sister-in-law to whom Forrest sends a message. "Tell Louisa to send me a letter or I'll complain to that blacksmith of hers that she uses her cousin ill." Louisa must have written, for apparently no complaints were made, and the blacksmith came home and married her. They set up housekeeping and he opened a blacksmith shop in East Beekmantown. Louisa lived to be a very old lady; in the last year of her life she inquired with interest and affection for Will and Forrest and Barnett and the other Beekmantown boys who went to the war in the sixties.

One of the most interesting letters in the collection contains a small, carefully smoothed splinter of wood. It is accompanied by a note which reads, "This is a sliver of wood from the oak tree under which the noble Pocahontas saved the life of Captain John Smith." This would not seem remarkable save that in 1942 my younger brother (who had never seen these letters) was stationed for a while in Virginia. One of the letters he sent home contained a small splinter of wood with the attached message, "This is a bit of wood from the oak tree where Pocahontas is said to have saved John Smith's life."

These are nothing unusual or startling. They are perhaps rather commonplace as letters go. But they give you a glimpse of the GI behind the letters. ▰

♛ GEORGE MORGAN OF RAQUETTE FALLS

By W. H. Burger, *North Country Life,* Spring 1952

Ruddy-cheeked, white haired, vivacious, cultured, gallant, George Morgan would have been thoroughly at home in a dowager's drawing room on Park Avenue, and she would have been charmed by him. Yet it is doubtful if he had graced such surroundings for a quarter of a century before his death.

My recollections of the people at Raquette Falls before the spring of 1925 are very vague. Then one day in June, Jack Olwine and I found George Morgan in charge. He invited us up to his log cabin on the knoll. As we talked, our eyes were dazzled by the great stack of books, shelved clear to the ceiling. We hadn't expected to find a private library of such dimensions that far back in the Adirondack wilderness. And the years held other surprises.

When the old two-story house burned down, George replaced it with a replica of a lumber camp. It was an affair of huge logs, containing living room, dining room, bedrooms, bath and a huge kerosene refrigerator in the kitchen. A meal in the dining room was served with the éclat of a first class hotel—lovely dishes, waiter in white jacket, and all the trimmings. In front of the open porch was a well-kept lawn. A canoe paddle bearing the legend "Raquette Falls Lodge" was suspended between two young pines.

But the biggest surprise was George himself. We presently learned that he had retired from a law practice in New York and that he and his wife were living at Raquette Falls the year around. He lived there alone in later years, except for a couple who worked for him during the summer. He was well past 70, and it seemed strange and unfortunate that he should be alone, miles from the nearest road and house, especially during Adirondack winters.

He had a passionate love for the place where he lived. I'll never forget my last evening with him. He and I were alone in his cabin. We sipped a little, talked some, and I read to him from DeVoto's *The Year of Decision.*

(Since the preceding December, because of increasing blindness, he had been unable to read). It was late as we stepped off the porch out into the gorgeous moonlight. Spread out below us were the lodge and clearing with deep woods banked all around. A luminous mist rose from falls and rapids, and the only sound was the gentle murmur of water running over rocks. George took my arm as he said, "Can there be anything in the world more beautiful than this?" He could see it but dimly, but how he could feel the beauty of that night!

What courage he had! The winter before he died, though he had high blood pressure, a double hernia, and very poor vision, he cut and drew

George Morgan at Raquette Falls. Photo taken the day Billy Burger and Jack Olwine visited Raquette Falls. *Photo by William H. "Billy" Burger*

all his wood. Rather, he cut and rode the logs a half-mile down a winding road on a sled of skis he had rigged up. Once the contraption hit a tree and he almost broke his neck. But he laughed as he told about it.

How he could laugh and quote poetry and prose by the hour, and what stories he could tell! Here is a sample.

One day when a case he was trying in a New York court was recessed for a while, he went into a neighboring courtroom to pass the time. A man was up for bigamy. He was a little man, weighing possibly 100 pounds. The first witness against him was a big, florid woman with tawny hair, baby blue eyes, and an immense bosom. As George said, "When she sat on the witness chair, she spilled over." Yes, she was married to this man. Any evidence? Yes, the marriage certificate. It was passed around and seemed okay. The next witness was built like a lead pencil. Yes, she was married to the defendant. Any evidence? Yes, a marriage certificate. It, too, was passed around.

Then the big and handsome lawyer for the little man got up, and placing his hands on the head of his client, said, "Now, Henry the Eighth, it's your turn." On the stand it was evident he didn't know the score. The judge quickly charged the jury. They retired and were soon back. It seemed like a closed case. The judge smiled as he asked for the verdict, but was furious when the response was "not guilty." All the members were polled. Same result. There was nothing for the judge to do but dismiss the case. On the way out, George sidled up to a couple of the jurors. As he had suspected, "Now, Henry the Eighth, it's your turn" did the trick. George said it was one of the cleverest stunts he had ever seen done in a courtroom.

Once when we were spending a memorable night at the lodge, George told us how he had rescued two damsels in distress the year before. One day he heard a call for help from across the river just below the last rapids. He rowed over in his skiff and found two girls standing on a rock with little on but shorts and bras. Because of high water they had missed the carry a mile above, had been sucked into the rapids, and had lost the canoe and all their duffle. Characteristically, George fed and clothed them and gave them money to get home. Their chief worry was the canoe which they had rented at Old Forge. Here again George came to the rescue with a suggestion. Said he, "If you write the canoe people that you've lost the canoe, they'll bill you for 60 to 70 dollars. But if you write that you've had a wonderful trip and despite the fact that it leaks a little, you've fallen in love with the canoe and want to buy it, they'll charge only 25 dollars." They followed George's advice, and that is precisely what happened!

George used to say Raquette Falls is the "last frontier in the Adirondacks." While there are a few other places as remote, or even more so, it is 17 miles by boat to Long Lake, the nearest village up river and lake in one direction, and Tupper Lake is 25 miles by water downstream. There is no road or even summer trail to the Falls. In winter you can snowshoe out to the post office in a house at Coreys, but it's almost eight miles and plenty rugged.

Mrs. Billy and I had said goodbye to the Bryans on the dock of Plumley Camp near the foot of Long Lake. They were very close friends of George Morgan and had been spending a few days with him. Now they were on their way to their home in New York, where Mr. Bryan was a ship builder.

We stepped into our canoe and pushed off for the eight-mile run to Raquette Falls Carry, the walk across, and the visit with George we had been promising ourselves. It was a gorgeous mid- September day, mild and sunny.

As we crossed the clearing to the lodge, we noticed the flag wasn't up—an indication that George was alone. The front door had never had a lock on it. We went in and started back through the dining room, but stopped suddenly on the threshold. On the table was an unfinished meal—steak and all the trimmings. Three places had been set, evidently for dinner the night before. On the floor was a blanket with something under it. Then we saw this note on a chair: "Thursday, 6:30 AM. We have gone to Coreys to notify authorities. T.H. Rome."

"Is it murder?" flashed through my mind. We went back into the kitchen. There were three empty soup plates and a pot of cold coffee on

Noah John Rondeau on dock at Plumley's Landing. George Morgan, Billy Burger,
Jim and Carl Plumley and Noah enjoyed random meetings at Plumley's Point House.
Courtesy Jim Plumley

the stove. While Mrs. Billy walked back to the porch, I hurried up to George's private cabin on the hill. No sign of him there. Back at the lodge, I finally screwed up my courage to look under the blanket. Sure enough, there was George, dead. I joined Mrs. Billy on the porch. The lunch we tried to eat tasted as dry as sawdust.

Coreys is eight miles from the Lodge by canoe and road. Whoever Rome was, he and whoever was with him had left six hours before. Someone should be showing up soon. We sat in the lean-to out front and watched the river below the falls.

Finally it was 2:30, and we decided that we should start the nine miles up river and lake to Plumley's to telephone the Bryans in New York and others, for who could tell what had happened to "Rome" on the way down. I wrote a note and left it with the other on the chair. As we came out of the lodge, we saw a boat being rowed up to the landing. I recognized the oarsman as Mr. Bryan, to whom we had said goodbye in the morning. In the boat were the coroner from Tupper Lake and Ross Freeman of Coreys. Another boat followed with the embalmer and Mrs. Bryan.

The story was soon told. Despite his near blindness and other infirmities, George Morgan had driven his own boat the tricky six and a half miles to Axton the day before, walked the mile and half to the post office, phoned for a taxi to Tupper Lake ten miles away, spent the day there and returned, arriving at the lodge with supplies in the late afternoon. As he was resting on the porch, a young couple, the Romes, whom he had never seen before, came by with their packs. He invited them to spend the night. I can imagine what he said: "I've just bought a fine steak in Tupper. Let's eat it together." So it was a gay trio that got the meal.

They set the table with the lodge's fine dishes, lit the big lamp, and served and ate the soup. After George had carved the steak and they had started to eat it, he said, "Excuse me," rose from the table, started for the living room, lay down on the floor and was dead in five minutes. Of course, the Romes couldn't eat and I don't believe they slept, for none of the beds had been used. At daybreak they started down the river for help.

The funeral and burial were next day, and of course we stayed. Since the men who came from Coreys seemed to be busy at other tasks and since Mr. Bryan, who it turned out was executor of George's estate, wanted to have the funeral promptly, he and I dug the grave the next morning out in front of George's cabin. The shipbuilder and little I must have presented quite a spectacle as we spelled each other every five or ten minutes, and how George would have chuckled if he could have seen us!

While the twenty friends of George's who gathered in the living room for the funeral were keenly sorry he had gone, we couldn't really mourn, for his death, we knew, was a welcome release from serious physical infirmities, old age, sorrow, loneliness, and misfortune. We had been greatly concerned about his living there alone, especially in winter, and had tried to get him to leave, but he loved this beautiful deep woods spot too much.

Now a tablet set in a boulder marking the last resting place of his mortal remains, bears this inscription: George E. Morgan, 1870–1944. Scholar, Woodsman, Friend, Resident of This Place 1919–1944. And George Morgan's spirit will hover above the spot as long as the river runs over the falls, for to him it was heaven. ◼

⬟ELKANAH WATSON, PIONEER

By David M. Ellis, *York State Tradition*, Fall 1972

Elkanah Watson, the founder of the county fair and a prime mover in promoting the Erie Canal, was also a pioneer in the Lake Champlain region. Who would imagine that a prominent figure who had graced the salons of Paris in 1780 would become a pioneer in the Adirondacks after he had reached the Biblical age of 70!

Born in Plymouth, Massachusetts, on January 22, 1758, Watson at 15 became an apprentice to John Brown, the wealthy Providence merchant. No doubt Watson received a thorough schooling in Puritan virtues as well as in merchandising. When Brown, in 1793, bought his 210,000-acre tract in the Fulton-Big Moose area, he selected appropriate names for his townships: Industry, Enterprise, Perseverance, Unanimity, Sobriety, Frugality, Economy, and Regularity. Watson was to exemplify most of these virtues during his long life.

Observing Watson's business talent, Brown soon entrusted him with responsibility. During the Revolution, in which Brown took an active role on the patriot side, he sent his apprentice to Paris with dispatches for Benjamin Franklin. Watson soon organized his own business partnership and spent much time traveling to Italy and the Low Countries. Peace, however, brought hard times and then bankruptcy to Watson's firm. He returned to America, where he married a Yankee girl.

After several false starts, including running a plantation in North Carolina, Watson moved to Albany in 1789. The vanguard of the Yankee invaders of that city, Watson created turmoil by denouncing Dutch lethargy and ignorance and demanding improvements such as paving the streets and cutting projecting waterspouts from the roofs. He agitated for all kinds of public enterprise—canals, turnpikes, schools, banks, and agricultural improvements.

In 1807 he retired to Pittsfield, Massachusetts, where the town square became the scene of the first county fair in America. He took as his mission the task of "showing Americans how to farm." In 1816 he moved back to Albany, where he carried on the crusade for agricultural societies and fairs.

County fair oratory, a blood brother of Fourth of July spread-eagle speechifying, has largely vanished, at least in the northern states. A fine example of this genre is a portion of Watson's address to the Otsego County fair in Cooperstown in 1817:

> *"Ladies of Otsego! Should you be thus inspired, I promise myself, if my life is protracted to your next anniversary, to be in the midst of you with many friends; and I fondly hope to witness a proud display of your industry, and ingenuity; and that of the ladies generally throughout this wealthy and respectable county*

...How glorious it will be for you, in cooperation with the ladies of Berkshire, to furnish such a patriotic example, thus contributing essentially to the prosperity and happiness of your beloved country, so dear to us all. Our flax and wool are as fine as those of Europe. Cotton is one of the principal staples of our country, of which Europe is deprived. You well know how to convert them into the useful and ornamental.

"Let us then, young and old, male and female, spontaneously assemble at the next anniversary, with joyous and grateful hearts. The grave, to promote the best good of the whole. The matrons, to return with rewards of 'honourable testimony.' The young, to mingle, and enliven this annual farmers' holiday. Let them come forth decorated in homespun. If ornaments more brilliant are required, to add to their native charms, let them seek the lilies of the valley, and the flowers of the field, in the true pastoral style of former ages."

Steamer approaching Hotel Champlain on Bluff Point, Lake Champlain, 1893.
A Seneca Ray Stoddard photo. Courtesy Maitland DeSormo Collection

Watson made several trips to western New York and he noted that improvements at Little Falls and Rome would greatly facilitate water transportation to the interior. In 1792 he called on Philip Schuyler, a state senator, and asked him to support a proposal for improving the Mohawk River. Schuyler agreed to work for two companies: The Western Inland Lock Navigation Company to open passage to Lake Ontario; and the Northern Inland Lock Navigation Company to improve navigation between the Hudson River and Lake Champlain. Schuyler became president of both companies and Watson a director. These companies, although they received state loans, were not very successful and skirted the edge of bankruptcy for years.

Watson's interest in northern lands was a byproduct of his interest in the Northern Company. He bought 500 acres in Clinton County. In 1805 he examined both sides of Lake Champlain to select good places to invest. He acquired 5,500 acres just west of the village of Union in Clinton County. He was impressed with the "good" land of the township of Peru, where Quakers from Dutchess County had settled, near the "Great River AuSable." [sic. He means the Little Ausable.] He commented:

> "This country it is said abounds in iron ore of the best quality in the world; and as this River has a continued succession of fine Mill Sites from its sources to its very outlet—it would seem that God of Nature has destined from creation these at present inhospitable Cold regions to become in time the Sweden of America, especially when accessible by water transportation to the head of Navigation in the Hudson River."

Watson and his sons Charles and Winslow concentrated their interests on their holdings in the Lake Champlain region. In 1823 Charles Watson opened a furnace to smelt the iron ore. Two years later Elkanah joined his sons at Port Kent, a name selected to honor Chancellor James Kent, the eminent jurist. Interestingly enough Winslow C. Watson, who wrote The Military and Civil History of the County of Essex, New York in 1869, makes no mention of his father's activities at Port Kent. Indeed he pays little attention to his brother's ventures in iron manufacturing, although his book contains a long chapter on the subject.

Port Kent in 1825 had three daily stages and a steamship which crossed to Burlington four times a day. Although there were only two or three houses in the settlement, Elkanah decided to construct a permanent home there. He described Port Kent in 1826 as the "best harbour—the most delightful locality" with the "best wharfs [sic] and warehouses" on Lake Champlain.

Watson realized that his community would never prosper without transportation connections. He petitioned Congress for a daily mail service between Keeseville and Burlington via Port Kent. His request was granted. Obviously the settlement needed a link with the interior but even a canal enthusiast (and Elkanah Watson was certainly one) could see that only turnpikes or a railroad could penetrate the rugged interior. Watson agitated for a turnpike to Hopkinton.

John L. Sullivan, a civil engineer of New York City, planned a railroad route across northern New York. He enlisted the support of Watson, who enjoyed a national reputation for his promotional activities. Watson could see that Port Kent could never attract population and business unless it secured rail connections.

Meanwhile the stone house, fifty feet square, was finished in October, 1828 and Watson brought his family to the new home. His plan was to spend his last years "in my red night cap and easy chair which I caused to be made expressly to indulge the old Gentleman at length to take repose after 50 years of constant effort by night and by day—in which time I have done enough to fill up the space of four lives."

Winters in Port Kent were (and are) severe. To add to his misery, Watson lost nearly all his teeth and contracted various ailments common to the elderly. Worst of all, his beloved Port Kent did not prosper. On January 22, 1831, he confided to his journal:

"Port Kent is now at its lowest ebb—one half the houses abandoned—and the few remaining inhabitants for the most part poor and depressed. To add to the gloom of this winter no snow yet, and the lake as free from ice as in the summer. The truth is— the dreadful inundation of July 1st has half ruined the interior—and we do not yet begin to feel the effects of the Hopkinton road altho nearly completed; and yet I feel as sanguine as ever that Port Kent must rise to eminence and importance—eventually a great city."

Watson continued his agitation for a railroad. He attended a convention at Montpelier, Vermont, on October 6, 1830, which was urging a Boston-to-Ogdensburg route. He was shocked when the Convention elected Luther Burbank of Malone as Chairman. Perhaps the delegates did not want to put Watson in a commanding position. Clearly Port Kent was not on a direct land route between Boston and Ogdensburg.

Meanwhile Watson was promoting a local railroad from Port Kent to the Forks of the AuSable. His plan called for construction of three sections: Port Kent to Keeseville; Keeseville to Clintonville; Clintonville to the Forks. Canny capitalists refused to subscribe for stock in this venture. Fearing loss of the charter, Watson subscribed for the entire amount of the stock which he finally unloaded in 1835 at the height of the speculative boom. Watson forged ahead and employed an engineer to lay out the route. The railroad, however, did not come into being.

In 1840 Watson petitioned Congress for a million dollar grant for a military railroad from Port Kent to Ogdensburg. His petition did not emerge from the House Committee on Military Affairs.

He enjoyed somewhat more success in stimulating the formation of Agricultural societies. He helped to send delegates to Albany, where they formed the New York State Agricultural Society in 1931. He was the mainspring behind the movement in 1833 to create an agricultural society for Essex and Clinton counties. He was offered but refused the office of President.

Watson died in Port Kent in his 85th year. Over his grave is a simple obelisk with the inscription (his own composition):

Here lies the Remains
of
Elkanah Watson
The founder and first President of
The Berkshire Agricultural Society
May generations yet unborn
Learn by his Example
To Love their country ◼

⚫ ARTHUR COUTURE, THE STRONG MAN OF ROUSES POINT

Author unknown, *North Country Life*, Winter 1947
Reprinted from *The North Countryman*

One of the best of the old-time local stories is about the late Arthur Couture, former proprietor of the Hotel Montgomery at Rouses Point. As a young man, the old-timers say, Mr. Couture was exceptionally strong. He frequently visited the local blacksmith shops and, just for exercise, toyed with the smiths' anvils much as the ordinary man would handle a pair of wooden dumbbells.

One day young Couture, so the story goes, strolled down to the old O.&L.C. railroad wharf, where a gang of stevedores were transferring a shipment of anvils from a freight car to a canal boat. The men were obliged to carry the anvils a distance of about fifty feet and then out over a plank between the dock and the boat. Each of the anvils weighed 110 pounds.

The local man stood around a few moments and became restless. It irked him to have to watch two men carrying each anvil. Finally he walked up to the gang and inquired:

"What's the matter with you fellows? Can't one of you carry one anvil?"

"No, one of us can't," was the reply, "and what's more you can't either."

"Bet you twenty dollars that I can carry two anvils at a time and load them on the boat," said Couture.

"You're on!" sang out the leader. "Just cover this money."

Then Mr. Couture walked over to the car and picked up two of the anvils by the horns. They were like toys in his hands even though their combined weight was 220 pounds. He started toward the boat and reached the end of the dock in safety. Then he began the trip over the plank to the side of the vessel. The plank broke in the middle, and Mr. Couture and the two anvils went to the bottom of the lake.

The stevedores began running around in circles looking for a rope to throw to the man struggling in the water. The latter had come to the surface once and had gone down again. As his head emerged for a second time he blew a stream of water from his mouth and yelled:

"If you blankety-blank-blank fools don't hurry up and throw me a rope, I'll have to drop one of these anvils!"

MELVIL DEWEY

By W. H. Burger, *North Country Life*, Spring 1951

In a few months—on December 10, to be exact—one hundred years will have passed since Melville Louis Kossuth Dewey was born in Adams Center (Jefferson County).

That he was a genius there can be no doubt. If his amazing intelligence and capacity for work had been channeled into one outlet or possibly two, he would have achieved international distinction. As it turned out, he gained eminence in several and ordinarily unrelated fields. His keen interest in everything that was going on around him and his urgent impulse to do something about it resulted in diffusion of genius, but the social gains were probably greater than if he had achieved paramount excellence in one field.

His twin passions for time-saving phonetic spelling resulted in shortening the name to plain Melvil Dewey just as soon as he had anything to say about it. His driving energy, which was an outstanding characteristic throughout his life, appeared in childhood. From then on he lived as if he were always catching trains. While generous in every other respect, he was miserly with time. He saved it by some weird devices, including a code of abbreviations which he used in memoranda and correspondence. One wonders what strange angels or devils drove him so hard.

As a boy his activities ranged from school work through cleaning the yard, making shoes, picking up stones, plowing the garden, playing chess, fishing, playing ball, reading Macaulay's *History of England*, doing chores, classifying his mother's preserves, helping his father with the store books, to earning and saving ten dollars with which he walked from Adams Center to Watertown (a distance of twelve miles) to buy Webster's unabridged dictionary. It is characteristic that when the book turned out to be too heavy to carry back, it hurt him cruelly to have to take the train. He just couldn't accept fatigue or any other limitation.

Out of his dissatisfaction with mediocre and inefficient arrangements came one of his two major contributions to modern society. When he went to Amherst as a student, the library appalled him. Here were the books he loved, arranged without rhyme or reason. It was the practice in those good old days for libraries to classify books according to author's names, or titles, or even according to size and color! Imagine the librarian or student trying to locate a book under these conditions.

Here was a challenge to the reformer-improver soul of young Dewey. He couldn't accept it or laugh at it. He must change it. So we find a mere student at Amherst creating and developing the Decimal System of Classification, which has been accepted throughout the library world as standard procedure.

It was inevitable that "librarying" should open up to him as a profession. So we presently find him at Columbia University as librarian and later at Albany as State Librarian and secretary to the State Board of Regents. In both situations he was soon in hot water—at Columbia, because of his insistence that women students should be included in his Library School, and at Albany, because his vision regarding the services the State Board of Regents should render the youth of the state failed to coincide with the schemes of his politically-motivated opponents.

He was Member No. 1 of the American Library Association, the moving spirit in its publications and conventions, and arch initiator and developer of education for librarians. It is probable that no man has made more outstanding contributions in the American library field.

It was during the Albany days that Melvil's hay fever and his wife's rose cold drove them to seek relief in the relatively pollen-free air of the high Adirondacks. As Morris Longstreth has put it, "The Lake Placid Club was sired by a sneeze." They looked about a bit, sampled Keene Valley among other places, talked with such outstanding Adirondackers as Paul Smith, and finally settled upon Lake Placid. In so doing they joined the small and select group of "Makers of the Modern Adirondacks," for without the Club, Lake Placid might not have got much further than Keene Valley or Wilmington. It certainly would never have had the winter Olympics, for it was Melvil Dewey's son, Godfrey, who put that over.

It was characteristic of Dewey that he couldn't just settle down all by himself and family for four months every year. He must create something for a larger group. We find him buying five acres on the shores of Mirror Lake and building Lakeside. This was in 1895. The "hotel" could accommodate thirty guests. How the lofty and gargantuan Stevens House on the hill across the lake must have looked down on this tiny upstart! The original Lakeside was added onto seven times before it was taken down several years ago. In its way it typifies the development of the Lake Placid Club. From five acres of land the property has grown to 9,000. From one building accommodating thirty guests it has increased to 300 buildings, 88 of which can accommodate members and their friends. The largest number of guests housed at any one time was 1,600 during the Olympics in 1932.

The Club owns seven farms, Adirondack Lodge at Heart Lake, two 18-hole and one 9-hole golf courses, a fine school for boys, and innumerable other features and appurtenances. The buildings and equipment have been valued at $3,800,000.

A walk through Forest, which is now the principal and largest building, is a revealing experience. As one enters the lobby, he sees the large hotel office, which looks like a bank. Turning left, he passes through one of the several lounges, past a post office (the Club has its own) and into another lounge, which is flanked on one side by a row of stores.

If he were to continue straight through, he would pass into a huge game room, past locker rooms and athletic directors' offices, more stores, and out on to tennis courts in summer and skating rink in winter. If one turned left, he would pass a huge tea room on his right and through another lounge into the Agora, a beautiful auditorium seating 1,200 people, several hundred of whom may sit in huge wicker arm chairs on the main floor. Should the Club organist be playing the four-manual $30,000 organ, he would be entranced by the lovely tone of what is probably the finest and largest instrument of its kind in Northern New York.

Should our visitor be sufficiently bold, he may mount the steps to the stage, and turning right through the wings, emerge into a lovely chapel with charming stained glass windows and beautiful chancel. If he is in tune with the place, he will linger for a while and then seek an exit which will lead him back past the Agora gallery and between yet another lounge and the dining room, which can be stretched to seat 900 guests, although not more than 200 ever seem to be in sight of each other. Ahead there is another lounge with huge bird cages and a striking view through glass of winter shrubbery and snow. Turning toward the front, he passes the library and reading room, a fine music room, and eventually to some stairs which lead to the place whence he started.

Of course, we haven't seen the whole Club. There is a winter wing we haven't even entered. But we've been through its heart, and if we have sufficient insight, have sensed its genius, which brings us back to the founder.

Melvil Dewey was a professional intellectual. He wanted to create a resort for his fellow professionals. But being a person of limited means, he could not afford the more expensive hotels, at least for very long. So he started his project with this purpose in mind. Of course, as it expanded, it cost more to run. That is the way with beneficent institutions, whether they are colleges or camps. Therefore, we find him organizing not only the Lake Placid Club but also the Lake Placid Company, and finally the Lake Placid Foundation. One of the express purposes of the last was to subsidize the cost of entertaining educational, social and religious workers, so that persons of very limited means might enjoy the privileges.

While physical recreative facilities abound, the Club is unique in its continuing emphasis upon educational recreation. Its big library, the symphony concerts during the summer, the musical festivals for schools, drama, and pageantry, both indoor and outdoor; even motion pictures, the daily chapel service, and the fine Northwood Preparatory School for Boys are all expressions of this fundamental concern.

In common with similar organizations, the Club has never accepted Hebrews or Negroes as members or guests. This inevitable concession to practicality constrains me to comment that it seems too bad that we fail to make enough strong friendships among people who are only superficially different from ourselves to want to play as well as work with them. Until we do, we shall not attain social maturity or international peace.

After the Club was under way, Dewey continued to give leadership to the manifold library interests he had fostered and to such reforms as simplified spelling and the introduction of the metric system into the United States. Despite his earnest espousal of both of these, the inertia and at times the perverted sense of humor of the people he tried to convert were too much.

My personal recollections of Melvil Dewey cluster about his help in staging his Indian pageant at Camp Dudley. The pageant had been given at the Club for years and was largely, if not wholly, his creation. I made a date to see him in Lake Placid in March, 1914. He met me at the station, drove me behind a pair of ponies to the Club, where we had lunch. I was a bit overwhelmed and bewildered by his brilliance and feverish energy. He was most gracious, however, and offered to lend his cast, including himself, for an initial performance on Lake Champlain in late July of 1914. It went off beautifully and was adopted by the Camp as a regular feature. Ironically enough, the triumph of the peace forces in the Iroquois pageant was followed within 48 hours by the outbreak of the First World War in Europe.

When northern winters began to irk him, Dewey founded the "Lake Placid Club" in Florida and died there the day after Christmas in 1931 at the age of 80. Nothing is more in character than his attempt to transplant Lake Placid to Florida. ✒

A. FITZWILLIAM TAIT, AN ADIRONDACK ARTIST

Author unknown, *North Country Life*, Winter 1947

When one thinks of Currier and Ives lithographs, he thinks of the cheap calendar reproductions that do so little to glamorize the wall of a home. When the firm was doing a large business during the 1850s, they were buying paintings from the best-known artists of the time. One of these was an Englishman by the name of Arthur Fitzwilliam Tait (1819–1905). Born in Liverpool, England, he learned to paint outdoor scenes there. At the age of 31, he journeyed to America, which was to remain his home until the time of his death.

Being ambitious to paint sporting scenes, he built a camp near Long Lake in Hamilton County. With the mountains as scenic material, and his comrades as characters, he produced some of the classic works devoted to the North Country. Travelers through the area often told of meeting a tall handsome stranger, armed with a palette and canvas rather than a rifle.

Collectors of today are willing to pay several hundred dollars for copies of "Sunrise on Saranac Lake" and "Brook Trout Fishing." "A Good Chance," and "Still Hunting in the Adirondack" are other well-known paintings on stone by A. Fitzwilliam Tait. ▰

☠ THE GIANT HERMIT OF THE ADIRONDACKS

Author unknown, *York State Tradition*, Winter 1971

"So, Sid; I knew you didn't have no warrant for me, but I'd just as soon go to jail as have my picture took."

The words were those of old "Bill" Smith, sometimes called the "Giant Hermit of the Adirondacks," to Sidney W. Barnard, Sheriff of Essex County, who had consented to accompany a visitor on a trip to the home of the grizzled mountaineer, who has lived alone for many years in this little cabin on what is known as the "Oregon Plains," six miles from Bloomingdale, NY.

The arrival at the cabin built by "Bill" Smith's own hands fifty-six years ago, was announced by the fierce barking of three dogs that ran out from a little shed at the rear, and threatened the visitors with rows of wolfish teeth and even more wolf-like eyes. Neither of the visitors ventured from the carriage, but they were contented with uttering loud and repeated "Whoas!" to the already halted horses. It was evident, both from the action of the dogs and the appearance of the pathway leading in from the main road, that visitors were few. All things about bespoke a wild environment, and the thought that a human being was the lord and master of the lonely domain almost prepared one for the uncouth figure, which at length partially revealed itself in the half open doorway, and said:

"Wa-al?"

"Hello!" One visitor ventured, "Is that you, Mr. Smith?"

"Mister Smith nothing!" came the voice, with more than a trace of sarcasm, "No Mister Smith here. Bill Smith's at home though. What do you want?" Then Sheriff Barnard spoke, and the old fellow came out and extended greetings. A word from the hermit, and the dogs returned to their kennel.

"Bill" was even more of a wonder than the tales of the country-side had pictured him. Almost a giant in stature, with a great mass of tangled hair falling a foot below massive shoulders, and a beard so full and long that it had to be tied up with strips of cloth upon his expansive chest, he presented a sight that was ample reward for a long journey.

"Oh, Sid," urged the hermit, at the same time taking the county official's arm and completely ignoring the stranger, "come enter the house and sit awhile, and we'll talk over the picture business by-m-by." And then we followed the old giant into the cabin, without being compelled, like him, to duck our heads going through the doorway. A fire was burning slowly in the old-fashioned cook stove, the top of which was covered with rust and a number of pans and kettles. "Bill," looking at a clock upon the wall that was not running, explained that he was preparing his breakfast.

"I eat twice a day, just about this time and again when I'm going to bed. Been in this habit for over twenty years, and I feel that it is just as good as three times."

"Most people eat too much," was ventured.

"Yes, and drink too much, and smoke too much, and talk too much," responded "Bill." "Folks who is always a-speaking about only once to live are just the ones that cram themselves so full of grub and nonsense that they don't half live while they're here. I don't know whether it's the grub or the nonsense that knocks them out first, perhaps both working together, for you'll notice that the ones that ain't got no brains is the ones that'll pile all kinds of rubbish into their stomachs. As for me," and "Bill's" voice betrayed much pride, "I ain't never gone too far in nothing except well, never mind," and he turned away and began to "tidy up" things in the little board pantry in the corner. The time seemed opportune for a question that would lead on to the narrative desired.

"You do think, then, that you have carried some things too far, do you Bill?"

"Wa-al, sometimes I think I have, and again I think I haven't. Some questions are never settled just right in my mind. But I ain't much different from lots of people, I guess; for as well as I can make out there are lots of people in the world that never know what they want nor how they want it. If they get it most times they're sorry it wasn't something else. But, here I am doing more talking than I have in years before; but it's all on account of you, Sid," and he slapped the big Sheriff familiarly on the shoulder.

"We want you to talk, Bill, and tell us about yourself—this is a newspaper man, you know."

"'Twas talking that made the first trouble in our family," "Bill" went on musingly, "and women started it. I was happy 'til then, but I ain't a-been happy—what you call downright happy—in many a long year; not since Lizzie died. You see, my son Henry went and married Emmy Bosley before he had a handkerchief of his own, and of course he fetched her to the house here. Wa-al, them two women got to sassin' back and forth, and Hen he always stood up for Emmy. Things got tarnal hot, and for some time his wife and him would eat by themselves. Then, one day they up and moved out, going up the Bloomingdale road and hirin' a house. We had a little peace after that, but then Lizzie died, and I was left alone.

"The other child, a little girl, had died some years before and I had no one to care for but Henry, and he didn't care a snap about me. Didn't have the manness, even, to come and visit me after his mother had been laid away."

Then, in the rush of memories "Bill" seemed to forget us. We were fearful lest our host get away from his train of interesting narrative, and at this point made a request that he undo his beard and let it down full length.

"It's a measly job putting it back again, but I'll do anything for you, Sid," and the old fellow good-naturedly began to untie the knots of cloth, and untangle the coils and twists of beard that formed a great mass upon his bosom. A comb and brush helped to smooth it out somewhat and then "Bill" stood up before us in his six feet four inches of length and with a beard the ends of which rested on the cabin floor.

"How did you come to let it grow, Bill?" asked the Sheriff.

"Wa-al, I'll tell you. You see, when Henry was to home he always used to shave me and clip my hair. I never liked to feel the beard on my face nor have my hair grow long, and you can know that I missed him when he moved out. One day about two months after he'd gone, I says to Lizzie: "Lizzie, I guess I'll go up to Hen's and get a hair clip." "Don't you do it, Will," she says, "Emmy I'll think I'm hankering to make up with her and that your going is just an excuse. Don't do it, Will." And of course I wouldn't go when Lizzie didn't want me to.

"But there come a time—this was after Lizzie died—that my hair was getting too long. I could keep my beard cut pretty well, but that was all. I was a-thinking hard of going up to Hen's, but I thought of the way him and Emmy had acted and I stayed home. Then one day I just happened to meet him on the road. He was a-going right by, but I stopped him and spoke. Still, he wasn't very good natured, and when he was a-going down the road I says: "Say, Henry, don't you think you'd better come down and give your old dad a hair clip?" "No, I don't," he snapped back; "cut it yourself!" I never was so mad in my life, and I just swore. I said, "I'll be damned if I will! I'll let it grow first!" And it's a-been a-growing ever since."

This, then, was one of the things, without a doubt, that "Bill" would have classified under the heading of "overdone" by himself, for his great beard and mass of hair must make him uncomfortable, particularly in the summer season. But he refused to clip either the one or the other because Henry years ago made the prediction that "The old man will come around some of these days asking me to give him a clip, and I'll tell him just as I did before."

"It's been a-growing this way for forty-odd years," said Bill, "and I guess I can stand it till the time comes to turn in for good."

"Bill," who is seventy-three years old, never works out, but he cultivates a strip of land in the heart of the big woods, and has a fair sized bank account. For fifteen years he has not drawn out a cent of his deposits in the Saranac Lake Bank, but always has money to pay for the little articles he buys of peddlers from time to time. In years gone by he was a tireless huntsman, and most of his savings have been from the sale of hides, furs and game.

"Bill" insisted upon "dressing up" when he at length consented to accompany his visitors to Bloomingdale to have his picture taken, although he had been told that a snapshot of him in his everyday rig would be as good if not a little better.

"No," he said, with an emphasis that brooded no further bickering, "I ain't ever a going to have my picture took again and we may as well make a decent job of it this time." ◾

★DANIEL DODGE

By Marjorie L. Porter, *North Country Life*, Fall 1959

Once upon a time—there lived at Monkton, Vermont, a spindly boy called Daniel Dodge. He was the son of a Baptist minister, John A. Dodge, and the grandson of a second minister of the same persuasion.

Daniel went to school—perhaps too much! After studying at the "common" school, Ferrisburg, Vermont, at Sherman Academy, Moriah, New York, at Troy Conference Academy, Poultney, Vermont, at Colgate Academy, Hamilton, New York, and at Madison University, he went home—when he was 28 (in 1848)—too exhausted to help his father (also "ailing") do farm chores. Dan had certainly lost strength, for in his teens he had accomplished a seven-year stint at blacksmithing.

Daniel Dodge's body may not have been up to par at that period of his life, but his mind was more active than ever along mechanical lines and worked without delay to the benefit of the Dodge family. He invented a horseshoe nail machine!

In 1848 farmers, including John Dodge, made horseshoe nails and cut nails laboriously, pounding them out on an anvil a few at a time. This irked young Dodge, who aimed to make farm work less arduous, and he succeeded in turning out a small model that would make miniature nails from bars of lead or copper. In 1849 a full-size machine was made and operated, though it needed frequent repair and turned out non-uniform nails. The ex-blacksmith tried again, and in June 1852 secured a patent, the first of a series, for it took Dodge more than sixteen years to evolve a satisfactory nail machine.

Keeseville, on the Great AuSable, was the scene of the horseshoe nail machine experiments—the family had long since moved to New York State—and his machines came into use there in 1857. In 1862 he began selling them at varying prices—from $40 to $500 each. Twenty-five of the machines went to the Jacob D. Kingsland plant in Chicago, Illinois, that year. Then on January 1, 1863, a firm, the AuSable Horse Nail Co., was established at Keeseville with Dodge as vice president and a trustee. The company became nationally known, and the machines invented by Daniel Dodge put their mark on Keeseville as the "home of the horse-shoe nail."

Mr. Dodge was the first president of the village of Keeseville upon its incorporation in 1878, was a stockholder in the Keeseville, AuSable Chasm and Lake Champlain Railroad, a stockholder and director of the Keeseville National Bank, and a trustee and deacon of the Keeseville Baptist Church, as well as a large land owner in North Dakota, where he spent considerable time at one period of his life.

Mr. Dodge married Eunice Reed of Vermont in 1852, and although they had no children of their own, they brought up as a cherished daughter the child of Eben R. Merrill of Merrillsville in Franklin County. The infant's mother had died in the Midwest, and her father brought the baby back to his home, cradled delicately on a pillow.

The three-story sandstone building (one of many in Keeseville) adjacent to the river, formerly the headquarters of the AuSable Horse Nail Co., is still in use. Extant is a photograph of Mr. Dodge standing by the building, which adjoins the old stone bridge, but no monument or marker in the village tells the story of Keeseville's famous citizen. Mr. Dodge died there on February 5, 1901. ▨

▨ THIS WAS PAUL SMITH

By Gayle Carman, *York State Tradition*, Spring 1965

Nestled in a small village on St. Regis Lake in the Adirondacks once stood a hotel to which came many of the wealthy and famous men of the United States. It had no great beauty, inside or out, but it did have a mystical charm, which, according to Donaldson's History of the Adirondacks, may be traced to the personality of the owner—Paul Smith.

Apollos Smith was born in Milton, Vermont, on August 20, 1825. He was soon nicknamed "Pol," which eventually became "Paul." He did not come from a wealthy family; he was just a poor New England boy who loved the woods. It was his love of the outdoors that started him on his road to success.

In 1852 he bought 200 acres of land near Loon Lake. Here he built a primitive lodge called "Hunters' Home." It was strictly a man's retreat, but it attracted a select patronage, primarily doctors. The men, however, soon wanted to bring their wives to enjoy the wilderness. The idea was mentioned to Paul.

In 1858, with financial aid from a friend, Dr. Hezekiah B. Loomis, Paul Smith was able to build a hotel which was comfortable and to which the men could bring their wives. This hotel on St. Regis Lake, in which only

Paul Smith. *Courtesy Special Collections, Feinberg Library, SUNY College at Plattsburgh*

simple and direct methods were employed, became a fad with people of wealth. Its fame grew to the point that one reporter for the *Adirondack Enterprise* commented, "... to visit Adirondacks without seeing him (Paul Smith) or his place was but a visit incomplete, not a real visit to the Adirondacks."

What kind of man could build such fame for himself? In stature he was tall, broad framed, big boned, and powerfully built. Yet he was well poised and balanced. His attitude toward men could be summed up as sunny skepticism, and his spirit one of mockery as is illustrated by his comment when he was told that a train coach of passengers had been held up after its departure from his hotel. He laughed heartily and said, "Fool of a highwayman! Holding up passengers after they've left here! What did he expect to find on them?"

Paul Smith was not a reader, and he held education in contempt. He believed that men were born with shrewdness and the ability to learn by

Paul Smith's Hotel, 1870. *A Seneca Ray Stoddard photo. Courtesy Maitland DeSormo Collection*

experience. If they were not shrewd or did not profit from experience, he believed that education would be of no use to them. His words to Dr. Edward Trudeau are typical of his philosophy: "No fool like an educated fool!"

In spite of his straightforward character, Paul Smith had many friends. He was, however, no respecter of men for their station in life. In his eyes all were the same. He made friends with the common as well as the rich and famous. He was well acquainted with such people as President Grover Cleveland and P. T. Barnum. Though he was quick to make friends, he was just as quick to dislike people. It is well known that if a man came to his hotel whom he did not like, he would ask the man to leave.

In all his life he was never adversely influenced by his popularity and wealth. He remained simple and unaffected in his nature, tastes, and habits. On his 85th birthday he received many beautiful, expensive gifts. The one which he chose to comment about and the one which gave him the most pleasure was an elaborate red tie, which had been hand-made by a lady guest at his hotel. As she was making it, Paul had admired it. The lady had said she intended to give it to the best man she knew.

One cannot comment on the character of Paul Smith without mentioning his story telling. It was his ability in this field that drew many friends to him. There was nothing that gave him more pleasure than to sit down and swap tales with someone. He enjoyed sharing his tales so much that a series of them were published in the *Adirondack Enterprise*.

Paul Smith was a success at every endeavor he undertook. He began his career as a caterer and a guide. As time passed he was lumberman, real-estate salesman, postmaster, merchant, electric light and power company owner, road builder, and railroad man.

Common sense was the basis of his life. To him it meant "the capacity a man has to regulate his appetite for food and drink, to know when to go to bed and when to get up… to know a good bargain after ascertaining the facts and how to go after it and get it; how to hold on to what you have and how to be square with all people on all sorts of matters." This was Paul Smith.

☑ CATHERINE R. KEESE

By Marjorie L. Porter, *North Country Life*, Winter 1960

"There is a hill in mine own land" a song reminds one. So might Friends at the Quaker Union have thought affectionately of Hallock Hill. Like the Indians before them, from this hill they looked down, northward to a sort of promised land—promised in 425-acre pieces to the first comers of their group, as payment for surveys completed for the post revolutionary proprietor, Zephaniah Platt; westward to the Adirondacks; southward to the valley of the Great Ausable River; eastward to Lake Champlain and the Green Mountains of Vermont. At the foot of the hill, to the west and north, lay the winding Little Ausable and its forested level valley, white pine country.

Into this uninhabited and seasonally forbidding yet beautiful land came pioneering Quakers from Dutchess County, among them William, Stephen, and Richard Keese and their father, John Keese. Stephen had eleven children. It was the seventh, Samuel, who married in 1847, his second wife, Catherine Robinson.

Catherine was 41 before the Quaker Union became her home. She was born April 4, 1806, in the city of New York and was brought up as a member of the New York Meeting. As a young woman she chose teaching as her work and was remarkably successful, largely because of her unfailing affection for her pupils. There seemed to be no discipline bugaboo in her schoolrooms whether in Philadelphia, Wilmington, or Poughkeepsie.

After a career of about twenty years as "teacher," Miss Robinson, then in her late thirties, felt she should become a preacher. She dreaded public appearances and said, in reference to the change in her life, "I rebelled long, and feel even yet that it would be easier to sacrifice my life than walk in the path which is laid out before me."

Samuel Keese [sic: Stephen Keese Smith], like other Friends at the Union in the town of AuSable, Clinton County, visited Dutchess County occasionally to attend the New York Yearly Meeting (until the Peru Monthly

Meeting was established), and in the case of Samuel Keese, whose home was a station on the Underground Railroad, to plead antislavery measures. It was doubtlessly on one of these trips that Catherine was seen, admired, and—courted! (He had been a lonely widower for nearly two years.)

The marriage was accomplished in accordance with Quaker custom, a committee of the Society having reported there was "nothing to hinder," and a second committee, that the marriage "was in good degree orderly accomplished." Samuel was 54 and had retired from the operation of his farm. He spent his time largely as a preacher and as an ardent Abolitionist. He later championed women's suffrage.

Among the advantages which marriage brought to Catherine Keese was official recognition as a minister. The Peru Monthly Meeting recommended her as such in April, 1849. She continued to preach, as she had for several years, so eloquently and forcibly that she held the attention of both Quaker audiences and others. Throughout Clinton County, including Clinton Prison at Dannemora, and in parts of Canada, Western New York, and Pennsylvania, Mrs. Keese was known and loved.

In the late 1850s Mr. Keese was financially embarrassed to such an extent that Mrs. Keese once more resumed teaching, this time conducting a private school in their home. Her work was suddenly interrupted when she was taken ill and died March 27, 1860, at the age of 54. She was mourned by the entire community, regardless of age or religious belief. Hers was an example, set also by other women of the Quaker Union who preached and traveled miles on horseback along dim forest trails to bring medical assistance and comfort to anyone in need.

Compiler's note: As a point of interest. Catherine Keese was the great-great-great aunt of Neal Burdick. ◼

♛ WILLIAM L. MARCY

A Capsule Biography of an Eminent Statesman of the Early 1800s
By Frederick C. Marcy, *North Country Life*, Spring 1955

The highest peak of the Adirondack mounts is Mount Marcy (5,344 feet), called by the Indians "Cloud Splitter." The name "Marcy" was given this mountain to honor one of New York State's great men, William L. Marcy.

Marcy was born at Sturbridge, Massachusetts, December 12, 1786. As a boy he was bad, unruly, and uncontrollable, but Salem Towne, his teacher, encouraged him to study and he rose rapidly.

After attending Brown University, he became a teacher, a lawyer, and an officer of the volunteers in the War of 1812, capturing the first prisoners and the first flag at St. Regis, Canada. He became editor of the *Troy Budget* and the leading member of the famous "Albany regency," a group of able Democratic politicians who exerted a powerful influence throughout the state. He was in turn comptroller of the state of New York, judge of the state Supreme Court, and United States senator. He was three times in succession elected governor. President Polk appointed him secretary of war and President Pierce made him secretary of state. He was noted as an authority on international law. He was one of the four founders of Rochester University.

Marcy died at Ballston Spa on July 4, 1857. He gave credit for his achievements to his early teacher. "Whatever I have attained," he said, "I owe to Salem Towne, my teacher. Towne made me." ✄

♦ FATHER MAC

By W. H. Burger, *North Country Life*, Summer 1952

Once in a while the more fortunate of us enjoy contact with a person who is too big-spirited to be walled up in an institution, whether it be church, party, or welfare state. Such a man was the Rev. Father Edwin H. McCarthy, an Ogdensburger, who for 32 years was pastor of St. Philip's in Westport and St. Elizabeth's in Elizabethtown.

Some years before his death Father Mac, as he was affectionately known to his fellow citizens of the two communities he served, was stricken with coronary thrombosis.

Doctor, Bishop, and friends of all faiths and none urged him to take it easy. But his free spirit would not submit, so there was another attack, then a third, nearly fatal, and a slow running down. He knew the signs but would not give in. He carried on to the end, which occurred December 9, 1950.

During the preceding summer, he got his intimate friend, Carl Huttig of Elizabethtown, who was to die himself very soon, to take what he knew would be his last picture. Then in the early fall he wrote a sermon message for the officers of the Adirondack Hi-Y clubs, who were in Training Conference at the Boy Scout Camp Bedford. Its spiritual horizon is so wide and its mood so tender that we quote from the closing paragraphs. Here in essence is Father Mac, so far as can be expressed in words.

> *"Let each one here make a resolution to seek diligently to find just what God wants of him, what type of love and service he wants of him and in which church he will find best exemplified the teachings of Christ—so that he will know what his own church teaches and why it teaches it and have an intelligent foundation for his particular belief in and service to his God. It is obvious, of course, that every person should go to church if he is to know about God. And it isn't a matter of going just when it's convenient. Everyone should go every Sunday. That's what the church is for and that is why God instituted a ministry to teach men God's will and to keep constantly before men's minds the necessity of its close contact with God. (And will you try always to keep in mind that you should never be critical of the beliefs of another. It is every man's privilege to believe as he will—provided he knows why he believes it and is convinced in his heart that that is what God wants of him.)*
>
> *"Before we leave this gorgeous spot made by God's hand, let's raise our eyes and our hearts to heaven and try to see God face*

to face—let us tell Him honestly that we shall try to live this
year—every day of it—close to Him and His Divine Son, asking
Him each morning just what He wants of us 'this day.' Let us
strive to fulfill His Holy Will in our own personal regard and
to strive unselfishly to influence those about us to do likewise.
God love you."

Father Mac is permanently enshrined in the hearts of people who knew him, and it is particularly significant that the physical remembrances which have been erected to his spirit are not stained glass windows but two social, recreational buildings in Westport and Elizabethtown. These will be known as the Father Mac Memorials and will express in physical forms his infinite capacity not only to appreciate fun but to create it. All of us will long remember his delightful flair for comedy. It was spontaneous, irrepressible, and irresistible.

One day he was to meet at the train two priests who were coming to conduct a mission in his church. He dressed incognito and greeted his guests with "Taxi? Taxi?" They said "Yes," so he put them into his car and asked where they wanted to go. "The church," they replied. "Okay," said the driver. But instead of stopping at his own church, he drove through the village and pulled up in front of the Baptist edifice. As they got out, he said, "Fifty cents, please." Instead of forking over the cash, they started the following colloquy:

"This isn't the church."
"What do you mean, it isn't the church?"
"It isn't the church."
"It's a church, isn't it?"
"Yes."
"What church do you want?"
"The Catholic."
"Oh!"

With that driver and driven got in and backtracked nearly the whole way to the station, finally stopping at St. Philip's. As men and bags got out, the driver said, "A dollar, please."

This incited heated recriminations. When the argument had about worn itself out, the driver said, "That's all right. I'm Father Mac. Glad to see you. Come in."

He laughed as he told me about an encounter with and old Irish cop who was a former parishioner of his in Port Henry. It was early morning. Father Mac was muffled up in hunting clothes, and the cop was half asleep. Father Mac pulled up and asked the cop how to get to Ticonderoga. "Straight ahead," said the minion of the law. Father Mac thanked him, drove around the block and inquired the way to Mineville. "Right up the hill." "Okay, and thank you," said Father Mac, as he again started around the block. This time he said, "I'd like to go to Westport." By now the old fellow was sufficiently awake to recognize his former curate and responded with "You go to hell."

While none of the Catholic clergy could excel him in his devotion to the Christian religion and the Mother Church, his liberality of spirit and his love of fun transcended any sectarian or creedal boundaries. To him these never mattered enough to shut him off from the closest fellowship with his host of Protestant friends and admirers. It was typical of him to give the minister of the Federated Church in Westport a farewell dinner in his home when the latter left town. And it wasn't the first time he had had the minister and his wife at table for one of the feasts for which St. Phillip's was famous. Some of the rest of us Protestants have also been there. And he and his sister Margaret, a retired public high school teacher, were with us every Christmas they were able to come to our house.

To see him downtown getting his noon mail was "a sight for sore eyes." Good to look at, well set up and quick stepping, with white hair and ruddy cheeks, his rich, resonant voice sounded a greeting for everyone, including the summer folks, some of whom he kidded mercilessly.

This compassion recognized no limits. It was typical of him to visit a Protestant woman who was mortally ill for months and to take her little delicacies, such as venison, and finally at her funeral to sit beside the Protestant minister who conducted it in her home. When his friend, the state secretary of the Y.M.C.A., was invalided to Westport, he became his most frequent visitor. He knelt by the casket of a Protestant neighbor. These instances could be multiplied many times.

Born in Ogdensburg November 13, 1883, he was ordained in the priesthood at St. Mary's Cathedral in 1913. His first assignment was to St. Patrick's in Port Henry as assistant. For a brief period thereafter he was administrator of St. Cyril's at Alexandria Bay and came to Westport and Elizabethtown in 1918. For several years he was Diocesan Director of the Society for the Propagation of the Faith and gave many missions and retreats during his priesthood.

I can attest to the earnestness and depth of his convictions as they were revealed to me during many conversations, as could some of his other friends, including at least two professed atheists. Beneath his face of banter there was tremendous faith and loyalty. This was recognized by such a religious leader as Dr. S. Parkes Cadman, who never failed to call on Father Mac whenever he was in Westport. A promising young Episcopal clergyman of my acquaintance had frequent and very rewarding "bull sessions" with Father Mac.

At his invitation, my family and I with some other Protestants attended Midnight Mass at Christmas, two confirmations and some special services. As a result of these experiences, we got a new appreciation of the Roman Catholic Church and a deep feeling that during the years of his priesthood in our twin communities, he was the priest of us all. From time to time he used to jokingly invite me to Confession. Sometimes I wish I had gone!

His sister Margaret, the last of eight children, survives him. She is older and an invalid. I have never seen a more devoted couple, even in marriage. They literally lived for each other. The last time I saw him he knew he was near the end, although he was still on his feet and walking with that brisk firm step, which was so characteristic. His chief concern was whether he should go to bed at her home or in the hospital, all on account of Margaret. I can imagine him exchanging a quip or two with

St. Peter as he enters the pearly gates, but he won't venture far beyond until Margaret shows up. Then they will approach the great white throne hand in hand. ✘

🐦GRANNY RHOADES OF EARLY WASHINGTON COUNTY

Developed by William J. O'Hern, from an article
that appeared in *North Country Life*, Summer 1958

According to Chrisfield Johnson's *History of Washington County*, "Dr. Nathaniel Rhoades was an early settler on Pike Brook. He was a practicing physician for many years, dying about 1858 or 1859. His wife, Mrs. Anna Rhoades, is still living (1878) and has reached the age of 103 years." North Country native Fred T. Stiles recalled his great-great-grandparents.

Fred Stiles' great-great grandparents, Dr. Nathaniel and Anna Rhoades, had died long before he was born, but Fred's memory of his ancestors was rekindled by Johnson's words and by the many stories his mother, Rachel Tracy had told about her Great-Grandmother Anna.

"As Mother was growing up, she loved to listen to the stories told by 'Granny Rhoades,' as she was called by everyone who knew her," Stiles wrote in "Granny Rhodes of Early Washington County." His family recollection appeared in G. Glyndon Cole's *North Country Life*, Summer, 1958 issue.

After developing his Granny Rhoades' article, Fred began to write other rural memories that occurred within the Adirondack Park as well as historical accounts that took place in and around Fort Ann, his home, located just outside the Blue Line that denotes the border of the Adirondack Park.

Fred's recollections were the kind of accounts historian Glyndon Cole found significant. Fred's family's narratives might not have been chosen for inclusion in a New York State history textbook for school children, but they were unquestionably the kind of chronicles Cole believed needed to be preserved for future generations of interested history enthusiasts.

Following Stiles' first story, he offered "Legends of Furnace Hollow" in the spring issue of *North Country Life*, followed by "Dieskau's March thru South Bay," which appeared in the Summer 1959 issue of *North Country Life*.

At this point, Stiles became a prolific regular contributor to Cole's magazine with "Tales of Rogers and His Rangers," *North Country Life/York State Tradition*, Fall 1959; "Tales of Old Canal Days" *North Country Life*, Winter, 1959 and a string of other well-developed stories: "Hogtown," *North Country Life*, Spring, 1960; "On the Road to Shelving Rock," *North Country Life/York State Tradition*, Summer, 1960; "Recollection of the Knapp Estate, Part I, *North Country Life/ York State Tradition*, Fall, 1960; "Peddlers I Remember," *North Country Life/York State Tradition*, Winter, 1960; "Recollection of the Knapp Estate, Part II," *North Country Life/ York State Tradition*, Winter, 1961; Recollection of the Knapp Estate, Part III," *North Country Life/ York State Tradition*, Spring, 1961; "1755–59 in the Champlain Valley: Fort Carillon," *North Country Life/York State Tradition*, Summer 1961; "1755–59 in the Champlain Valley: Massacre at Fort William Henry" *North Country Life/York State Tradition*, Fall, 1961; "The Stiles Name in Early New York," *York State Tradition*, Spring 1963; "Tales of Lake George" *York State Tradition*, Summer, 1963; and "More About South Bay," *York State Tradition*, Fall, 1963.

Some of Stiles' stories preserved a part of northern New York's history that might otherwise have passed into relative obscurity. These accounts required research. Others simply ripened from the pleasant memories and musings of older generations.

Stiles was as interested in regional history as he was in family history. In "The Stiles Name in Early New York," he wrote, "Though Robert Stiles, the first of our line to come to America, settled in 1639 with the Ezekiel Rogers Company at Rowley, Massachusetts, many of his descendants were early settlers in the State of New York. Research on the family tree reveals that they settled in at least seven different counties, mostly in the northern area."

Vanishing Adirondack and North Country Americana inspired Stiles and others to write pieces that recounted the old days. It was a new world and some old timers thought it was not necessarily a better one. Stiles' stories took readers back to humble farm and roadways. His writing echoed down the corridor of years.

Perhaps Fred Stiles believed the machine age had hijacked much that was picturesque, even though the old ways and days were more laborious. The horse, covered wagon, stage coach and carriage were gone. The stitching horse and shaving horse—both once common hand tools of tradesmen—were now trappings of the past. Wooden barrels produced in a cooper shop were no longer common household items. The butter churn and the spinning wheel were relics of the past. Grist mills stood silent.

Glyndon Cole knew Stiles loved history, and he accepted every story Stiles submitted about the past. I believe Stiles and other *North Country Life* and *York State Tradition* contributors shared a common goal with Cole. What literature needed, along with reports of amazing progress, was a reminder of what the old days held. They appreciated the small things that had been lost to the past—the final run of a train whose whistle traveled far across the ice of Lake George, sounding for all the world like the angel Gabriel blowing his horn; the taste of freshly-churned butter; the self-satisfaction of making a good life in a rough land.

In the 1960s, Howard C. Mason "discovered" Stiles.

"I had heard of Mr. Stiles through articles he had written for historical and nature lovers' magazines and I decided I must meet this man," Mason wrote in *Backward Glances*, Volume II, 1964. Howard Mason entitled his piece about Stiles "The Vanishing American" because "Fred Stiles is just exactly that."

Mason explained that Stiles lived like the typical small *and* upland farmers...what I call subsistence farmers." He observed the Stiles family "produced on their own land everything possible for their own use. If there was a surplus of anything, they might sell it or exchange it with neighbors."

Beyond the Stiles family's lack of dependence on the outside world for their livelihood, Mason emphasized Fred Stiles "was not an eccentric mountain hermit." While he only left his extensive upland ground twice a year for supplies that "were not produced on their land," Stiles demonstrated an acute aptitude for current events and self-improvement. "While he had very little formal schooling," Styles "kept up on world events by radio and television." He was a voracious reader and enjoyed writing. Mason concluded Styles "did a good job" of being a learned man.

Years later Fred Stiles's writing projects were assembled in two volumes titled *From Here to Now* (1978) and *Old Days, Old Ways* (1984) by the Washington County Historical Society.

TED HAMNER, BUILDER OF ADIRONDACK GUIDE BOATS

By Ed Schulz, *North Country Life*, Spring 1957
Reprinted from the *Schenectady Union-Star*

Old Ted Hamner, 97, cups his hand around your ear and says in a wavering, fading voice, "Will's still the best boat-builder in these parts."

And Ted knows. He held the title for 60-odd years.

Ted Hamner of Saranac Lake didn't build the first Adirondack guide boat but the Hamner family has laid a hand to more good ones than any other woodsman.

"It takes a woodsman to build a woodsman's boat," Ted says.

For a fact, no one seems to know where the Adirondack guide boat originated. There isn't the vaguest hint—with the exception of an observant traveler who posted a card from Norway with a museum view of Eric the Red's trim craft; that's as close as anyone has come to pin-pointing the origin.

The guide boat resembles Eric's canoe-like contraption, peaked fore and aft without any thwarts (cross-members) running between the gunwales. Everyone in the North Country knows, though, that a good guide boat can mean life and death in the Adirondacks; it can mean "gittin' or not gittin' where you're goin'," the old guides say.

It is the fastest transportation for a trapper, hunter or camper. It will shoot rapids as well as a canoe and is more durable; it is light enough (40-lbs) for one man to carry when portage afoot is necessary; on a still lake, a good man can paddle a guide boat over a mile of water in four and one-half minutes.

To Ted Hamner, who gave up driving a stagecoach to guide in the wilderness and later to build the boats, it meant a living. He has passed the craftsmanship down to his son Willard, 55, who still builds the rugged, lightweight craft in a shop next to his home at Saranac village.

He uses power tools—that's all that has changed.

Ted, until recent years, used to go over to his son's shop to help out, to work the stiffness out of his fingers. The new-fangled contraptions Will used meant nothing to him, except possibly a passing era, and he continued to use hand-shavers and a pen-knife to put the boats together. The whirring sanders, electric saws and drills might speed up the operation a bit but they don't do it any better. Ted holds that they don't do it as well but he never went in for outboard motors to push a boat either. ◼

⚡ SENECA RAY STODDARD, A PIONEER PHOTOGRAPHER

Author Unknown, *York State Tradition*, Spring 1963

Sixty years ago, Seneca Ray Stoddard would have needed no introduction to readers of *York State Tradition*, for his name was commonly known throughout the East and was linked particularly with the Adirondack region. People knew him as a lecturer, world traveler, author of Adirondack guidebooks, and pioneer photographer. He was also a talented artist with ink, oils and watercolor, a writer of both prose and poetry, and an inventor, according to Maitland C. DeSormo, an authority on Stoddard's life and work.

Stoddard was born in 1844 on a farm in Saratoga County. At the age of 16, he left home to work for the next four years at painting numbers on freight cars and decorative scenes on the interiors of passenger coaches. When he was 20, he located in Glens Falls and began taking stereopticon views of the town. Then, traveling on foot, by bicycle, and by train, he took pictures of Lake George, Ticonderoga, Crown Point, Lake Champlain, and Ausable Chasm. Later picture-taking trips took him over a wide area of the Adirondacks.

Chateaugay Lake looking south from Merrill's Hotel.
Photo by S.R. Stoddard. Courtesy Special Collections, Feinberg Library, SUNY College at Plattsburgh

He set up a store in Glens Falls from which he sold these pictures and a series of guidebooks and maps of Lake George, Lake Champlain, and the Adirondacks, which he published from 1873 to 1914.

Though the main interest in Stoddard today lies in the photographic record which he left of the Adirondacks in the 19th century, he traveled far beyond that region. He made trips to other parts of New York State, New England, Florida, Cuba, the Far West, Alaska, the Holy Land, and Europe. Everywhere he traveled his camera went with him, and each voyage to a distant land resulted in lectures illustrated with stereopticon slides.

None of his lectures were more popular, however, than those on the subject of the Adirondacks, by which he took his audience, according to an account in the New York *Mail and Express* following an appearance in New York City in 1893, "into the forest's depths, across carries, into club preserves, up mountains and down rapids. He hunted with them, fished with them, introduced them to camp life, to lumber and mining camps, to the noted guides." Through these lectures, he not only publicized the Adirondacks but was influential in persuading the state legislature to create the Adirondack Park in 1892.

In 1906 Stoddard started another venture, which proved to be short-lived—the publication of his *Northern Monthly*. Early issues of the magazine were full of Adirondack articles and photographs. Through this medium, he attacked the current despoliation of the mountain forests by lumber and power interests, pollution of the streams, and the lax enforcement of the game laws. The contents of later issues was not confined to the Adirondacks; in fact, in these, greater space was often devoted to faraway places. Circulation shrank and he was forced to cease publication in September 1908.

Stoddard died in Glens Falls in 1917, but his work lives on. His photographs—mountain guides, lumbermen and sportsmen; lakes, rivers and mountains; camps and hotels; guideboats, steamboats and stage coaches—still frequently appear in books and magazines. ◼

⫸ AFTERWORD ⫷

Debra Kimok, Special Collections Librarian, Feinberg Library,
SUNY Plattsburgh, October 2011

In 1960, Dr. Allan Everest, SUNY Plattsburgh history professor, and Dr. M. Frances Breen, Director of SUNY Plattsburgh's Benjamin F. Feinberg Library, decided to build the North Country Historical Research Center (NCHRC). They knew they needed a local and state history expert to help with the development and organization of the enterprise, and an enthusiastic expert they found in G. Glyndon Cole.

Mr. Cole writes in his *Manuscripts for Research: Report of the Director, 1961–1974*, that "Dr. Everest conceived of [the NCHRC] as a means of enriching his course in New York State history," and that he "spent many hours" researching locally-held collections to add to it. By 1974, the NCHRC, under Cole's stewardship, had received major donations from over 125 individuals and families, and smaller donations from "hundreds of donors," and included a wide variety of formats.[1]

Subsequently, the NHCRC was renamed the "New York History Collection" and later "Special Collections," and has grown to include more than 4,000 linear feet of manuscripts, maps, pamphlets, clippings, audio/visual materials, photographic materials, periodicals, and books, and is the largest collection of North Country history in the region. We continue to collect historical materials of significance for Clinton, Essex, and Franklin Counties, and the Adirondack and Lake Champlain regions. We also have a large collection of books about New York State history, developed by Cole and Everest, but due to space limitations, we no longer add to this collection. Our materials are used by college students and professors, amateur historians, and genealogists—locally and from afar. Over the years the collection was moved from a small space in Redcay Hall to a larger vacated gymnasium in Hawkins Hall in 1974, and finally to its current space on the first floor of the Feinberg Library building on Draper Avenue.

Cole not only oversaw the building of the collection—he also made a very large portion of it accessible to researchers. In the process of creating access to the collections, librarian Connie Pope was hired to help with the indexing and organization of the materials. Together they created a card catalog of manuscript collections, pamphlets, and periodical articles that remains in use in the Special Collections reading room to this day. This catalog is now also available online in our P.O.L.A.R.I.S. database and is the collection's most often used finding aid.

Possibly Cole's greatest contribution to making regional historical materials accessible was his compilation of the *1968 Historical Materials Relating to Northern New York: A Union Catalog*, which lists the printed materials holdings (items published prior to 1961) of "92 libraries and other institutions in six Northern New York counties." Long before online access tools were in use, this catalog enabled researchers of Northern New York history to find, in one publication, the list of "books, pamphlets, leaflets (folded broadsides), maps, newspapers, and magazines" in libraries that held materials pertaining to the region, were written by a resident of the region, or were "Northern New York imprint[s]." [2] The 307-page volume is topically arranged, with additional sections for specific formats, i.e. maps and surveys, and each entry includes information about the holding libraries. Both author and title indexes are also included.

The revised and updated 1976 edition includes the holdings of eight additional libraries and one additional county, and titles published through 1968. In addition to the formats included in the 1968 edition, this one also lists masters' theses and doctoral dissertations. The arrangement is also expanded to provide more detailed information about materials relating to specific localities. [3]

Without Glyndon Cole's expertise, Special Collections would exist, but it would not be the large, valuable, accessible collection that it is today. He was the right person for the job and has been followed through the years by others inspired by his great efforts and knowledge—Bruce L. Stark, Joseph Swinyer, Michael Burgess, Wayne Miller, and now me. I think I can speak for all of us when I thank Mr. Cole for his dedication to the development of these very Special Collections and the monumental contributions he made to making them accessible for research. ◾

⯈ POSTSCRIPT ⯇

William J. "Jay" O'Hern

My complete collection of G. Glyndon Cole's *North Country Life and York State Tradition* magazines was revisited time and again in the process of compiling this book. Rereading each monthly issue can be just as interesting as the initial call. There is the satisfaction of boosting my memory by reviewing past events of Adirondackiana coupled with the bonus that comes of noting the additional memorabilia that initially went unnoticed—all mirroring the historical past of the vast mountainous region.

When the original body of work was completed, the manuscript was massive. It was much too large to be contained in one book.

The voluminous Fall 1946 through Summer 1974 body of diverse articles speaks with authority and with more than passing interest of this land which preserved a way of life that otherwise would have been scattered and lost with the passage of time. It was just for that reason that Glyndon Cole took on the personal challenge to develop, finance and self-publish the Adirondacks' first regional magazine.

Cole was a researcher at heart. He saw libraries as a treasure-house. Drs. Everest and Breen recognized Cole's ability and knew that with his interest and enthusiasm, SUNY Plattsburgh's Benjamin F. Feinberg Library would fast become organized, catalogued and microfilmed, a valuable resource always available for researchers.

I remember my conversation with Glyndon when I approached him with my concept to highlight his publishing career and put a spotlight on what one person can do to preserve history. He was interested in something new that would focus attention on his long-out-of-print magazines. He felt it would provoke the interest of a new generation of readers who were unfamiliar with the old days. I suspected there might even have been a wry grin across his face as I passionately described the kinds of topics

Algonguin House, Saranac Lake. "One of the most beautifully situated hotels in the Adirondacks." —Alfred Donaldson. *Photo: S.R. Stoddard. Courtesy Special Collections, Feinberg Library, SUNY College at Plattsburgh*

and subjects the book might cover. "A story of the two-holer." "Oh, yes, an *objet d'art* and very important to the life and times of old-timers."

Each time I reexamined the bulky volume I had developed. I found it impossible to eliminate any of the memorabilia. Everything was so interesting. The range of subjects and stories was diverse. It was like being one of the touring public visiting The Adirondack Museum at Blue Mountain Lake.

And, because the museum is such a worthwhile place that no one should plan to spend less than a day seeing the exhibitions, I decided I would rework the original manuscript into an interesting mix of themes. To that end, I plan to follow Adirondack Kaleidoscope with Adirondack Memories and Campfire Stories. The follow up will feature articles about Adirondack communities, places of interest, transportation, exploration, thrillers, adventure and true and fictional tales in the mountains.

⇒ ACKNOWLEDGMENTS ⇐

William J. "Jay" O'Hern

I would first like to thank G. Glyndon Cole, who gave his vote of confidence for this project when I spoke with him in March 1989. Without his support this project would never have been started. It has been a privilege to honor his commitment to regional history. A special thanks to his daughter, Carolyn Trivilino, who shared background material and rounded out my collection of *North Country Life* and *York State Tradition* magazines.

This book would never have been completed without the interest and support of a wide variety of helpful people. Enormous gratitude goes to all those who contributed to *North Country Life* and *York State Tradition* over the years, and to those who generously backed my effort to share the historical significance of Cole's out-of-print magazine.

The author extends his expression of gratitude to: The Adirondack Museum at Blue Mountain Lake and Librian, Jerry Pepper; Daniel E. Alexander, President and Publisher, Denton Publications, Inc.; Edward Blankman; Elizabeth Folwell, Creative Director, *Adirondack Life* magazine; Caroline Kehne, Editor of *Lake Champlain Weekly*; Joe Kelly, editor and publisher of the *Boonville Herald & Adirondack Tourist* and host of the Joe Kelly Show on WUTR-TV; Jenna Kerwin, staff writer at the New York State *Conservationist*; Cathleen Kittle, Bureau Director, Division of Public Affairs and Education of the New York State Department of Environmental Conservation; Rob Igoe Jr., President, North Country Books, Inc.; John J. Kettlewell, Publications and Marketing Director of the Adirondack Mountain Club; Debra Kimok, Special Collections Librarian, Plattsburgh, State University of New York; Jennifer Kuba, Assistant Director, Archivist/Curator at the Adirondack history Center Museum, Essex County Historical Society; Stan Linhorst, Senior Managing Editor of the *Syracuse Post-Standard*; M. Dan McClelland, Publisher, *Tupper Lake Free Press*; Ellen McHale, Executive Director of the New York Folklore Society; and David H. Nelson, Editor, NYS *Conservationist*.

Grateful Acknowledgement is made to Anthony F. Hall, editor/publisher of the *Lake George Mirror*, who, on behalf of his family, has relinquished all or any literary rights and interests in *North Country Life/York State Tradition* that his father, Robert F. Hall, acquired from Glyndon Cole.

A special heartfelt thank-you goes to my daughters Susan Steverman and Kerry Suppa, whose nimble fingers eased the labor of some keyboard work for their father.

The assistance of my dedicated editors, Mary L. Dennis and Neal Burdick, was invaluable. They shared the work of copy correcting as only those with their skills can do. Their insightful questions and suggestions gave me confidence to carry forward.

Grateful acknowledgement is made for permission to use Edna West Teall's "Mother Was an Optimist," original material that appeared in *Adirondack Tales, A Girl Grows Up in the Adirondacks in the 1880s*, copyright *Adirondack Life*, 1970 and 2001.

For permission to reprint the following material, grateful acknowledgement is made to the New York State *Conservationist*. Regrettably, G. Glyndon Cole did not cite all of the original issues of the *Conservationist* in which these articles appeared: *Inferno in the Adirondacks* by Harry W. Hicks, *Verplanck Colvin and the Great Land Survey* by Roland B. Miller, and *The Adirondack Guide Boat* by Roland B. Miller.

For permission to use material by William J. O'Hern that previously appeared in *Adirondack Life* magazine, grateful acknowledgement is made to *Adirondack Life* magazine and Elizabeth Folwell, Creative Director.

For permission to use material that previously appeared in The *Ad-i-ron-dac*, grateful acknowledgement is made to the Adirondack Mountain Club.

For permission to use material that previously appeared in The *Syracuse Post-Standard* grateful acknowledgement is made to The *Syracuse Post-Standard* and Stan Linhorst, Senior Managing Editor.

For permission to use "'Pants' Lawrence of the Adirondack," that previously appeared in *New York Folklore Quarterly* grateful acknowledgment is made to the New York Folklore Society.

I have made every effort to acknowledge the assistance of everyone who helped with this project; any ommision is an unintentional oversight.◢

⇒ CONTRIBUTORS ⇐

William J. "Jay" O'Hern

Glyndon Cole was closely acquainted with many of his contributors, and for them it is possible to list *biographical* notes. For others, we know nothing more than where they lived. For still others, nothing is known beyond a name. Readers are encouraged to provide additional information for inclusion in subsequent editions.

➡ **E. EUGENE BARKER**, Albany, N.Y. Worked as a landscape architect for the Office of New York State Architecture.

➡ **DAVID H. BEETLE**. His work as long-time columnist for the *Utica Sunday* and *Daily Observer Dispatch*, the *Utica Daily Press*, and other newspapers in the Gannett group, gave him wide readership. Beetle is the author of *West Canada Creek, Along the Oriskany, Up Old Forge Way* and *The New York Citizen*.

➡ **JOHN G. BROUGHTON**, Assistant New York State geologist.

➡ **GLADYS R. BROWN**, Saranac Lake, N.Y.

➡ **WILLIAM "BILLY" H. BURGER**, Westport, N.Y. Burger acted as Associate Editor of *North Country Life*. He authored a long-running "The Adirondacker" column for *The Record-Post*, Au Sable Forks, N.Y., throughout World War II. Burger counted Noah John Rondeau, the famed Adirondack hermit, among his closest life-long friends.

➡ **GAYLE CARMAN** wrote the character sketch of Paul Smith in 1964, when she was a senior at State University College, Plattsburgh. It was done as an assignment in Dr. Allan Everest's class in New York State history and government.

➡ **L. E. CHITTENDEN**, Terrytown, N.Y. and Burlington VT. was an author, lawyer, businessman, politician, political activist and served as Register of the U.S. Treasury in Lincoln's first administration.

➡ **G. GLYNDON COLE** compiled and published the quarterly *North Country Life* (later called *York State Tradition*) from 1944–1974. Cole operated on a shoestring and set up his pages on a manual typewriter, faithfully printing the stories of his friends and reader-contributors. Throughout

New York and across the United States, fans made the quarterly digest a much-anticipated periodical. He included poetry, art and literature, and interesting reprints of old newspaper and periodical stories, true backwoods tales, true pioneer tales, military history and much more.

➡ **FREDERICK H. COWLES**, Santa Barbara, California

➡ **DAVID M. ELLIS**

➡ **MRS. R. L. FOOT**

➡ **MARION S. FRESN**

➡ **TERRY JAMES GORDON**, Plattsburgh, N.Y. (1951–2001). Chief clerk for Supreme and County Courts of Clinton County, he served there until his death.

Gordon was a member of the New York State Court Clerk's Association, a director of Murray's Raiders (Revolutionary War Re-enactment Group), Clinton County Historical Association, Plattsburgh *Press Republican*, and writer and author of numerous articles in various magazines.

➡ **HELEN IRELAND HAYS**, Johnstown, N.Y. An author and poet, Hays was a graduate of Wellesley College and member of the Albany County Poetry Society. A number of her poems have appeared in various publications including *York State Tradition*, the *Christian Science Monitor* and the *National Parks Magazine*.

➡ **MARK HEMENWAY**

➡ **HARRY W. HICKS**. Glyndon Cole reported Hicks "lived in Lake Placid for many years and knows the North Country as well as any man alive. He also knows—from bitter experience—what fire can do to it."

➡ **EDNA GREEN HINES**, Watertown, New York. (1888–1957). Hines was an American author and poet. According to her obituary she was a graduate of Syracuse University, where she majored in English and Latin and was a member of the Boar's Head Dramatic Society. In addition to her work as a poet she taught Latin in the Watertown, New York schools for many years and offered private tutoring. Hines was the poet of *The Valley of Blue Moon* (1939); *Underneath the Bough* (1940); *Candle in the Night* (1942); *The Endless Trail* (1946); *White Butterflies* (1949); and *Captured Dreams* (1957). Edna Hines and

Glyndon Cole shared a friendship, a love of literature and a deep affection for history and the North Country.

➡ **RALPH S. HOSMER**, Professor of Forestry, Cornell University, N.Y.

➡ **GRACE L. HUDOWALSKI**, Albany, N.Y. Born in 1906, she was one of the founders of the Forty-Sixers and first president of the Adirondack Forty-Sixers. She worked as a promotion supervisor for New York State and held numerous positions in various organizations following retirement, including past president of the New York Folklore Society, lifetime historian of the Adirondack Forty-Sixers, secretary of the Adirondack Park Association, past editor of the Adirondack Mountain Club publications and editor of *The Adirondack Forty-Sixers* (1958) and *The Adirondack High Peaks and the Forty-Sixers* (1970 and 1971). Grace was the first woman to climb all forty-six Adirondack High Peaks.

➡ **EDWIN A. JUCKETT**, Hyde Park, N.Y. Juckett was principal of the Keene Valley schools from 1927 to 1939.

➡ **JANE KELTING**, Malone, N.Y.

➡ **DEBRA KIMOK**, Special Collections Librarian, Feinberg Library, State University of New York at Plattsburgh.

➡ **LEE KNIGHT**. Raised in the Adirondacks, Lee became interested in folk music while in high school. During college, he became familiar with the music and stories of the Southern Appalachian Mountains, as well as of the Adirondacks. He wanted to learn the music and stories from traditional sources—people who had known them as part of their culture and community for generations.

Lee currently works as a folk singer and story teller and guides whitewater raft trips.

He is currently working on a book of Adirondack ballads and folk songs as recorded by Marjorie Lansing Porter in the 1940's and 1950's. Read more about Lee at: www.leeknightmusic.com.

➡ **EMIL G. KRAELING**, New Canaan, Connecticut. Author, *The Brooklyn Museum Aramaic Papyri: New Documents of the Jewish Colony at Elephantine* (New Haven: Yale University Press, 1953).

➡ **S. R. LEONARD, SR.** Oneida, N.Y. Stephen was born in the Oneida Community and always worked for Oneida Ltd., successor to Oneida

Community when it changed from its social organization to a stock corporation in 1881. He served in positions of considerable responsibility in the company and for more than 50 years had been a member of its Board of Directors. Fishing, hunting, and camping have been his life-long hobbies.

➡ **CARROLL V. LONERGAN**, Teacher, Crown Point Central School, Crown Point, N.Y.

➡ **FREDERICK C. MARCY**, Boonville, N.Y.

➡ **ROLAND B. MILLER.** MILLER wrote many articles for the New York State *Conservationist* magazine during the 1950s.

➡ **REV. FREDERICA MITCHELL**, Keene Valley, N.Y.

➡ **CHARLES L. MOONEY**, city editor of *The Knickerbocker News*, Albany, N.Y.

➡ **GLENN NEVILLE.** Editor of *The New York Mirror* from 1954 to 1963, when that paper ceased publication. At the time of his death in June 1965, the New York Times referred to him as "a shirtsleeve newspaper-man who spent more time in the newsroom than in his large office." Though born in the West and educated at the University of Denver, he had "found" the Adirondack country and died in his Keene Valley home, where his widow continued to reside. He wrote "The Old Kitchen Stove" for *York State Tradition* only a few weeks before his death.

➡ **MARJORIE L. PORTER**, Keeseville and Keene, N.Y. Associate Editor of *North Country Life & York State Tradition,* she died in 1973 at the age of 82. Up to the time of her death, she wrote newspaper columns on folklore and historical subjects, wrote and published several histor-ical pamphlets, and was a frequent speaker before historical groups. In addition, she served at various times as Essex County historian, Clinton County historian, and Plattsburgh city historian. In July 1972 the New York State Historical Association presented her with an award of merit "in recognition of long service to local history and the folk-lore of the Adirondack area."

Mrs. Porter willed to the North Country Historical Research Center, State University College, Plattsburgh, her collection of local history and folklore consisting of books, pamphlets, manuscripts, notes, photographs, clippings, and more than 100 tapes and records. The tapes and records are recordings of folk songs and interviews with North Country residents. Her collected works are undoubtedly the largest in Northern New York.

➡ **SAMUEL IRENAEUS PRIME** (1812–1885), author of *Under the Trees*, 1874. Prime was an American clergyman, traveler, and writer. He was born at Ballston, N. Y., and graduated from Williams College in 1829. Three years later he entered Princeton Theological Seminary, was licensed to preach in 1833, and in 1835 was installed pastor of the Presbyterian Church at Ballston Spa, N. Y. For a time he was principal of the academy at Newburgh, N.Y. In 1840 he entered upon the chief work of his life as editor of the New York *Observer*, a paper of which he afterward came to be the principal owner. His brother and then his son, Wendell Prime, carried on the editorship after his death. He was the founder of the New York Association for the Advancement of Science and Art, president and trustee of Wells College, and a trustee of Williams College. (From Widipedia, the free encyclopedia)

➡ **DOROTHY PITT RICE**, Crown Point, N.Y. First wife of Harold Rice who worked as a logger and scaler for International Paper Company and as a carpenter.

➡ **C. R. ROSEBERRY.** C. R. Roseberry's books documented the histories of Albany, N.Y., aviation and steamboats. Roseberry died at the age 88 in 1990. Roseberry's work as a reporter, critic and columnist at newspapers in Albany, Ithaca, Buffalo and Rochester spanned five decades.

➡ **MICHAEL J. RUSHMAN**

➡ **ED SCHULZ**, a 40-year photojournalist with the Schenectady *Union-Star* and *The Gazette*. While still an adolescent, his son Marc apprenticed with his father at *The Gazette* as a contributing photographer and became a full-time staff photographer in 1983.

➡ **CLAYT SEAGEARS**, first director of the Division of Conservation Education and chief architect in 1946 of its new publication, *The New York State Conservationist*. Al Bromley, a former editor of *The Conservationist* said, "No one who ever heard Clayt talk...ever forgot him." Seagears, knowns as "Mr. Conservation" was a showman who loved the 1940s–50s New York Sportsmen's Show. He was admired for his natural history-conservation field of illustrated writings, sketches, drawings, cartoons, oil and watercolors as well as his *Conservationist* series, "The Inside on the Outdoors."

➡ **FRANCES B. SEAMAN**, Long Lake, N.Y. Francis Boone Seaman is the author of *Nehasane Fire Observer*. Her publisher, Nick Burns, reports Frances "was a very nice lady and talented." Early in her life she worked as a commercial artist in New York City, drawing women's fashions for newspapers and magazines. *Nehasane Fire Observer* is about her time in the 1940s as a fire tower observer at Nehasane Park. She functioned as the historian of Long Lake for decades before her passing.

➡ **JULIA GARDEPHE SIMMONS**, Rouses Point and Saranac, N.Y.

➡ **CYNTHIA SMITH**, Malone, N.Y.

➡ **DONNAL V. SMITH**. Smith served as President of the State Teachers College at Cortland, N.Y.

➡ **FRED T. STILES**, Fort Ann, N.Y. Fred was a long-time contributor of early rural Adirondack memories.

➡ **EDNA WEST TEALL** (1881–1968). Born in Essex on Lake Champlain, Teall grew up in nearby Lewis. She was a self-taught painter and journalist. She was employed with the Newark (New Jersey) *Evening News* for more than thirty years as a reporter and Women's Page editor. In her retirement, she returned to the North Country she knew so well as a child. The familiar scenes were satisfying. They brought back memories of life as it was lived in the Adirondacks in the 1880s. Wanting to preserve those cherished memories, she wrote the four-part series "Mother Was an Optimist: Essex County Life in the 1880s." Published in *North Country Life* in 1953–54, her memorabilia mirrored the past of the Adirondack region. The piece refreshed the memories of those who lived during that time, satisfied her desire to revisit the past and inspired her to expand her memorabilia regarding Adirondackana. In 1970, *Adirondack Life* magazine published Teall's *Adirondack Tales*. The 2001 reprint includes an excellent biography of Mrs. Teall by Christine Jerome.

➡ **LEROY H. WARDNER, M.D.**, West Hartford, Connecticut. Wardner was born in St. Regis Falls on Jan. 19, 1910. He grew up in upstate New York and graduated from Saranac Lake High School. Wardner later attended Cornell University and Cornell University Medical School.

After practicing family medicine with his father in Saranac Lake, he completed his internship at the Hartford Hospital and his residency at the University of Pennsylvania. In 1949 he began his 35-year practice in Obstetrics and Gynecology at the Hartford Hospital.

Wardner was on the forefront of women's issues, including planned parenthood, legalized abortion, and childbirth education.

Doctor Wardner's interests included music, history, genealogy, gardening, and all things Adirondacks.

➡ **LOUELLA WATERMAN**, Philadelphia, PA. and Croghan, N.Y.

➡ **LEILA M. WELLS** (1880–1984). Leila was born in John Brown's farmhouse in North Elba, N.Y. Her family was renting the farm at the time. Her granddaughter, Donna M. Wells shared, "There is a little story in one of her books about John Brown's grave which is on the farm. Apparently, pilgrims to the site would pick up a stone from the grave as a remembrance and when there were no more stones on the grave, Leila and her siblings would go down to the brook or river and gather up some more stones to scatter on the grave."

Leila, like many contributors to Cole's magazine, wrote about her North Country reminiscences. At age 90, she published her first book describing her life as a child and young woman living in the Adirondacks. Memories of the *Good Old Days; Once Upon a Time;* and *Times Have Changed* is a three volume book of Wells' Adirondack memories. Publisher Kellscraft Studio reports: "Her writing is filled with imagery from her childhood: a visit to her Grandfather's homestead; shopping at the local country store; childhood games; attending school and later as a teacher. She was active through her long life, enjoying quilting, sriting, and cooking. She died at the age of 104."

➡ **ELSIE WILKINS** (1905–unknown), Utica, N.Y., contributed poetry to *North Country Life* for eight years.

➡ **JOHN WILKINS**—former fire observer on West Mountain near Raquette Lake.

☰ SOURCES ☰

BOOKS

Beetle, David H. *Up Old Forge Way/West Canada Creek.* Lakemont & Old Forge, NY: North Country Books, 1971.

DeSormo, Maitland C. *The Heydays of the Adirondacks.* Saranac Lake, NY: Adirondack Yesteryears Inc., 1974.

Donaldson, Alfred L. *A History of the Adirondacks: Vol.II.* Harrison, NY: Harbor Hill Books, 1977.

Horrell, Jeffery L. *Seneca Ray Stoddard: Transforming the Adirondack Wilderness in Text and Image.* Syracuse, NY: Syracuse University Press, 1999.

Nyber, Mae. *Siblings, Scribblings and Borrowed Children.* Boonville, NY: Boonville Gaphics, 1978.

O'Hern, William J. *Adirondack Characters and Campfire Yarns: Early Settlers and Their Traditions.* Cleveland, NY: The Forager Press, 2005.

O'Hern, William J. *Adirondack Stories of the Black River Country.* Utica, NY: North Country Books, 2003.

MAGAZINES

_____. "Arthur Couture, the Strong Man of Rouses Point." North Country Life, Winter, 1947. Reprinted from *The North Countryman.*

_____. "A. Fitzwilliam Tait, Adirondack Artist." *North Country Life,* Winter 1957.

_____. "An 1842 Fishing Trip to Moose River." *York State Tradition,* Spring 1963.

_____. "Seneca Ray Stoddard." *York State Tradition,* Spring 1963.

_____. "Ice Harvest." Reported in the *Utica Saturday Globe,* February 15, 1890. Reprinted in *York State Tradition,* Winter 1964.

_____. "President Cleveland in the Adirondacks." Reprinted from *Frank Leslie's Illustrated Newspaper,* 1885 in *York State Tradition,* Summer 1968.

_____. "The Giant Hermit of the Adirondacks." *York State Tradition,* Winter 1971.

_____. "The Philosopher's Camp." *York State Tradition,* Fall 1972.

Barker, E. Eugene. "Father's Last Decoration Day." *North Country Life,* Spring 1950.

Broughton, John G. "Adirondack Fundamentals." *North Country Life,* Spring 1949.

Brown, Gladys R. "Ice Fishing in the Adirondacks." *North Country Life,* Winter 1958.

Burger, William H. "Some Conservation Men." *North Country Life,* Summer 1950.

_____. "Melvil Dewey." North Country Life, Spring, 1951.

_____. "George Morgan of Raquette Falls." *North Country Life* Spring 1952.

_____. "Father Mac." *North Country Life,* Summer 1952.

_____. "The First Adirondackers." *North Country Life,* Spring 1953.

_____. "Tom Peacock, Adirondack Guide." *North Country Life,* Winter 1953.

_____. "George Webster, An Adirondack Minister." *North Country Life* Summer, 1954.

Carman, Gayle. "This Was Paul Smith." *York State Tradition,* Spring 1965.

Chittenden, L. E. "Mitchell Sabattis." *York State Tradition,* Spring 1964. Reprinted from Personal Reminiscences, 1840–1890.

Cole, G. Glyndon. "Summer in the North Country." *North Country Life,* Summer 1948.

_____. "Adirondack Murray." *North Country Life,* Spring 1958.

Cowles, Frederick H. "Recollections of the Adirondacks." *North Country Life,* Fall 1952.

_____. "Recollections of the Adirondacks." *North Country Life,* Fall 1953.

_____. "Recollections of the Adirondacks." *North Country Life,* Winter 1953.

Ellis, David M. "Elkanah Watson, Pioneer." *York State Tradition,* Fall 1972.

Fresn, Marion S. "The Lion Couchant." Reprinted from the *Ad-i-ron-dac*, publication of the Adirondack Mountain Club. *North Country Life*, Winter 1954.

Gordon, Terry James. "Jacques Suzanne—Man of the North." *York State Tradition*, Spring 1973.

Hays, Helen Ireland. "Pants Lawrence in New York City." (poem) *North Country Life*, Winter 1963.

Hemenway, Mark. "The Hand of Nature." (poem) *North Country Life*, Spring 1955.

Hicks, Harry W. "Inferno in the Adirondacks." Reprinted from New York State *Conservationist* in *North Country Life*, Fall 1948.

Hines, Edna Greene. "Rendezvous With Beauty." (poem) *North Country Life*, Spring 1957.

Hoffman, Elmer Owen. "Adirondack Hermit: Ferdinand Jensen." *North Country Life*, Winter 1956.

Hosmer, Ralph S. "Our Forest Preserve… A Rich Inheritance." *North Country Life*, Spring 1947. Condensed from the Bulletin to the Schools.

_____. "Franklin B. Hough, Father of American Forestry." *North Country Life*, Winter 1955.

Hudowalski, Grace L. "Marcy Kaleidoscope." Reprinted from *The Ad-i-ron-dac* in *North Country Life*, Spring 1954.

Juckett, Edwin A. "An Early Adirondack School." *North Country Life*, Winter 1952.

Kelting, Jane. ""From the Editor's Mail." *York State Tradition*, Summer 1973.

Knight, Lee. "Three Literary Greats on Ampersand Bay." *York State Tradition*, Spring 1963.

_____. "The Philosopher's Camp." *York State Tradition*, Fall 1972.

Kraeling, Emil G. "Old Man of the Mountains." *North Country Life*, Spring 1955.

Leonard, S. R., Sr. "The Mattesons and Their Sweet Mountain Home." *North Country Life*, Spring 1951.

Lonergan, Carroll V. "The Country School at the Crossroads." *North Country Life*, Fall 1946.

Marcy, Frederick C. "William Marcy." *North Country Life*, Spring 1955.

Miller, Roland B. "The Adirondack Guide Boat." Adapted from the New York State *Conservationist* in *North Country Life*, Fall 1950.

_____. "Verplank Colvin and the Great Land Survey." Reprinted from the New York State *Conservationist* in *North Country Life*, Spring 1956.

Mitchell, Rev. Frederica. "Old Mountain Phelps." *North Country Life*, Summer 1951.

Mooney, Charles. "North Country Bootlegging Days." *North Country Life*, Spring 1959.

Neville, Glenn. "The Old Kitchen Stove." *York State Tradition*, Winter 1966.

Porter, Marjorie L. "It All Belongs to Me." *North Country Life*, Fall 1948.

_____. "Number Please!" *North Country Life*, Summer 1949.

_____. "The Passing of the Pigeons." *North Country Life*, Fall 1950.

_____. "A Log Cabin Speaks." *North Country Life*, Fall 1955.

_____. "Daniel Dodge." *North Country Life*, Fall 1959.

_____. "Catherine R. Keese." *North Country Life*, Winter 1960.

Prime, Samuel Irenaeus. "A Vist to Adirondack Country." An excerpt from *Under the Trees*, published in 1874. In *York State Tradition*, Winter 1967.

Rice, Dorothy Pitt. "The One-Room Country School." *York State Tradition*, Winter 1967.

Roseberry, C.R. "T. R.'s Midnight Ride." *York State Tradition*, Winter 1969.

Rushman, Michael J. "Creation of the Adirondack Park (Part One), *York State Tradition*, Fall 1973.

_____. "Creation of the Adirondack Park (Part Two), *York State Tradition*, Winter 1974.

Schulz, Ed. "Ted Hamner, Builder of Adirondack Guide Boats." *North Country Life*, Spring 1957. Reprinted from the *Schenectady Union-Star*.

Seagears, Clayt. "The Hermit of Cold River." Reprinted from New York State *Conservationist*, October-November, 1946 in *North Country Life*, Spring 1947.

Seaman, Frances Boone. "Mountain Moods." *North Country Life*, Winter, 1953.

_____. "The Adirondack Guide Boat." *North Country Life*, Winter 1958.

Simmons, Julia Gardephe. "Adirondacks." *North Country Life*, Spring, 1948.

_____. "GI, 1863." *York State Tradition*, Winter 1964.

Smith, Cynthia. "The Sky Was Too Blue— a True Tale of the Great Blizzard of 1888." *North Country Life*, Winter 1948.

Smith, Donnal V. "'Pants' Lawrence of the Adirondacks." *North Country Life*, Fall 1953.

Stiles, Fred T. "Granny Rhoades of Early Washington County." *North Country Life*, Summer 1958.

Teall, Edna West. "Mother Was an Optimist: Essex County Life in the 1880s, Part I." *North Country Life*, Spring 1954.

_____. "Mother Was an Optimist: Essex County Life in the 1880s, Part II." *North Country Life*, Summer 1954.

_____. "Mother Was an Optimist: Essex County Life in the 1880s, Part III." *North Country Life*, Fall 1954.

_____. "Mother Was an Optimist: Essex Country Life in the 1880s, Part IV." *North Country Life*, Winter 1955.

Wardner, M.D., LeRoy H. "Adirondack Medicine." From *New York State Journal of Medicine* in *North Country Life*, Fall 1949.

Waterman, Louella. "My Friends." *North Country Life*, Spring 1955.

Wells, Leila M. "Lake Placid Childhood." *York State Tradition*, Spring 1972.

Wilkins, Elsie. "Woodsloafer" (poem) *North Country Life*, Summer 1956.

_____. "Holiday Time" (poem) *North Country Life*, Spring 1958.

Wilkins, John. "Life on an Adirondack," reprinted from The New York State *Conservationist* in *North Country Life*, Summer 1956.

NEWSPAPERS

Schwarz-Kopf, Rebecca. "For the Love of History." *Lake Champlain Weekly*, February 20, 2002.

OTHER DOCUMENTS AND PAPERS

Rondeau, Noah J. Journals for 1946, now property of the Adirondack Museum, Blue Mountain Lake, N.Y.

⊨ END NOTES AND SOURCES ⊨

Three Literary Greats on Ampersand Bay

1. Ralph Waldo Emerson, "The Adirondacks," in Alfred L. Donaldson's *A History of the Adirondacks*, Friedman, 1963. v. 2, p. 271

2. E.W. Emerson, *The Early Years of the Saturday Club*, Houghton, 1918. p. 173.

3. William James Stillman, *The Autobiography of a Journalist*, Houghton, 1901. p. 256.

4. Graham Balfour, *The Life of Robert Louis Stevenson*, Scribner, 1901. p. 39.

5. Walter H. Larom, "Mark Twain in the Adirondacks," in *The Bookman*, January, 1924. p. 537.

6. Charles A. Sleicher, *The Adirondacks: American Playground*, Exposition Press, 1960. pp. 222–233.

7. Larom, op. cit.

8. Ibid.

9. Ibid.

10. Henry W. Raymond, *The Story of Saranac*, Grafton Press, 1909. p. 66

The Philosophers' Camp

1. William James Stillman, *The Autobiography of a Journalist* (Cambridge, 1901), p. 240.

2. Ibid., p. 248.

3. Ibid., p. 241.

4. William J. Stillman, *The Old Rome and the New and Other Studies* (Cambridge, 1898), p. 270–271.

5. Stillman, *Autobiography*, p. 248.

6. Paul F. Jamieson, *The Adirondack Reader* (New York, 1964), p. 76.

7. Stillman, *Autobiography*, p. 256.

Creation of the Adirondack Park, Part One

1. *Laws of New York*, 95th Session 1872. Vol. 2, Chap. 848, Sec. 2, p. 2006

2. State of New York, *Senate Documents* 1873. No. 102, p. 2.

3. Ibid., pp. 9–15

4. Joel T. Headley, *The Adirondacks, or Life in the Woods.* pp. 459–61

5. Charles Z. Lincoln, *Messages of the Governors.* Vol. 3, p. 720.

6. State of New York, *Assembly Journal* 1883. Vol. 1, p. 194.

7. State of New York, *Assembly Documents* 1883. No. 130, pp. 1–7

8. *Laws of New York*, 106th Session 1883. Chap. 13, Sec. 1, p. 10.

9. The preceding relies heavily upon Darwin Benedict, *The New York Forest Preserve— Formative Years*, 1872–1895. pp. 42–44

10. C.S. Sargent, "Forest Destruction," *Harper's Weekly*, XXIX (January 24, 1885), p. 58.

11. *Laws of New York*, 108th Session 1885. Chap. 283, Sec. 7–8, p. 482.

Creation of the Adirondack Park, Part Two

1. Alfred L. Donaldson, *A History of the Adirondacks.* Vol. 2, p. 182

2. Gurth Whipple, *Fifty Years of Conservation in New York State 1885–1935.* p. 59.

3. "For a State Park—Report of the Forest Commission to the Legislature," *New York Tribune*, January 23, 1891, p. 3.

4. *Laws of New York*, 115th Session 1892. Chap. 700, p. 1459.

5. Alfred L. Donaldson, Vol. 2, p. 190.

6. Ibid.

7. *A Revised Record of the Constitutional Convention of 1894*, Vol. 2, p. 1201.

8. "To Go Before the People," *New York Tribune*, September 14, 1894, p. 1.

   Uncle VanDyke's Place, Sand Lake photo. John Van Dyke is featured in the chapter "A Near Homicide" in *Adirondack Stories of the Black River Country* by William J. O'Hern

Elkanah Watson, Pioneer

1. The most scholarly account of Watson's life is Hugh Meredith Flick, *Elkanah Watson—Gentleman-Promoter, 1758–1842* (Columbia University dissertation, 1958.).

2. Quoted in Ulysses Prentiss Hedrick, *A History of Agriculture in the State of New York* (Albany, 1933, reprinted 1966), pp. 127–128.

3. Original Journal, E, 91, Watson Papers, New York State Library, as quoted in Flick, p. 319

4. Edward Chase Kirkland in his monumental *Men, Cities and Transportation; a Study in New England History 1820–1900*, 2 vols. (Cambridge, 1948).

5. Original Journal, D, 517–518.

6. Original Journal, E. 169, as quoted in Flick, p. 327.

This was Paul Smith

Donaldson, Alfred L. *A History of the Adirondacks*. Century Co., 1921

Seaver, Frederick J. *Historical Sketches of Franklin County*. J. B. Lyon Co., 1918

Wessels, William L. *Adirondack Profiles*. Hamilton Advertising Agency, 1961.

White, William C. *Adirondack Country*. Duell, Sloan and Pearce, 1954.

Adirondack Enterprise: August 25, 1910; August 24, 1911; May 9, 1912; December 19, 1912; January 3, 1913.

New York Evening Sun: December 16, 1912

Afterword

1. G. Glyndon Cole, introduction to *Manuscripts for Research: Report of the Director, 1961–1974* (Plattsburgh, N.Y.: North Country Historical Research Center, Benjamin F. Feinberg Library, State University College at Plattsburgh, 1974.), ii, iv.

2. G. Glyndon Cole, ed., *Historical Materials Relating to Northern New York: A Union Catalog* (Canton, N.Y.: North Country Reference and Research Resources Council, 1968).

3. G. Glyndon Cole, ed., *Historical Materials Relating to Northern New York: A Union Catalog* (Canton, N.Y.: North Country Reference and Research Resources Council, 1976).

⇒INDEX⇐

Adirondack High Peaks, 92, 356
Adirondack Lodge, 132, 133, 321
Adirondack medicine, 6, 193, 201
Adirondack Mountains, 19, 24,
    68, 91, 113, 276
Adirondack Murray, 7, 198, 230,
    233, 295, 361
Adirondack North Country, 14,
    368
Adirondack Railroad, 149
Adirondack trout, 291
Agassiz, Louis, 64, 68, 69, 70
Alexandria Bay, 191, 340
Algonquins, 99, 103
Ampersand Bay, 5, 64, 65, 66, 68,
    362, 364
anorthosite, 107, 108
Au Sable River, 34, 35
Ausable Forks, 35, 133, 189, 190,
    196
AuSable Horse Nail Co., 189

Barker, E. Eugene, 6, 153, 354
Barnes, Charles, 289
Bartlett's, 106, 236, 254, 257, 261
Becraft's Place, 78, 79
Big Brook Marsh, 25
Black Bear Mountain, 90
Black River, 3, 12, 73, 94, 100, 239,
    245, 361, 365
blizzard of 1888, 5, 29, 37
Blue Mountain, 47, 90, 91, 142,
    145, 147, 174, 351, 352, 363
Blue Mountain Lake, 91, 142, 351,
    352, 363
bootlegger 201, 202, 203
Brooklyn Constitution Club, 120,
    123, 126
Broughton, John G., 5, 106, 354
Brown, Gladys R., 5, 84, 354
Brown, John, 44, 46, 142, 259,
    311, 360
Burger, W. H., 5, 103, 258, 283,
    291, 305, 318, 336
Byrne, Peggy, 266

Calkins Creek, 286
Call, Joe, 51, 134, 178
Canadian Shield, 106, 107
Canton, 190, 191, 365
Carman, Gayle, 7, 330, 354
Cascade Lakes Hotel, 134
Champlain, Samuel, 104
Chateaugay, 180, 181, 190, 346
Chittenden, L.E., 7, 252

Civil War, 53, 72, 79, 118, 153,
    158, 196, 204, 239, 297, 343
Cleveland, Grover, 45, 120, 259,
    333
Clinton, DeWitt, 100, 179, 239
Cold River, 3, 7, 16, 17, 20, 267,
    270, 271, 285, 286, 298, 362,
    368
Cole, G. Glyndon, 4, 5, 7, 8, 10,
    13, 14, 23, 94, 95, 230, 233,
    348, 349, 350, 352, 353, 354,
    355, 365
Columbia University, 320, 365
Colvin, Verplanck, 5, 29, 102, 109,
    116, 142, 149, 236, 240, 259,
    297, 298, 353
Conservation Department, 98,
    103, 136, 241, 265, 271, 273,
    283, 284, 285, 286, 287
Cooper, James Fenimore, 239
Coreys, 284, 308, 310, 311
Cornell, Alonzo B., 118
Couture, Arthur, 7, 317, 361
Cowles, Frederick H., 6, 139, 141,
    145, 148, 355
Cranberry Lake, 148, 149, 150, 151
Crown Point, 42, 143, 153, 156,
    158, 159, 222, 223, 224, 256,
    345, 357, 358
Crown Point Center, 223, 224

Dannemora, 123, 132, 335
David Beetle, 77
Decoration Day, 6, 94, 153, 155,
    156, 157, 361
Dewey, Melville Louis Kossuth,
    318
Dix, John A., 118
Dodge, Daniel, 7, 328, 329, 362
Donaldson, Alfred L., 54, 58, 101,
    215, 364
Dresden, 42, 341, 342, 343
Dunning, Alvah, 90, 226

East Beekmantown, 302, 304
Elizabethtown, 48, 108, 113, 132,
    191, 195, 202, 252, 254, 336,
    337, 338, 340
Ellis, David M., 7, 311, 355
Emerson, Ralph Waldo, 64, 68,
    364
entertainment, 19, 23, 24, 291

Father Mac, 7, 336, 337, 338, 339,
    340, 361

Fire Observer, 98, 173, 359, 360
Fisher, Cornelius, 302
Fisher, Forrest, 302
Flower, Roswell P., 126
Folensby Pond, 65
Foot, Mrs. R. L., 94, 355
Forest Commission, 123, 125,
    126, 241
forest fires, 78, 118, 122, 130, 131,
    135, 136, 137
Fort Ann, 294, 341, 359
Fort Ticonderoga, 24, 159, 182
Franklin, Benjamin, 205, 312
Fresn, Marion S., 94
Fulton Chain, 12, 49, 90, 187, 219,
    226, 245
Fulton Chain of Lakes, 12, 90, 219

Glens Falls, 41, 42, 203, 294, 297,
    345, 346, 347
Gordon, Terry James, 7, 263, 355
Gouverneur, 107, 231
Grand Army of the Republic, 156
Granny Rhoades, 341
great blizzard of 1888, 5, 37
griddlecakes, 164
guide boat, 6, 71, 183, 184, 185,
    186, 187, 188, 261, 344, 345,
    353, 362, 363

Hamner, Ted, 7, 344, 345, 362
Harper's Ferry, 259
Harvard University, 241
Hathaway, "Old Mel," 289
Hays, Helen, 7, 243
Headley, Joel T., 117, 364
Heart Lake, 31, 132, 133, 134, 321
Hemenway, Mark, 5, 22, 355
Hermit of Ampersand, 283
Hicks, Harry W., 5, 130, 353, 355
High Peaks, 16, 92, 96, 108, 280,
    356
Hines, Edna Greene, 6, 140, 355
Hoevenberg, Henry Van, 133, 136
Hoffman, Charles Fenno, 29, 296
Hoffman, Elmer Owen, 7, 272,
    355
Hoffmeister, 80, 82, 213, 227
Holmes, John, 65, 69, 70
Holmes, Oliver Wendell, 65, 68,
    69, 70
Hosmer, Ralph S., 5, 7, 99, 237,
    355
Hough, Franklin B., 7, 101, 237,
    239, 362

Hudowalski, Grace L., 5, 27, 356
Hudson River, 41, 102, 110, 118, 179, 190, 227, 314

ice fishing, 5, 15, 84, 85, 87, 88, 226, 361
ice harvest, 5, 41, 361
Indian Lake, 91, 185, 189, 294
Inlet, 90, 91, 92, 105, 143, 160, 175, 232
Ironville, 158
Iroquois, 29, 99, 103, 194, 195, 323

J. & J. Rogers Company, 133, 189
John Brown farmhouse, 46
Johnson Hall, 104
Johnson, Sir John, 104
Joques, Father, 104, 194, 195
Juckett, Edwin A., 6, 215, 356

Kahil, MaryLee, 92
Keene Valley, 29, 43, 98, 132, 133, 178, 203, 209, 215, 218, 271, 320, 356, 357
Keese, Catherine R., 7, 334, 362
Keeseville, 34, 35, 70, 189, 190, 197, 202, 236, 315, 316, 329, 330, 357
Kellogg, Orrin, 58
Kelting, Jane, 95, 356
Killdare Club, 272, 273, 276
Knight, Lee, 5, 64, 68, 356
Kraeling, Emil G., 7, 295, 356

Labradorian ice sheet, 108
Lake Champlain, 41, 42, 52, 55, 56, 84, 85, 100, 132, 142, 143, 194, 195, 202, 259, 291, 311, 313, 314, 315, 323, 329, 334, 345, 346, 348, 352, 359, 363
Lake Colden, 30, 56, 289
Lake George, 41, 42, 132, 194, 211, 245, 345, 346, 353
Lake Placid, 5, 16, 43, 45, 47, 108, 130, 132, 133, 134, 136, 196, 234, 260, 264, 265, 266, 320, 322, 323, 355, 363
Lake Placid Club, 260, 320, 322, 323
Lawrence, "Pants," 7, 12, 243, 244, 245, 246, 247, 251, 252
Leonard, Stephen R., 77, 356
Lonergan, Carroll V., 6, 220, 357
Long Lake, 24, 26, 104, 105, 110, 150, 151, 184, 185, 186, 187, 189, 235, 236, 252, 256, 257, 258, 270, 271, 286, 287, 288, 308, 323, 359

Longfellow, Henry Wadsworth, 65, 68
Longstreth, Morris, 320
Louie, "French," 263
Lowell, James Russell, 64, 68
Lower Saranac, 64, 68, 71, 236, 254, 261, 270
Lower Saranac Lake, 64, 71, 260, 270
Lowville, 237, 239, 243
Lynch, Dan, 113, 298, 300
Lyon Mountain, 94, 182, 189

Malone, 55, 132, 190, 191, 202, 316, 356, 359
Marcy, Frederick C., 7, 336, 357
Marcy, William L., 336
Marion River, 90, 235
Martin's, 64, 65, 68, 71, 197, 236, 260
Martinsburg, 239
McCarthy, Rev. Father Edwin H., 336
McKeever, 90
McKinley, William, 54
McLane, Fred, 271
measles, 45, 46
Miller, Roland B., 5, 6, 109, 183, 353, 357
Milton, J. Elet, 94
Minerva, 30, 295, 300
Mirror Lake, 45, 47, 48, 142, 260, 320
Mitchell, Rev. Frederica, 7, 279, 357
Mohawk River, 100, 194, 314
Mooney, Charles, 6, 201
Moose River, 5, 22, 73, 74, 90, 210, 227, 361, 368
Morehouseville, 77, 78, 80, 227
Morgan, George, 7, 305, 306, 308, 309, 310, 311, 361
Mother Johnson's, 236
Mount Marcy, 8, 27, 29, 34, 300, 336
Mt. Matumbla, 274
Mulholland, M. D., 288
Murray, Reverend William Henry Harrison, 233

Neville, Glenn, 6, 203, 357
New York Board of Trade and Transportation, 120, 123, 126
New York State Forest Commission, 241
New York State Museum of Art, 266
Newcomb, 133, 184, 189, 252, 255, 273

Noah, 3, 12, 17, 20, 56, 263, 266, 267, 268, 269, 270, 271, 287, 309, 354, 363, 368
North Creek, 54, 56, 57, 58, 59, 300
North Elba, 45, 260, 360
Northwood Preparatory School for Boys, 322

O'Connor, Walt, 295
O'Donnell, Thomas C., 210
Ogdensburg, 191, 316, 340
Ogdensburger, 336
Old Forge, 90, 91, 105, 175, 184, 189, 230, 290, 308, 354, 361
Olmstedville, 288, 289, 295, 296
Oneida Community, 77, 356
Oval Wood Dish Company, 274, 276
Owl's Head Mountain, 287

Paulus, Marjorie Porter, 93
Peacock, Thomas L., 258
peddler, 48
Petty, Bill, 285, 286
Phelps, Old Mountain, 7, 28, 29, 31, 33, 98, 279, 281, 282, 283, 362
Phelps, Orson, 279
Phelps, Orson Schofield, 29
pigeon, 178, 179, 180, 181, 182, 183
pigeons, 6, 178, 179, 180, 181, 182, 183, 362
Pinchot, Gifford, 29
Piseco, 12
Plattsburgh, 41, 42, 47, 50, 51, 61, 105, 110, 141, 154, 158, 189, 190, 191, 192, 201, 202, 331, 346, 348, 350, 351, 352, 354, 355, 356, 357, 365
Port Henry, 42, 133, 190, 266, 339, 340
Port Kent, 314, 315, 316, 317
Porter, Marjorie L., 5, 6, 7, 49, 97, 178, 189, 328, 334, 357
President Pierce, 336
Prime, Samuel Irenaeus, 5, 34, 358

Raquette Falls, 7, 105, 305, 306, 308, 361
Raquette Lake, 12, 69, 104, 184, 189, 235, 245, 360
Redfield, William C., 27, 111
Revolution, 50, 100, 104, 153, 159, 195, 312
Revolutionary War, 13, 95, 355
Rhoades, Anna, 341
Rhoades, Dr. Nathaniel, 341

Rice, Dorothy Pitt, 6, 223, 358
Rice, Walter Channing, 283, 284
Richardson, Albert, 181
Richardson, Pigeon, 181
Rocky Peak, 90
Rondeau, Noah John, 3, 12, 17, 263, 266, 267, 269, 309, 354, 368
Roosevelt, Theodore, 29, 54, 55, 58, 261
Roseberry, C. R., 5, 54, 358
Rouses Point, 7, 190, 201, 317, 359, 361
Rudd, Gordon, 92
rural school, 220, 221
Rushman, Michael J., 5, 115, 123, 358
Russell, Lucius, 286, 287, 288

Sabattis, Mitchell, 7, 184, 187, 252, 254, 255, 257, 258, 361
Santa's Workshop, 90
Saranac Lake, 26, 64, 65, 66, 68, 69, 71, 72, 104, 132, 133, 136, 184, 185, 189, 190, 193, 196, 197, 199, 200, 258, 260, 262, 263, 270, 284, 285, 323, 328, 344, 351, 354, 360, 361
Schulz, Ed, 7, 344, 358
Seagears, Clayt, 7, 267, 287, 358, 362
Seaman, Frances Boone, 5, 6, 24, 185
Seward Range, 25
Seymour, Louie, 12
Sharp, Donald E., 247
Shattuck's Clearing, 286, 287
Simmons, Julia, 5, 97
Simmons, Julia Gardephe, 7, 302, 359
Skiff, Vic, 287, 288

Smith, "Bill," 324
Smith, Cynthia, 5, 37, 359
Smith, Donnal V., 7, 244, 359
Smith, Paul, 7, 36, 320, 330, 331, 332, 333, 354, 361, 365
South Bay, 42
Special Committee on State Lands, 120
Speculator, 246, 247, 249, 250
St. Huberts, 133, 136
St. Regis House, 236
St. Regis Lake, 36, 330
Stafford, Lawrence, 272
stagecoaches, 48, 64
State University Teachers College at Cortland, 245
Stevenson, Robert Louis, 64, 65
Stiles, Fred T., 7, 341, 359
Stillman, William James, 64, 364
Stoddard, Seneca Ray, 7, 28, 44, 106, 132, 147, 234, 263, 281, 313, 332, 345, 361
Suzanne, Jacques, 7, 12, 263, 266, 362
Syracuse University, 210, 284, 355
Tahawus, 29, 56, 57, 58, 65, 142, 266, 297
Tahawus Club, 56, 57
Tait, Arthur Fitzwilliam, 323
Teall, Edna West, 6, 160, 163, 167, 171, 353, 359
telephone, 55, 176, 178, 189, 190, 191, 192, 193, 310
Thousand Islands, 24, 107, 191
Ticonderoga, 24, 30, 142, 143, 159, 182, 190, 339, 345
Totten and Crossfield Purchase, 110, 149

Trudeau, Dr., 199, 200
Trudeau, Dr. Edward L., 198
tuberculosis, 198, 199, 200, 201, 236
tuberculous, 198
Tupper Lake, 69, 105, 132, 180, 186, 191, 192, 196, 260, 272, 273, 276, 308, 310, 352
Twain, Mark, 64, 66, 364

Uncle Palmer's, 236
uranium, 107

War of 1812, 95
War of Rebellion, 50
Wardner, Le Roy H., 193
Waterman, Louella, 6, 214, 360
Watertown, 55, 239, 319, 355
Watson, Elkanah, 7, 311, 315, 317, 361, 365
Webb Road, 149, 152
Webster, George, 7, 291, 294, 361
Webster, George Orlia, 291
Wells, Leila M., 5, 43, 360
West Canada Creek, 77, 79, 227, 229, 354, 361
West, Clint, 288, 289, 290
West, Clinton, 288
Westport, 48, 336, 338, 339, 340, 354
Whitaker Lake, 250
White Face Mountain, 62
White Lake, 89, 90
Whitehall, 41, 42, 143, 343
whooping cough, 45
Wilkins, Elsie, 7, 232, 360
Wilkins, John, 6, 173, 360
Wilmington, 90, 320, 334
Wilmurt, 15, 78, 79, 80, 81, 82, 225
Woodgate, 89